2 vols
The Second (Best) edition

W. Hoare delin.   B. Baron Sculp.

BLADUD,
To whom the GRECIANS gave the Name of
ABARIS.

A DESCRIPTION OF BATH,

WHEREIN

The ANTIQUITY of the CITY, as well as the EMINENCE of its FOUNDER; its Magnitude, Situation, Soil, Mineral Waters, and Physical Plants; its BRITISH Works, and the GRECIAN Ornaments with which they were adorned; its Devastations and Restorations in the Days of the BRITONS, ROMANS, SAXONS, DANES, and NORMANS; with its New Buildings, Baths, Conduits, Hospitals, Places of Worship, and other Public Edifices; its Gates, Bridges, Walks, and Streets, &c.

Are respectively Treated of:

The Gods, Places of Worship, Religion, and Learning of the Ancient BRITONS

Occasionally considered:

And the Limits of the City in its present State; its Government, Trade, and Amusements

Severally pointed out.

ILLUSTRATED WITH
The Figure of King BLADUD, the First Founder of the City;

TOGETHER WITH
Proper Plans and Elevations from Twenty-two COPPER PLATES.

By JOHN WOOD, Esq;

The SECOND EDITION, Corrected and Enlarged.

In TWO VOLUMES.

LONDON:
Printed for W. BATHOE, in the *Strand*; and T. LOWNDS, in *Fleet Street*. MDCCLXV.

PREFACE.

AN Opinion hath almoſt univerſally prevailed that every thing Recorded of *Bladud,* one of the Antient *Britiſh* Princes, the ninth King of our Iſland in the Line of *Brute,* and the firſt Diſcoverer of the Hot Fountains of *Bath,* is meer Fable and Romance; but none that I know of have yet undertaken to prove it to be ſo!

THIS Reflection naturally led me to collect ſuch Circumſtances as would amount to a Probability, at leaſt, of the Reality of King *Bladud*; and from thoſe Circumſtances the *Britiſh* Prince appears to have been a great Prophet, and the moſt Eminent Philoſopher of all Antiquity: He was the Renowned *Hyperborean* High Prieſt of *Apollo* that ſhined in *Greece* at the very time *Pythagoras* flouriſhed; He was a Diſciple and a Colleague to that celebrated Philoſopher; and among the *Grecians* he bore the Names of *Aithrobates* and *Abaris*; Names implying the exalted Ideas

PREFACE.

which that Learned Race of People had of his great Abilities.

To this famous Prince, Prieſt, and Prophet, the City of *Bath* owes her Original: An Original ſo Illuſtrious that no City upon Earth can boaſt of a greater, ſince with it the *Druids* of the Weſtern World ſeem manifeſtly to have taken their Riſe: It is a City placed in a Situation agreeable to the ſupreme Wiſdom of the Antients: And therefore it was only Popular Prejudice and Ignorance that, of late Years, Decreed this eminent Place to be a City ſtanding in a Hole, and built on a Quagmire; to be Impenetrable to the very Beams of the Sun; and to be ſo confined by almoſt inacceſſible Hills, that People can hardly come at it without danger of breaking their Necks; or, when in it, Breathe or Converſe beyond the Smell of their own Excrements.

These falſe and malicious Repreſentations I thought it highly neceſſary to Explode; and in Exploding them I have endeavoured to ſhew that, during the Times of Paganiſm, *Bath* was not only the Summer

PREFACE.

mer Seat of *Apollo* himself; but the Place where the *British Druids* Worshiped that God with greater Pomp and Ceremony than he appears to have been ever Honoured in any other Part of the World.

THE chief Seat of *Apollo*, must of Course become the chief Seat of his Priests; and upon that Consideration no Pains have been wanting to collect such Things as are necessary to prove the City of *Bath* to have been the Metropolitan Seat of the *British Druids*; whose University having been Founded by King *Bladud*, the Building still so far exists within eight Miles of our Hot Fountains as to prove the Work to have been a stupendous Figure of the *Pythagorean* System of the Planetary World.

THIS glorious Monument of Antiquity undeniably proves the *Britons* to have been a more Civilized People before the *Romans* came into our Island, than the Stream of Historians have represented them; and it likewise proves that our Sacred Edifices were composed of Marble, even when the *Romans* themselves had aspired no higher, in their Works of Architecture, than to build their
Temples

PREFACE.

Temples with common Clay: It is a Monument that *Egypt* herself might boast of amidst her proudest Structures; and it is a Monument that confirms what *Cæsar* says of the *Druids* in respect to their Astronomical Learning.

THE Reader is desired to amend any literal Faults he may meet with in the following Sheets; and in page 3, line 42, for *must* to read *much*; in p. 10, l. 27, for *Gothick* to read *Gallick*; in p. 17, l. 2, to alter the *Period* to a *Comma*; in p. 34. l. 27. to dele *more*; in p. 93, l. 14, for *parted from* to read *parted at*, and in l. 29, for *Jou* to read *Iou*; in p. 96, l. 38, for F G to read D E; in p. 106, l. 16, for *to the Mother of Venus within*, to read *to Venus, the Mother, in*; in p. 127, l. 4, and 31, p. 137, l. 22, p. 168, l. 4, and p. 173, l. 12, for *Rocks of Solis* to read *Rocks of Sol*; in p. 217, l. 30, to read *Kilkhampton*; in p. 224 after *Autumn* to add *of the next Year*; in p. 226, l. 11, for 1710 to read 1711, and l. 14, for *following* to read *same*; and in p. 229, l. 32, for *my* to read *any*.

CONTENTS

OF THE

FIRST VOLUME.

PART the FIRST.

CHAP. I.
THE Introduction, Page 1

CHAP. II.
Of the Antiquity of Bath, p. 7

CHAP. III.
Of the Reality and Eminence of King Bladud, the first Founder of Bath, p. 24

CHAP. IV.
Of the general Magnitude of Bath in its Antient, Middle, and Modern State, p. 40

CHAP. V.
Of the various Names of Bath, p. 43

CHAP. VI.
Of the Situation of Bath; of its Vales; and of its Hills, p. 49

CHAP. VII.
Of the Soil of Bath, and the Fossils peculiar to it, p. 57

CHAP. VIII.
Of the Mineral Waters of Bath, p. 63

CHAP. IX.
Of the first Discovery of the Mineral Waters of Bath, and their having Medicinal Virtues, p. 71

CHAP. X.
Of the Physical Plants of Bath, p. 82

CHAP. XI.
Of the general Form and Size of the Body of the City of Bath, p. 83

CHAP. XII.
Of the Shape of the detached Parts of Bath; with their Situations, Bearings, and Distances from the hot Springs of the City, p. 89

CONTENTS.

PART the SECOND.

CHAP. I.
The Introduction, Page 105

CHAP. II.
Of the Gods, Places of Worship, Religion and Learning of the antient Britons, p. 109

CHAP. III.
Of King Bladud's Works at Bath, and their constituting the Metropolitan Seat of the British Druids, p. 117

CHAP. IV.
Of King Bladud's Works near Bath, and their constituting the University of the British Druids, p. 147

CHAP. V.
Of the Grecian Ornaments with which the antient Works of Bath, and in its Neighbourhood, were adorned, p. 159

CHAP. VI.
Of the Devastations as well as Restorations of Bath in the Days of the antient Britons, p. 162

CHAP. VII.
Of the Devastations as well as Restorations of Bath in the Days of the Romans, p. 166

CHAP. VIII.
Of the Devastations as well as Restorations of Bath in the Days of the Saxons, Danes, and Normans, p. 180

CHAP. IX.
Of the Additional Works to Bath, between the End of the Norman Government and the Removal of the Episcopal See to Wells, p. 189

CHAP. X.
Of the Additional Works to Bath, between the Removal of the EpiscopalSee to Wells and Vesting the City in the Hands of the Laity, 197

CHAP. XI.
Of the Additional Works to Bath, between Vesting the City in the Hands of the Laity and the Election of its present Titular King, p. 205

CHAP. XII.
Of the Additional Works to Bath, between the Election of its present Titular King and The Year 1727, p. 222

AN ESSAY

TOWARDS A

DESCRIPTION of BATH.

PART the FIRST.

WHEREIN

The Antiquity of the City, as well as the Reality and Eminence of it's Founder; the Magnitude of it in it's Antient, Middle, and Modern State; the Names it hath borne; it's Situation, Soil, Mineral Waters and Physical Plants; the general Form and Size of it's Body; and the Shape of its detach'd Parts

Are respectively Treated of.

CHAP. I.

The Introduction.

DINOCRATES, the celebrated *Macedonian* Architect, having formed a stupendous Design, for cutting Mount Athos into the Figure of a Man, holding in one Hand a large City, and in the other a great Bason to receive the Water of all the Rivers of that lofty Island before it should pass into the Sea, as a Work suitable to the Taste, and worthy the Grandeur of *Alexander* the *Great*, when his conquering Arms had rendered him Master of the chief Part of the Eastern World; he determined to lay it before the Victorious Monarch; and following him into *Asia*, got an Audience of the King while he was sitting on his Throne, in the midst of his Army, administring Justice, by the Novelty of his Appearance in the Habit of an *Hercules* crowned with Poplar.

In this Dress our Architect, who was comely and tall, presented his Design; and the King, struck with the Magnificence of the Invention, expressed the highest Approbation of it; but, at the same time, asked the Inventor, whether there would be Land enough about the intended City to raise Corn for the Subsistence of the Inhabitants? *Dinocrates* answering there would not, *Alexander*, as *Vitruvius* writes in the Preface to his second Book, assured him, that though he much admired his Design, he nevertheless disapproved of the Place where it was proposed to be put in Execution; telling him, "That as an Infant can't be nourished, or grow, without a Nurse that has Milk; so a Town can neither subsist it's Inhabitants, much less increase and grow larger, without having plenty of Necessaries about it." The King, however, retained *Dinocrates* in his Service, and employed him in turning his gigantick Ideas from the Figure of a Man, to that of a Soldier's Coat, disposed into such Lines of Building as should be necessary to constitute a City for the chief Seat of his Empire.

When our Architect had compleated a new Design according to the King's Direction, and *Alexander* had got himself declared the Son of the *Ammonian Jupiter*, and therefore intitled to Divine Honours, the Hero, eager to raise some stupendous Work on Earth to perpetuate his Name, and give Mankind an Opportunity of idolizing him, directed it to be carried into Execution on a low Situation in *Egypt*; lining out the Streets with his own Hand; and then dignifying the City with the Title of *Alexandria*, from his own Name.

This famous City, according to the Accounts given us of it by *Diodorus Siculus*, extended five Miles in Length; and, by the great Art of *Dinocrates*, it was rendered a healthy Place of Habitation; our Architect contriving the Streets so as that the Etesean Winds should pass through them; and, with their comfortable Breezes, refresh and purify not only the publick Ways, but every other Part of the intended Capital of the World.

Such was the Idea of the Antients, concerning the Situation proper for a City; such was their Art to render a City in the lowest Situation, tho' open to the Sea, and backed with Marshes, as *Alexandria* was, perfectly healthy to it's Inhabitants; and from hence we find that the Cities in the most early Ages of the World were generally placed on Ground that lay low for the sake of it's Fertility, and for the Advantage of Water.

Chap. I. A Description of BATH.

THE antient Cities in general appear to have had but very small Beginnings, each one making no more than the Habitation of a few Families who had agreed to live together under the same Laws; and consisting of nothing but a small Group of Building, with a high Tower in the Middle, as a Mark to direct People, that wandered abroad, to the Place of their Abode, and for an Object of Religious Worship.

BABEL was just such a City when it was first built; and as the World increased the Towers in the new Cities that were founded became Places of Defence to the Citizens.

As soon as *Ishmael* took up his Abode in the Wilderness of *Paran*, a Name which points out to us a desolate Country, but beautiful and rich, he built a Tower, to which the *Arabians*, as Monsieur *Banier* writes in his *Mythology* of the Antients, gave the Name of *Acara*, signifying in general a Citadel; and his twelve Sons, as *Moses* tells us in the Book of *Genesis*, built each of them a Castle in that part of the Country which was assigned to them; round which they erected Houses for their Families; and then called those Castles, as well as Houses, by their own proper Names, to wit, *Nebajoth, Keder, Adbeel, Mibsam, Mishma, Dumah, Massa, Hadar, Tema, Jetur, Naphish,* and *Kedemah*.

THESE Names were most undoubtedly intended to point out to Posterity the former part of *Ishmael*'s Life; and, from a State of Sorrow, to shew that he was raised, by Degrees, to the highest pitch of Happiness; since *Nebajoth* seems to carry in it God's Promise to *Abraham*, as well as to *Ishmael* of making him the Father of twelve Princes, and a great Nation; *Keder* seems to express the melancholy State which *Ishmael* must have been in on his settling in a desolate Country; and *Kedemah* being a Name importing not only that Quarter of the Heavens where the Sun begins to dispell the Shades of Night, but a Transaction of former Time, it seems to have been designed to set forth the Joy naturally ensuing the Birth of his twelfth Son; which he must have looked upon as the End of the Promise, in respect to the Number of his Sons, and as the opening of the Day of Prosperity to himself and his Family.

THE Quantity of Land assigned by the Antients to a City, for the immediate Subsistence of it's Inhabitants, will best appear from what the Prophet *Ezekiel* writes, concerning the new *Jerusalem*; for to that City he has allotted just five times as must Ground as the City is to stand upon, for the Use and Support of the Inhabitants: So that to every City of Old, we may suppose a Quantity of Land to have been appropriated for a Berton, or Demesne to it, equal to five times its Area; and that was undoubtedly sufficient to raise Corn, and yield Pasture, for the immediate Maintenance of the People; since the Cities, in the early Ages of the World, were composed of detached Houses fronting broad Streets, and large open Areas.

Now when the Inhabitants of any City had so increased, as to have made it necessary to transplant some of her Families to her utmost Borders, wherever a single Family pitch'd, that Place was called a Village, which very often increased to a large Town; and then some of the Possessors of that Town sent forth part of their People to found new Villages, subordinate to such Town, but, at the same time, dependant upon the Body of the City, and subject to the Laws for the Government of it.

By these Means, original Cities were soon surrounded with Villages; some of these grew into Towns; and then a City with her Towns became environed with new Villages: But the Berton, or Demesne Lands, for the immediate Maintenance of the Inhabitants growing more barren, the further any of the People were removed from the first fruitful Spot on which they pitched, the Towns, on that Account, had more Land for their Bertons, in proportion to their Buildings, than the City had; and so the Villages had still more Land for their Bertons, in proportion to their Buildings, than the Towns had; and consequently the further the Parts of a City were removed from the Center, the less populous we find such Parts to have been.

Few Cities preserved their Properties so long as to become environed with Towns and Villages; for though that Part of the Land of *Canaan* which was allotted for the Tribe of *Judah*, contained one hundred and sixteen Cities, as we read in the fifteenth Chapter of the Book of *Joshua*, yet there were but four of them, to wit, *Jerusalem*, *Ekron*, *Ashdod*, and *Gaza*, that were surrounded first with Towns, and then with Villages: But when Cities were thus doubly environed, they became so formidable as to support powerful Kings; nay *Nineveh* and *Babylon* were so potent, as to raise up two great Empires; and each, in it's Turn, subdued and made all the bordering Nations tributary to her.

That *Babylon* in her greatest Glory was no more than a large Group of Building, divided by a great River, and environed first with Towns, next with Villages, and then the whole

Chap. I. A Description of BATH.

whole enclosed with Walls and Ditches, will appear evidently from a Passage in the first Book of *Herodotus* concerning the Siege and taking of the City by the *Persians:* " *Cyrus*, says
" he, having posted one Part of his Army near the Place
" where the River *Euphrates* enters *Babylon*, and the rest in
" another Station below, where the same River leaves the
" City, with Orders to enter as soon as they should see the
" Channel passable; he went with the useless Part of his Men
" to the Lake which *Nitocris* had formerly made, at a con-
" siderable Distance above *Babylon*, and turned the Stream of
" the *Euphrates* into it, by which Means the River below
" subsided, and the Channel became fordable at the City.
" The *Persians* observing this, put their Orders into Execu-
" tion, and boldly entered *Babylon*, having the Water no
" higher than the middle of the Thigh; but the Extent of
" the City was such, that, if the *Babylonians* are to be be-
" lieved, when those who inhabited near the Center were
" taken, the People who dwelt about the Extremities heard
" nothing of their Disaster; but were celebrating a Festival
" that Day with Dancing and all manner of Rejoicings, till
" they received certain Information of the general Fate."

WITH this Festival the *Babylonian* Empire was determined; for the Prophet *Daniel* tells us, that *Belshazzar*, the King, having wantonly prophaned the sacred Vessels of the Temple of *Jerusalem*, while he was celebrating it in his Palace with the chief Lords of his Empire, with his Wives, and with his Concubines; God, in the very same Hour that they drank their Wine out of those Vessels, and, in Derision of him, praised their Idols made of Gold, Silver, Brass, Iron, Wood, and Stone, caused an Hand to appear against the Wall of the Banquet-House before *Belshazzar*'s Face, and to write thereon, in mysterious Words, that he had put an End to his Kingdom, divided it, and given it to the *Medes* and *Persians:* The Troops of *Cyrus* in a few Hours after this reached the King's Palace; *Belshazzar* was slain during the Recess of the same Night; and *Cyrus* immediately gave his Crown to *Darius* the *Median*.

NOTWITHSTANDING *Babylon* had been for a long Time besieged before *Cyrus* thought of his Stratagem to take it; and notwithstanding the *Chaldeans*, or *Babylonian* Priests, were eminent for their Knowledge in foretelling future Events; yet, while *Cyrus* was executing his Design against the City, the impending Danger was neither apprehended by the Soldiery,

nor

nor forefeen by the Prognofticators : So that Defolation came upon that renowned Place fuddenly ; and fhe fuffered the Lofs of Children and Widowhood in a Moment, in one Day, without knowing the Rife of thofe Evils, or having it in her Power to award the dreadful Blow, as Sacred Hiftory informs us the Jewifh Prophets had, for Ages before, foretold.

Now the great and ftupendous Cities of the Antients, that received their Increafe by Time, being duly confidered, fuch of them as were not the capital Seats of large Empires, can be juftly compared with nothing among us in the prefent Age but a good Borough-Town, or at moft a moderate City, ftanding on low and fertile Ground ; this twice furrounded with Villages ; and thofe Villages making that Divifion of the Country which we call a populous and fertile Hundred ; fuch as the HUNDRED of BATHFORUM, if fpread to it's original Bounds, would appear, at this very Day, to be.

SOME Hundreds have been divided fince their firft Inftitution ; others have been united ; while fome have been reduced by Liberties granted out of them: The firft and laft appears to have happened to the HUNDRED of BATHFORUM ; but neverthelefs the greateft Part of what hath been taken from that Region of Country ftill continues, with the prefent Hundred, as one Divifion of the County of *Somerfet* ; and the reft have been added to the neighbouring Counties of *Wilts* and *Gloucefter*: Counties themfelves having been likewife increafed and diminifhed fince their firft Inftitution ; fometimes by extending or contracting their utmoft Bounds ; and fometimes by taking a whole Diftrict in the very Body of one County, and making it Part of another.

THE undivided Region of Country originally bearing the Title of the HUNDRED of BATHFORUM, as it feems to have contained all the detached Parts of the City in it's middle State, and, at the fame Time, to have comprehended all thofe Monuments of Antiquity round about the Hot Springs that, in the Times of Paganifm, had any Relation to one another, fhall now be included under the Title of the CITY of BATH: The DESCRIPTION of which CITY will be the Subject of the principal Part of the following Pages ; while the Defcription of the *Britifh* Works in it's Neighbourhood, but lying within the Limits of the CITY in it's antient State, will be the Subject of the reft : A Work compofed at firft for no Motive fo much as to detect the IGNORANCE of fuch as have reprefented the CITY, in it's modern State, as ftanding, for the moft Part,

upon

Chap. I. A Description of BATH.

upon a Quagmire; and likewise the MALICE of the Author of a Tour through *Great-Britain* in afferting, in the third Volume of the second Edition of his Work, Page 43, that BATH is so confined a Place, that the Company frequenting it have scarce Room to converse out of the Smell of their own Excrements.

CHAP. II.
Of the ANTIQUITY of BATH.

SUCH of the Inhabitants of the Group of Building immediately surrounding the Hot Springs of *Bath* as formerly looked upon themselves to be *Aborigines* of the City, boasted of very great Antiquity, as well as Nobleness of Blood; and pretended that they were the Descendants of a Colony of the chief Subjects of the *Britannick* Island, who settled themselves near the Hot Fountains to constitute the Court of an illustrious King, that, by Accident, had discovered them; and in grateful Remembrance of Benefits received by the Waters, had made bathing Cisterns at the Heads of the Springs; and transferred the Seat of the antient *British* Monarchy to the healing Streams, as the properest Method to publish their Virtues, and make Mankind Partakers of them.

SEVEN and twenty Years are supposed to have elapsed between the Discovery of those Springs, and the Execution of the first Works about the Heads of them; for Doctor *John Jones* tells us, in the Epistle Dedicatory to a Book bearing Date the 13th of *May*, A. D. 1572. and published by him under the Title of *The Bathes of Bathes Ayde*, that the Waters had been tried for two thousand four hundred and sixty Years or thereabout; which he afterwards brings down from the Year eight hundred and ninety before the Incarnation of Christ; and most of our Historians, Antiquaries, and Chronologers, inform us, that the Baths were founded eight hundred and sixty three Years before the Commencement of the Christian Æra.

THIS Date hath appeared, from the remotest Times, in the publick Inscriptions touching the first Discovery of the Hot Waters, and the Antiquity of the City; and more particularly in an Inscription wrote upon a large Table of Wood, and formerly placed against the Wall that makes the South Side of the chief Bath, to inform the Publick by what Accident the

Hot

8   An ESSAY towards   Part I.

Hot Springs, and their Healing Virtues, firſt came to the Knowledge of Mankind.

But the Story thus exhibited to publick View appearing to ſome of the laſt Century as a legendary Tale, the Inſcription was therefore abridged, and, in reſpect to Time, brought down to the Year 1672; Doctor *Guidott* tranſlating it into *Latin* a few Years after, and inſerting it in his *De Thermis Britannicis*, a Book printed A. D. 1691.

The Wooden Table on which this Abridged Inſcription was wrote decaying with the Seventeenth Century, the Story was then engraved on a flat Stone, which now ſupplies the Place of the Table, and opens to us the Name, the Qualifications, and the Place of Education of the King to whom the City owes it's Original, as well as the Vulgar Æra of it's firſt Foundation; the Inſcription running thus:

BLADUD,
Son of Lud-Hudibras,
Eighth King of the Britons,
From Brute,
A Great Philosopher and Mathematician,
Bred at Athens,
And Recorded
The First Discoverer and Founder
Of these Baths,
DcccLxiii Years before Christ,
That is
MmdLxii Years, to the present Year, Mdcxcix.

Now this Æra of *Bath* carrying us into that Period of the *British* Hiſtory, too ſupinely called fabulous, the antient Writers of the Tranſactions of thoſe early Times have repreſented King Bladud not only as a Magician; but, by the Magical Art, making the Hot Waters of the City boil out of the Ground in three different Places: And even what they have delivered to this Effect was ſo far from being rejected by our great and learned Antiquary, Mr. *Camden,* that he leaves the Truth of it to others to determine; advertiſing us, at the ſame Time, with what *Pliny* writes relating to the high Pitch to which the *Britons* had raiſed the Magical Art; but concluding that he did not dare to attribute the Original of the Baths to that Art.

The

Chap. II. A Description of BATH.

The Truth of the Pagan Accounts touching the Origin of *Bath* coming thus recommended to our Enquiries; and Mr. *Camden* expressing the most earnest Desire to support the *British* History from *Brute*, to the Death of *Cadwallader*, in the Year of Christ 689, I will therefore recite the Substance of what the Author of that History writes concerning BLADUD, and his eight Predecessors in the Government of the Kingdom, as a Basis, at least, for ascertaining the ANTIQUITY of the CITY of BATH.

"WHILE the Mother of *Brutus*, says the *British* Historian, was with Child of him, his Grandfather *Scanius*, the Son of the famous *Æneas*, commanded his Magicians to consult of what Sex the Damsel had conceived: Satisfied of the Event, they told him she was big of a Boy, who would kill his Father and Mother; and after travelling over many Countries in Banishment, would at last arrive to the highest Pitch of Glory. Nor were they mistaken in their Prediction, for at the Time of Travel the Woman brought forth a Son and died at his Birth; but the Child having been delivered to a Nurse and called *Brutus*, he, after the Expiration of fifteen Years, accompanied his Father *Sylvius* in Hunting, and killed him undesignedly by the Shot of an Arrow; for which heinous Fact his Kinsmen were so enraged that they forthwith expell'd him *Italy*."

"THUS banished, *Brutus* flew into *Greece*, and finding the Posterity of *Helenus*, Son of *Priam*, kept in Slavery by *Pandrasus* King of the *Grecians*, he undertook to be their General, and free them from their Servitude. This he soon accomplished, for having defeated the *Grecian* Army and taken the King Prisoner, *Pandrasus*, to save his own Life, not only gave his eldest Daughter *Ignoge* in Marriage to *Brutus*, but permitted the *Trojans* to leave his Kingdom, giving them Gold, Silver, Ships, Corn, Wine, Oil, and whatever they found necessary for their Voyage to another Country."

"THE *Trojans* thus released, forthwith embarked in a Fleet consisting of three hundred and twenty-four Ships laden with all manner of Provision, and setting Sail with a fair Wind, in two Days and a Night they arrived at an Island called *Leogecia*: *Brutus* desirous to know who inhabited it, sent three Hundred armed Men ashore for that purpose; who returning to their Ships, reported that there was no human Creature to be met with; but that they
"had

" had found a desolate City, wherein there was a Temple of
" *Diana*, with a Statue of the Goddess in it, which gave
" Answers to those that came to consult her."

" The *Trojans*, tho' pleased with this Account, were so
" far from seizing upon the Island, that they thought it ex-
" pedient to consult the Oracle, and let the Goddess deter-
" mine what Country was allotted them for their Place of
" Settlement. To this end *Brutus* was advised to go to the
" City, and address the Deity of the Place; which he con-
" sented to do; and being attended by *Gerion* the Augur,
" and twelve of the antientest Men, he set forward to the
" Temple with all Things necessary to invoke the Goddess
" by Sacrifice to return him an Answer to the following
" Question,"

  " Goddess of Woods, tremendous in the Chase
  " To Mountain Bores, and all the Savage Race!
  " Wide o'er th' Æthereal Walks extends thy Sway,
  " And o'er th' infernal Mansions void of Day!
  " On thy third Realm look down! unfold our Fate,
  " And say what Region is our destin'd Seat?
  " Where shall we next thy lasting Temples raise?
  " And Choirs of Virgins celebrate thy Praise?"

" Brutus reposing himself before the Altar, and falling
" into a deep Sleep, the Goddess seemed to present herself
" before him, and thus deliver her Answer to the Hero's
" Question."

  " *Brutus* there lies beyond the *Gothick* Bounds
  " An Island which the Western Sea surrounds,
  " By Giants once possess'd; now few remain
  " To bar thy Entrance, or obstruct thy Reign.
  " To reach that happy Shore thy Sails employ:
  " There Fate decrees to raise a second *Troy*,
  " And found an Empire in thy Royal Line,
  " Which Time shall ne'er destroy, nor Bounds confine."

" Gerion and the Elders were so rejoiced with this Answer,
" that they urg'd *Brutus* to return to the Fleet, and, while
" the Wind favoured them, to hasten their Voyage towards
" the West in pursuit of what the Goddess had disclosed.
" Without Delay therefore they re-embarked, and setting
            " sail,

Chap. II. A Description of BATH.

"sail, a Course of thirty Days brought them to *Africa*, from
"whence they proceeded to the *Philenian* Altars, and to a
"Place call'd *Salinæ*; but sailing afterwards between *Ruscicada* and the Mountains of *Azara*, they there fell among
"the Pirates, whom they fortunately vanquished, enriching
"themselves with their Spoils: After this, passing the River
"*Malua* they arrived at *Mauritania*, where the want of Provisions obliged them to go ashore and lay the whole
"Country in Waste to store their Ships; which they had no
"sooner done than they steered to *Hercules*'s Pillars, but
"with the utmost Peril of their Lives; for some of the Sea
"Monsters, called *Syrens*, surrounded their Ships, and were
"very near overturning them."

"Escaping this Danger they came to the *Tyrrhenian* Sea,
"upon the Shores of which they found four several Nations
"descended from the banished *Trojans*, that had accompanied *Antener* in his Flight; and these People having been
"headed by a Person whose Name was *Corineus*, they readily
"joined themselves with *Brutus*: So that the whole Body of
"*Trojans* pursuing their Voyage, they next arrived at *Aquitain*; and entering the Mouth of the *Loire* there cast
"Anchor, and spent seven Days in viewing the Country."

"Goffarius Pictus having been then King of *Aquitain*, he was vastly alarmed at the Arrival of a foreign
"People with so great a Fleet upon his Coasts; and a War
"immediately commencing between them, *Brutus* soon
"routed the King, destroyed *Aquitain* with Fire and Sword,
"and enriched himself with the Treasures that were hid in
"the Cities burnt by him."

"In the midst of this Destruction *Brutus* coming to a convenient Place for a Camp, forthwith pitched one at it, the
"better to enable him to give Battle, a second Time, to *Goffarius*, and the twelve Princes of *Gaul* who had all joined their
"Forces against him; and in two days time after the Camp
"was compleated *Brutus* in a pitch'd Battle gained a compleat
"Victory over the united Force of the *Gauls* and *Aquitains*."

"In this Battle his Nephew *Turonus* was slain, and from
"him the City of *Tours* derived its Name, because he was
"buried there: This City was built where *Brutus* had
"pitch'd his Camp; and *Brutus* himself erected it as *Homer*
"testifies."

"The Success of this Battle gave *Brutus* a Pretence for
"an honourable Retreat from the Continent, to go in quest

" of the Island which the Goddess had pointed out to him;
" so that repairing to the Fleet, and lading it with the Riches
" and precious Spoils he had got, he, without any further
" Delay, set sail with a fair Wind towards the promised
" Island, and the first Place he arrived at was the Shore of
" *Totness*."

" ALBION was the Name which the promised Island then
" bore, and *Brutus* landing upon it, found that it was in-
" habited by none but Giants; he was nevertheless willing
" to fix his Habitation in it, being allured thereunto by the
" pleasant Situation of Places, by the Plenty of Rivers, and
" by the engaging Prospect of Woods; so that dividing the
" Country among his Company, and *Corineus* taking *Corn-*
" *wall* for his Share, they began to till the Ground and to
" build Houses; the Giants every where flying from them,
" and retreating to the Caves in the Mountains."

" WHEN this was done *Brutus* resolved upon erecting a
" City, and in order to it travelled thro' the Land to find
" out a convenient Situation, and coming to the River *Thames*
" he walked along the Shore, and at last pitched upon a
" Place very fit for his Purpose. Here therefore he built a
" City to which he gave the Name of *New Troy*; and having
" made Choice of the Citizens that were to inhabit it, pre-
" scribed them Laws for their peaceable Government."

" DURING these Transactions, *Brutus* had by his Wife
" *Ignoge* three Sons, whom he named *Locrin*, *Albanact*, and
" *Kamber*; and the King dying in the twenty-fourth Year
" after his arrival in *Britain*, his Sons buried him in the
" City he had built, and then divided his Dominions among
" themselves; each retiring to his Part of the Kingdom to
" govern it."

" LOCRIN, after a Reign of ten Years, was killed in
" Battle; and his Wife, the Daughter of *Corineus*, taking
" upon her the Government of the Kingdom in the Behalf
" of her Son *Maddan*, held the Scepter during his Minority;
" and at the End of fifteen Years delivered it to him;
" *Maddan* ruling the Kingdom in Peace for forty Years after:
" He was then succeeded by his Son *Menpricius*, a Tyran-
" nical Prince, remarkable for his having been devoured, in
" a horrible Manner, by a Multitude of ravenous Wolves,
" in the twentieth Year of his Reign: And *Ebraucus* his
" Son, a Man of great Stature, and wonderful Strength,
" next mounting the Throne, held the Government of the
                                                    " Island

Chap. II. A Description of BATH.

"Island full forty Years; during which Time he, by an Invasion of *Gaul*, enriched himself with an infinite Mass of Gold and Silver, and was thereby enable to build two Cities, *Kaerebrauc*, and *Alclud*, together with the Town of Mount *Agned*."

"EBRAUCUS was succeeded by his eldest Son *Brutus*, sirnamed *Greenshield*, who reigned twelve Years; and then the Crown descended to his Son *Leil*, a peaceable and just Prince; and he enjoying a prosperous Reign built the City of *Kaerleil*, at the same time that *Solomon* began to build the Temple of *Jerusalem*, and the Queen of *Sheba* came to hear his Wisdom. His Reign amounted to five and twenty Years compleat; but the King, towards the latter Part of his Life, growing remiss in his Government, his Neglect of Affairs quickly occasioned a Civil Dissention in the Kingdom: Nor was this composed till the Reign of his Son *Hudibras*; who succeeding him, and holding the Scepter nine and thirty Years, put an End to the Dissention among the People."

"HUDIBRAS built *Kaerlem*, *Kaerguen*, and the Town of Mount *Paladur*; and at this Place an Eagle spoke while the Wall of the Town was building; which Speech I should not have failed transmitting to Posterity, had I thought it true as the rest of the History. At this Time, *Haggai*, *Amos*, *Joel*, and *Azariah*, were Prophets in *Israel*; and when *Hudibras* died, his Son *Bladud* succeeded him, and reigned twenty Years."

"THIS Prince built *Kaerbadus*, and made hot Baths in it for the Benefit of the Publick, which he dedicated to *Minerva*; in whose Temple he kept Fires that never went out, nor consumed to Ashes, but as soon as they began to decay were turned into Balls of Stone: About the same Time the Prophet *Elias* prayed that it might not rain upon Earth, nor did it rain for three Years and six Months: And *Bladud* having been a very ingenious Man, taught Necromancy in his Kingdom; pursuing his Magical Operations, till he attempted to fly to the upper Region of the Air, with Wings he had prepared for that purpose; but falling down upon the Temple of *Apollo* in the City of *Trinovantum*, the King was thereby dashed to Pieces."

To the above Account I will add from the Writings of Mr. *Camden*, that the Speech of the Eagle was a Prediction of a great Change that would happen in the *British* Government;

ment: "But this Prediction, says our Author, was given, as "some think, by a Person named *Aquila:*" And to the same Account I will also add, "That *Bladud* sent for Necro- "mancers to *Athens* to enable him to effect his Works at "*Bath*; and that after his Death his Body was deposited at "*New Troy*," as the Reverend Mr. *Joseph Glanville*, formerly Rector of *Bath*, declares it to have been recorded in a couple of old Manuscript Chronicles, existing when he wrote the Letter now bearing his Name in the printed Transactions of the *Royal Society*, N 49. P. 978: One of which Chronicles, Doctor *Peirce* acknowledges to have been in his Possession when he published his *Bath* Memoirs, in the Year 1697.

The *New Troy* mentioned in these Chronicles, as well as the *Trinovantum* where *Bladud* met with his tragical Death, seems to have been one and the same Place; and this none other than the City of *Bath*; Doctor *Gale* most expresly declaring in his Commentary on *Antoninus*'s Itinerary, "That the Sun had a Temple in that City;" and Mr. *Slatyer* telling us in his *Palæ Albion*, published in the Year 1619, "That King *Bladud* practising Necromancy at *Bath*, decked "himself with Feathers, and, presuming to fly, broke his "Neck on the Temple he had there built to *Apollo*."

As for the Word *Trinovantum*, the Author of the *British* History declares it to be corrupted; and as Mr. *Sammes* in his *Britannia*, P. 164, as well as many others, omitting the *Latin* Termination, *um*, write it *Troy Novant*, we may suppose this Name to have been applied to *Bath* to point out its Situation: For the City stands in a quick turning Vale, which *Troy Novant* implies; *Troi* being a *British* Word for whatever makes a quick Curve Line, as *Nant*, or *Novant*, is for a Valley; and from the Word *Troi* Mr. *Vaughan* derived the Name of *Torques*, applied to the golden Wreaths worn by the Antients, when he composed the Account inserted in the last *English* Edition of *Camden*'s *Britannia*, P. 787, touching a wreathed Bar of Gold found in the Year 1692, by digging in a Garden near the Castle of *Harlech* in *North Wales*.

Now from the collective History of *Bladud* and his eight Predecessors it appears, that *Brute* landing with his Colony of *Trojans* at the South-West Corner of *Devonshire*, and surveying the Country to the opposite Sea, even to the Promontory of *Hercules*, his chief Companion, *Corineus*, chose the Land on the West Side of the River *Tamar*, *Brute* the Land

Chap. II. *A Description of* BATH.

on the East Side, and so settled themselves in that Part of the Island; the latter, in a short time, building a City on the Shore of the River that limited his Territories to the Westward; and his Posterity residing in it, or at least building no other City till the fourth Generation.

THEN we find *Ebraucus*, by an Acquisition of Riches, founding two new Cities and a Town; and after that his Grandson *Leil*, beginning another City at the very time that a Temple was begun to be built in the City of *Jerusalem:* And we also find the Son of this Prince giving Peace to his Subjects after a Civil Dissention amongst them, and building two Cities, with a walled Town; probably as places of Defence while those Troubles subsisted.

WHILE the Wall of this Town was about, a Prophet rose up in *Hudibras*'s Kingdom, and predicted a great Change that would happen in the *British* Government; and while that Prophet was prophesying in *Britain*, *Haggai* became a Prophet in *Israel*, and a strange Woman, one of the Sibyls according to *Pliny*, appeared in the Court of *Tarquinus Superbus*, at *Rome*, loaded with several Volumes of Oracles for sale: After which the Son of *Hudibras* built a City, made hot Baths in it, and then began to teach Necromancy in his Kingdom; which Circumstance seems to be a sufficient Demonstration that he was the Prophet that rose up while his Father was building the Wall of the Town of Mount *Paladur*.

THUS in the compass of nine Kings Reigns in a continual Succession from Father to Son, the Colony of *Trojans* that *Brute* brought into *Britain*, or such of them as came with him from *Greece*, appears to have founded no more than seven Cities, and two Towns; and to have extended their Territories no farther into the Island than the South-Westward Borders of *Wiltshire*, and *Gloucestershire:* So that between that Line and the River *Tamar*, we may safely place those Towns and Cities, instead of skipping from one remote Part of the Island to another with a Handful of People, and carrying *New Troy* into *Middlesex*, *Kaerebrauc* into *Yorkshire*, *Kaerleil* into *Cumberland*, *Kaerlem* into *Kent*, and *Kaerguen* into *Hampshire*, as some Interpolater of the *British* History has done; and thereby loaded it with Improbabilities.

WE may likewise look upon the River *Tamar*, dividing *Devonshire* from *Cornwall*, to be the *Thames* meant by the first Compiler of the *British* History, instead of making *Brute*
ramble

ramble to a River of the like Name, at so great a Distance from the Place of his first Landing on our Island as the *Thames*, the chief River of *England*, is situated.

THE Extent of the *British* Monarchy, in the Time of King *Bladud*, being thus reduced and brought to the Westward Promontory of the Island, known to *Diodorus Siculus* by the Name of *Belerium*, we may lower the Antiquity of *Brute*'s first landing on it very considerably, since it preceded the Inauguration of *Lud-Hudibras* but one hundred and eighty-six Years; and since *Hudibras* in *Britain* was Cotemporary with *Haggai* in *Israel*, who commenced a Prophet in the second Year of the Reign of *Darius Hystaspes* King of *Persia*; and consequently the Arrival of *Brute* at the Shore of *Totness* cannot reach higher than the Year 744, nor fall later than the Year 705 before the Birth of Christ, or a few Years later than the dreadful Assassination of *Romulus* at *Rome*, by the *Roman* Senators.

THAT *Brute* and *Romulus* were Cotemporaries, and Kinsmen, seems sufficiently demonstrated by the *British* Historian's making the former the Grandson or Great Grandson of *Æneas*; and by the first *Greek* and *Latin* Writers making the latter the Grandson of a Person of the same Name with the *Trojan* Hero.

FROM hence it must therefore appear more than probable that *Brute*, as the real or adopted Son of *Amulius Silvius*, was driven out of *Italy* by the Tyranny of the Founder of *Rome*; and that the Murder of *Amulius Silvius*, by his supposed Twin Sons, *Romulus* and *Remus*, when they were sixteen Years old, was applied to our exiled *Trojan*; the Author of the *British* History telling us, that after fifteen Years were expired from the Birth of *Brute*, the young Man killed his Father *Sylvius*, and that he was expelled *Italy* by his Kinsmen for that heinous Fact.

THE *Roman* Monarchy continued from the Year 748, to the Year 509 before our Lord's Nativity; but yet it grew to no greater Extent during the Reigns of seven Kings, than over a Territory of about forty Miles in Length, and thirty Miles in Breadth: A Territory inconsiderable to that over which the *British* Monarchy extended in the same Period of Time, and during the Reigns of nine of her Kings; the Western Promontory of the Island being at least forty computed Miles in Breadth, on a Medium; and extending one hundred and fifty computed Miles in Length from the Lands End

Chap. II. A Description of BATH. 17

End in *Cornwall*, to the Confluence of the Rivers *Severn* and *Wye* in *Gloucestershire*. Limiting that Arm of the *Irish* Sea which now bears the Name of the *Bristol* Channel.

HUDIBRAS in *Britain*, and *Haggai* in *Israel*, being represented by the Author of the *British* History as Cotemporaries; and the City of *Kaerleil*, and the Temple of *Jerusalem*, being represented also, by the same Author, as Works of the same Antiquity; if we turn to sacred History we shall find the like Interval of Time between *Haggai*'s prophesying, and the commencement of the Work of the Temple of *Jerusalem*, that there was between *Hudibras*'s holding the *British* Scepter, and his Father's beginning the City of *Kaerleil*; it being expresly declared in Holy Writ, that God raised up *Haggai* in the Reign of *Darius Hystaspes*, to excite the Governor, the High Priest, and the Elders of the *Jews* to compleat the Temple begun by them fifteen Years before, by the Authority of *Cyrus* the Founder of the *Persian* Empire.

THE Structure so began was the Temple built by *Zerubbabel* on the same Spot of Ground that King *Solomon* long before erected his Temple: And that the Temple of *Jerusalem* always retained the Name of it's first Builder, even after it was taken down in the seventeenth Year before Christ, and then rebuilt, a second Time, by *Herod* the *Great*, is a Truth so well known that it needs no Demonstration: So that the Compiler, the Transcribers, and the Translators of the *British* History may be very well excused for putting the Name of *Solomon* to a Work that really belonged to *Zerubbabel*; and for accompanying the Name with a Circumstance that really attended it in the Visit which the Queen of the South made the King of *Israel*, after he had compleated those Works which drew People from all Parts to *Jerusalem* to view them.

SOLOMON's Temple was compleated just one thousand Years before the Birth of Christ; and *Nebuchadnezzar* defeating the *Jews* in the three hundredth and ninety third Year after, sent many of them Captive to *Babylon*, with an Order that some of the wisest of the Royal Seed should be taken into the King's Palace, and there instructed in the Language and Learning of the *Chaldeans*, to make them eligible for the Priesthood of that Nation; which was then composed of four Orders of Men, stiled in our present Bibles Magicians, Astrologers, Soothsayers or Sorcerers, and Chaldeans, a Name common to the *Babylonian* Priests in general.

D   FOUR

FOUR of the *Jews*, *Daniel*, *Hananiah*, *Mishael* and *Azariah*, appearing vastly superior to any of the rest, were committed to the Care of a particular Officer; and at the End of three Years Time the King, conversing with them, found that they were ten times better qualified to disclose the hidden Secrets of Futurity than all the Magicians and Astrologers of his Realm: So that it was not long before *Daniel* was appointed Governor of the Governors of the Priests of *Babylon*; or rather Arch-Chaldean of that stupendous City, under the Name of *Belteshazzar*, according to the Name of the God of the King.

DANIEL was also appointed Governor of temporal Affairs over the whole Province of *Babylon*; his Commission thereby exceeding that of the famous *Belesis*, whose spiritual and temporal Government, in the Reign of *Sardanapalus*, extended no farther than over the City itself: But *Daniel* resigned his temporal Government to his three Companions, and the King confirmed them in it.

THUS the Supremacy of the *Babylonian* Priesthood was vested in the Hands of one of the Captive *Jews*; the Prophet *Daniel* thereby became acquainted with all the Artifices of the Priests; and in about fifteen Years after, in the Year 588 before the Birth of Christ, *Nebuchadnezzar* totally destroyed the Temple of *Jerusalem*, after it had subsisted four hundred and twelve Years from the Period of it's Completion by King *Solomon*.

The Arch-Priesthood of *Babylon* continued in the Hands of *Daniel* till the first Year of the Reign of *Cyrus*; and the Prophet was moreover raised to the highest Honours, in temporal Affairs, in the sixty seventh Year of the Captivity of the *Jews*, and a few Hours before *Cyrus* executed his Stratagem and took the City, as above: For on the very Day that his Troops entered *Babylon*, *Belshazzar*, the King, advanced *Daniel* to be his chief Minister of State, cloathed him in Scarlet, and put a Chain of Gold about his Neck, as the proper Ensigns of his high Office: This was but just done when the *Persians* entered the Heart of the City; for in the Night they became Masters of the Royal Palace, and slew the King.

DARIUS, the *Median*, succeeding to the Crown of *Babylon*, continued *Daniel* in the Office to which *Belshazzar* had advanced him; and the King dying after a Reign of two Years, *Cyrus* succeeded to all his Dominions; this Monarch then

then joining the Realms of the *Medes* and *Babylonians* to thofe of the *Perfians*, and thereby conftituting the *Perfian* Empire in the Year 536 before the Birth of Chrift; and twelve Years after he had made himfelf Mafter of all the Wealth of *Crœfus*.

The new Imperial Monarch is faid to have honoured *Darius*'s prime Minifter above all his Friends; and as the Time of the Captivity of the *Jews*, predicted by the old *Jewifh* Prophets, was nearly accomplifhed on *Cyrus*'s Acceffion to the Throne of the *Perfian* Empire; fo *Daniel* refolved to magnify the God of *Ifrael* before the King; and to give him the higheft Proof that no Divinity prefided in the *Babylonian* Idol that *Cyrus* adored and worfhipped, under the Name of *Bel*, as a living God, daily fed with a vaft Quantity of Food and Wine.

The Fallacy of the eating and drinking Quality of the Brazen Idol, the Prophet, as he was of the Sacerdotal Order himfelf, and, confequently, acquainted with all the Artifices of the *Chaldean* Priefthood, foon detected; and *Cyrus* thereupon flew the whole College of Priefts, their Wives, and their Children, that were concerned in the Cheat; delivered *Bel* into *Daniel*'s Power; and the Prophet, after deftroying him and his Temple, fhewed *Cyrus* the Prophecies of the Prophet *Ifaiah*, which fpoke of him by Name, one hundred and fifty Years before he was born, as one whom God defigned to be the Reftorer of *Jerufalem*, as well as of it's Temple; as one that fhould fubdue Nations before him; and as one that fhould releafe the Captive *Jews*, and re-inftate them in their native Country.

Josephus informs us in the firft Chapter of the eleventh Book of his Antiquities of the *Jews*, that the King was fo tranfported upon reading the Divine Infpirations and Predictions of the Prophet *Ifaiah* concerning himfelf, that he immediately refolved to perform what had been fo long before foretold: And therefore this Monarch, in the firft Year of his Empire, fhook the very Foundation of the pagan Religion, by a Decree in favour of the *Jews* to releafe them from their Captivity, and to impower them to rebuild their Temple, that had been deftroyed by *Nebuchadnezzar* two and fifty Years before; which Decree was, by his Order, proclaimed throughout all *Perfia*; and afterwards written and entered among the Records of that new Empire in the following Words, extracted from the firft and fixth Chapter of the Book afcribed to *Ezra*.

"Thus saith Cyrus King of Persia,

"The Lord God of Heaven hath given me all the King-
"doms of the Earth; and he hath charged me to build him
"an House at *Jerusalem*, which is in *Judah*. Who is there
"among you of all his People? his God be with him, and
"let him go up to *Jerusalem*, which is in *Judah*, and build
"the House of the Lord God of *Israel*, he is the God,
"which is in *Jerusalem*. And whosoever remaineth in any
"Place, where he sojourneth, let the Men of his Place help
"him with Silver and with Gold, with Goods and with
"Beasts, besides the Free-Will Offering for the House of
"God that is in *Jerusalem*. Let the Foundation thereof be
"strongly laid, the Height thereof threescore Cubits, and
"the Breadth thereof threescore Cubits, with three Rows
"of great Stones, and a Row of new Timber; and let the
"Expences be given out of the King's House. And also let
"the golden and silver Vessels of the House of God, which
"*Nebuchadnezzar* took forth out of the Temple, which is
"at *Jerusalem*, and brought unto *Babylon*, be restored, and
"carried again unto the Temple which is at *Jerusalem*, every
"one to his Place, and place them in the House God."

By this Decree the God of *Israel* is declared to be the only and true God; and in pursuance of it, near fifty thousand Persons left the Province of *Babylon*, and went to *Jerusalem*; carrying with them no less than five thousand four hundred Vessels, which *Mithredath*, *Cyrus*'s Treasurer, stripped the Temple of the Pagan Gods in *Babylon* of, to adorn the Temple of the great God of Heaven and Earth at *Jerusalem*: Which Temple *Zerubbabel* set about in the second Month of the second Year after this Migration; several antient Men who had seen the Structure erected by *Solomon* having been then present; and *Daniel* having been then alive, and, perhaps, at *Susa*; where he is supposed to have died soon after.

Now if this Work commenced with the beginning of the Reign of King *Leil*, then *Bladud* must have ascended the *British* Throne in the Year 470 before the Birth of Christ; but if at the latter End of the Reign of King *Leil*, then his Inauguration was earlier by five and twenty Years: We may, however, circumscribe *Bladud*'s ascending the Throne with the Years 495, and 470; and suppose it to have happened between both, or about the Year 483 before our Lord and Saviour's Birth.

SACRED

Chap. II. A Description of BATH.

SACRED History informs us that the Foundation of the Temple was no sooner began, than the *Samaritans* began to obstruct the *Jews* in carrying on the Work; so that all that Zerubbabel was able to do in the Reign of *Cyrus*, and the beginning of that of his Son *Cambyses*, towards rebuilding that Structure, was only to compleat the Foundation; and while that was about the *Jews* made a great Progress in rebuilding the City of *Jerusalem*, as well as in setting up the Walls thereof: This was represented to *Cambyses* as a dangerous Proceeding to the State; and the King ordering the Work to be stopped, gave the *Samaritans* an Opportunity to stop the Work of the Temple also; nor did the *Jews* resume it for several Years after, on the Pretence that the time was not come that the House of God should be built.

FOR this Neglect God smote the Land with Barrenness, and restrained the Heavens from yielding Rain: Under which Calamity we find the Prophet *Haggai*, on the first Day of the first Month, in the second Year of the Reign of *Darius Hystaspes*, reproving the *Jews* for dwelling in ceiled Houses, while the House of God lay waste, and inciting them to proceed with the Building; which Zerubbabel resumed on the four and twentieth Day of the same Month, in the Year 519 before the Birth of Christ; and after that the Work was carried on with the greatest Rapidity, the Workmen, for Expedition, ROLLING the great STONES to the Building, instead of CARRYING them, as in the time of King *Solomon*; *Haggai* and *Zechariah*, by their Prophecies, encouraging them in it.

THESE Proceedings soon drew *Tatnai*, the King's Governor on that Side the River, to *Jerusalem*, to know by what Authority the *Jews* were building; and they having answered by a Decree of *Cyrus*, *Tatnai* forthwith wrote to *Darius* that the Records of the Empire might be examined, and the King's Pleasure sent him concerning the Matter: The Records were accordingly examined, *Cyrus*'s Decree was found, and *Darius*, as we read in the sixth Chapter of *Ezra*, sent *Tatnai* the following Answer to his Letter, as his final Decree.

" LET the Work of the House of God alone, let the
" Governor of the *Jews*, and the Elders of the *Jews* build
" it in it's Place: And to enable them to do so without the
" least Delay, let the Expences of the Work be forthwith
" given out of the King's Goods; even out of the Tribute
" beyond the River: And that which they have need of,
" both

"both young Bullocks and Rams, and Lambs, for the Burnt-Offerings of the God of Heaven; Wheat, Salt, Wine, and Oil, according to the Appointment of the Priests, which are at *Jerusalem*, let it be given them Day by Day without fail; that they may offer Sacrifices of sweet Savours unto the God of Heaven, and pray for the Life of the King, and of his Sons. Whosoever shall act contrary to these Directions, let Timber be pulled down from his House, and this being set up for a Gallows, let him be hanged thereon; and then let the House itself be made a Dunghill: And the God that hath caused his Name to dwell at *Jerusalem* destroy all Kings and People that shall put to their Hand, to alter and to destroy the House of God which is at *Jerusalem*: I *Darius* have made a Decree, let it be done with Speed."

TATNAI instantly performed every thing that *Darius* had ordered; the Work prospered; and the Temple was finished on the third Day of the twelfth Month, in the sixth Year of the King's Reign; and in the Year 515 before the Birth of Christ: But the *Samaritans*, soon after, growing remiss in furnishing the Supplies which *Darius* had ordered for the Sacrifices, the Senate and People of *Jerusalem* drew up a Complaint against them, and dispatched *Zerubbabel*, with four other eminent Persons, to the *Persian* Court with it: These Embassadors met with a favourable Reception; and, as *Josephus* informs us, l. 9. c. 4. the King immediately redressed the Grievances complained of.

THE four Persons who thus accompanied *Zerubbabel* seem to have been introduced into the *British* History, under the Character of Prophets; and by the Names of *Haggai*, *Amos*, *Joel* and *Azariah*: *Josephus* has given us the Names of no more than two of those Embassadors, *Ananias*, and *Mardochæus*; these were probably the *Amos* and *Joel*, or the Persons meant by those Names in the *British* History; and the *Azariah* mentioned in the same Book was undoubtedly one of those Elders to whom *Nehemiah* tells us the Care of re-instating the *Jews*, and rebuilding the Temple, was committed.

THE *British* History makes *Hudibras* to have lived till *Haggai* prophesied; so that if this Prophet began to prophesy at the beginning of the Reign of *Lud-Hudibras*, then *Bladud* became King of *Britain* in the Year 480 before the Birth of Christ, but if at the latter End of his Reign, then *Bladud's* Government began nine and thirty Years earlier.

THUS

Chap. II. A Description of BATH.

THUS the Time of *Bladud*'s Inauguration may be again circumscribed with the Years 519, and 480; which leads me to propose it as a PROBLEM, at least, that it really fell in the Year 483 before our Lord and Saviour's Birth as above; since this Æra fixes the Coronation of his Father in the eighth Year of the Reign of *Cambyses*; the time of *Haggai*'s prophesying in the third Year of the Reign of *Lud-Hudibras*; and the beginning of the Temple of *Jerusalem* in the twelfth Year of the Reign of King *Leil*.

THE Æra thus proposed can't be advanced above three Years to preserve the historical Fact of *Bladud*'s Father having been Cotemporary with the Prophet *Haggai*; nor can it be lower'd above thirteen Years to preserve the other Fact in the *British* History, which makes the City of *Kaërleil* and the Temple of *Jerusalem* to have been Works of the same Antiquity, and both to have been begun in the Reign of the King's Grandfather: *Bladud*'s Inauguration must therefore have fallen between the Years 486 and 470 before the Birth of Christ; and most probably in the Year 483, as above.

THIS Æra fixes the Time of *Bladud*'s Journey to *Greece*, and carries it up to about the Year 506 before our Lord's Nativity, since there were seven and twenty Years between his Discovery of the Hot Waters of *Bath*, and his building the City; which we cannot suppose him to have compleated till three or four Years were expired from his coming to the Throne: Nor can it be supposed that he went to *Greece* the Moment he discovered the Hot Springs.

I will therefore propose it as an Addition to my PROBLEM, that *Bladud* began his Works round those Springs in the very Year that he ascended the Throne, though it lowers the ANTIQUITY of the CITY almost four hundred Years from what Chronologers make it; and from what the Inhabitants have always asserted in their publick Inscriptions concerning the Origin of the Baths, as well as of the City denominated from them.

BY this Æra the first Landing of *Brute*, on the *Britannick* Island, falls in the Year 708 before the Incarnation of Christ, and three Years after *Romulus* was torn in Pieces, by the *Roman* Senators, for his tyrannical Proceedings after the Death of his Grandfather *Numitor*, the last of the *Trojan* Race of Kings that governed *Italy*: And by the same Æra the Expulsion of the *Tarquins*, and thereby the Destruction of the *Roman* Monarchy, preceded *Bladud*'s Journey to *Greece*

about

about three Years; and happened in or about the fourteenth Year of the Reign of *Lud-Hudibras.*

The *British* Prince seems to have acted the Part of a Prophet full thirteen Years before he took that Journey; but whether he began to keep perpetual Fires in the Temple of *Minerva* before he went to *Greece*, or after his Return from thence, is uncertain: However it may very justly remain a Question, whether the Fires that were kept constantly burning in the Temples of the Antients, were of British or Persian Institution?

While the Work of the Temple of *Jerusalem* lay neglected, God smote the Land of *Canaan* with Barrenness, and restrained the Heavens from yielding Rain. This Calamity seems to have ended when *Zerubbabel* resumed the Work; and it was undoubtedly the Drought mentioned by the Author of the *British* History to have been brought upon the Earth by the Prayer of the Prophet *Elias*, about the Time that *Bladud* began to keep perpetual Fires in the Temple of *Minerva*; since the *Persian* Magi made an *Elias* to have flourished in the Age wherein the *British* Prince commenced a Prophet; and affirmed that *Zoroaster* was a Disciple to that very *Elias.*

Thus the Temple mentioned in the *British* History does not appear by any one Circumstance to be that which was erected by King *Solomon*; but, on the contrary, every thing unites to prove it to have been that which was built by *Zerubbabel*; and thereby to lower the Antiquity of Bath to about the Year 483 before the Birth of Christ, as above.

CHAP. III.

Of the Reality and Eminence of King Bladud, the first Founder of Bath.

THAT Part of *Britain* which produced the Metal called by the *Latins Plumbum Candidum*, by the *Greeks Cassiteron*, and explained by *Pliny* in the sixteenth Chapter of his thirty-fourth Book, to have been white bright Lead or Tin, was industriously concealed by the first Traders to it; for by their representing it sometimes as an Island of itself, sometimes as Islands under various Names, they so obscured it's Situation, that *Herodotus* knew nothing of it, under its Name of *Cassiterides*, as he himself most expressly declares in his
third

Chap. III. A Description of BATH.

third Book, after telling us that the Western Bounds of *Europe*, with the Sea beyond them, were so little known in his Time, that he was incapable of relating any thing with certainty touching the one or the other.

EVEN in *Cæsar*'s Days the Trade in the *British* Tin was carried on with all the obscurity that was possible; the *Britons*, as *Diodorus Siculus* informs us in the second Chapter of his fifth Book, sending their square Dyes of that Metal from the Inland Part of the Promontory of *Belerium* to the Sea Shore, and conveying them in Carts at low Water to the Isle of *Ictis*, supposed by Mr. *Camden* to be the *Vecta* of *Suetonius*, or the *Isle of Wight*, there sold them to the Merchants; who transporting them to *Gaul*, and, for thirty Days Journey, carrying them in Packs upon Horses Backs through the Body of that Country to the Mouth of the *Rhosne*, there embarked them for *Greece* and other Nations joining on to the *Mediterranean* Sea.

BY the general Mart thus held in the Isle of *Ictis*, *Britain* was rendered so very obscure to the Foreigners that traded to it, that when *Cæsar*, previous to his first Expedition, summoned a Council of Merchants from all Parts to give him an Account of the Island, they could inform him of nothing more than a small Part of the Southern Coast: Nor did *Cæsar* himself, after his second Expedition, get any certain Intelligence of the White Lead Mines; since he declares that it was the Midland Countries of the Island that produced the Tin.

THE important Uses of this Metal rendered it highly valuable to the Antients; for by what *Pliny* writes in the seventeenth Chapter of his thirty fourth Book, it appears that they applied it to their Brazen Vessels to preserve them from Rust; to render them sweet; and to make them look like Silver: With the same Metal they made their Mirrours; washed the Harness and other Furniture for their Horses; and garnished their Chariots and other Carriages: And by mixing Tin with common Lead they formed the compound Metals, called Argentine, Tersiarium, and Argentarium, wherewith they sodered their Conduit Pipes, and made such Vessels as were proper for the Kitchen; setting a Price upon those Vessels of more than five times the Value of the Metal contained in them.

THE great Estimation which the Antients had for Tin is carried up, by *Pliny*, so high as the *Trojan* War; and therefore an Expedition undertaken, a few Generations after that

War, to discover the Mines from whence so valuable a Metal was taken, must make the Story of *Brute*, with his Colony of *Trojans*, and, in consequence thereof, the REALITY of King BLADUD, as evident as any Fact in History dependant upon probable Circumstances, if the Name of that Prince had not been attended with any thing besides the Time of his Reign: But as it is accompanied with many remarkable Circumstances, that alone must destroy our Ideas of Fable, and make us conclude his History to have Truth for its Foundation; such as rendered *Britain* an Island renowned in the *Greek* and *Roman* Records long before *Pliny* wrote his Natural History, as he, in the sixteenth Chapter of his fourth Book, declares it to have been.

THAT Part of *Britain* which was the Source of her Fame, and disguised by the first Traders to it, does not seem to have been known, even to our great *Roman* Researcher into the Curiosities of the World; the *British* Island producing White Lead, or Tin, bearing the Name of *Mictis* in his History; and he, after placing it six Days Sail from *Britain*, assuring us that the *Britons* sailed thither in Winter Vessels covered with Leather.

"LEAD, according to the same Author, was of two
" Kinds, White and Black; the latter, says he, abounds
" in *Britain*: But the former was supposed to be fetched
" from the Islands of the Sea that bounded the Western
" Shores of the Continent of *Europe* and *Africa*; the In-
" habitants of those Islands, as it was commonly reported,
" conveying it in little Twiggen Boats, covered all over with
" Feathers."

DIODORUS SICULUS, writing before *Pliny*, gave the Name of *Belerium* to the Western Promontory of *Britain* producing Tin; and while one Part of the Inhabitants was described by *Solinus* under the Name of *Dunmonii*, *Ptolomey* distinguished the other by the Title of *Danmonii*; the first implying Miners of the Hills, or Lode-Works, and the second Miners of the Vales, or Stream-Works.

HERODOTUS, a much older Historian than *Diodorus Siculus*, calls the Islands that produced the White Lead in his Time *Cassiterides*; telling us they were so named from the Tin imported from thence to *Greece*; and the Prophet *Ezekiel*, writing before him, gives the Name of *Tarshish* to the Country from whence the *Tyrians* fetched the same Metal; probably from the hard Marble Rocks penetrated and examined for

the

the Ore, after the profoundeft Meditation; fince this is the import of the *Hebrew* Name.

THE *Tarſhiſh* of *Ezekiel*, and the other Penmen of Sacred Hiſtory; the *Caſſiterides* of *Herodotus*; the *Belerium* of *Diodorus Siculus*; and the *Miɛ́tis* of *Pliny*, being duly confidered, muft appear to have been one and the fame Part of *Britain*: And the Metal it produced feems to have been of fuch vaft Importance to the Inhabitants, as to have caufed the firſt Traders for it to pronounce them a bleſſed and happy People; and to have repreſented them as a People inhabiting a remote Ifland fituate beyond the Breezes of the North Wind: For what the Antients called the *Hyperborean* Ifland, could be none other than the Weſtern Promontory of *Britain* extending from the Eaſt end of the Ifle, or rather Peninfula, of *Purbeck*, to the Lands End in *Cornwall*, on one Side; and from the Mouth of the River *Severn* to the fame extreme Part of *Cornwall*, on the other; as the Situation of both, delivered down to us by the antient Hiſtorians, will clearly teſtify.

THE *Hyperboreans*, according to *Hecateus* and other antient Writers referred to by *Diodorus Siculus*, l. 2. c. 3. " Inhabit an Ifland as big as *Sicily* lying in the Ocean overagainſt " *Gaul*, and under the *Arɛ́tick* Pole:" And in like Manner our *Sicilian* Author tells us, l. 5. c. 2. " That *Britain*, as " well as the greateſt Part of *Gaul*, lies under the *Arɛ́tick* " Pole; that the former faces the Shore of the latter; and " that it is the largeſt of many Iflands in the Ocean fronting " *Gaul*."

Now the Length of the Weſtern Promontory of *Britain*, being compared with the Dimenfions which *Diodorus* gives us, l. 5. c. 1. of the Ifle of *Sicily*, it will appear that the former fhoots out as far Weſtward into the *Atlantick* Ocean, as the latter fhoots Weſtward into the *Mediterranean* Sea: And therefore as the Situation and Extent of the *Hyperborean* Ifland and the Promontory of *Belerium* is the very fame, they muſt inevitably appear to have been one and the fame Country.

FROM this Promontory of the *Britannick* Ifland, by its Name of *Caſſiteris*, *Midacritus* is recorded by *Pliny* to have been the firſt Man that brought Lead: And *Bochart* obferving that *Midacritus* is a *Greek* Name corruptly written for *Melcartus*, fignifying the King of the City, that is, faith he, of the City of *Tyre*, we may fairly afcend the Trade between the *Tyrians* and *Britons* as high as the firſt King of *Tyre*;

and, with the higheſt Probability, ſuppoſe the *Midianites* to have been furniſhed from the Weſtern part of our Iſland with the Bedil, or Tin, and the Ophereth, or Lead, that fell a Prey to the *Iſraelites* when *Moſes* defeated them, about the Year 1452 before the Birth of Chriſt; and that the *Phœnicians* giving the Name of *Barat-anac*, or *Bratanac*, to the Region of Country which produced the Metals, the ſame was, in ſucceſſion of Time, extended ſo as to become the Name of the whole Iſland, although, as Mr. *Sammes* remarks in the fifth Chapter of his *Britannia*, corrupted and diſtorted by the ſeveral Dialects it ran through.

Our Hiſtories give us a Race of *Celtick* Kings, that began a Monarchy in the Iſland 883 Years before the Acceſſion of *Phranicus* to the Crown; a Prince who, after a ſhort Reign, abdicated the Government, and retired to the Continent juſt before the Arrival of *Brute* at the Shore of *Totneſs* in the Year 708 before our Lord's Nativity; and conſequently the Inauguration of the firſt *Celtick* King of the Iſland was antecedent to the Defeat of the *Midianites*, and preceded it by one hundred and fifty Years, or thereabouts.

That *Tarſhiſh* was governed by the moſt renowned Kings of the Earth, ſo early as the Infancy of the *Jewiſh* Monarchy, ſeems ſufficiently evident from what King *David* writes in the ſeventy ſecond Pſalm; and that the *Jews* and *Tyrians*, in the Time of King *Solomon*, carried on a great Trade between the Head of the *Mediterranean* Sea and *Tarſhiſh* Weſtward; and between the Head of the *Red* Sea and *Ophir* Eaſtward, is ſtill more evident from what the Authors of the Books bearing the Titles of *Kings* and *Chronicles* have therein declared.

Every Eaſtern Voyage was performed in one Year, but every Weſtern Voyage took up three Years time; ſo that the Intercourſe between *Tarſhiſh* and *Ophir* required a Period of four Years; and *Pliny* telling us in the fourth Chapter of his ſixteenth Book, that the *Indians* having no Lead of their own took that Kind of Metal from Merchants in Exchange for their Pearls and precious Stones, is a Demonſtration that a Trade was carried on, from the remoteſt Ages, between *Britain* and *India*; and therefore, the further we ſearch into the dark Period of our Hiſtory, the more Truths we ſhall diſcover towards giving the higheſt Probability not only to the Race of *Trojan* Kings, but that of the *Celtick* Monarchs that governed *Britain*.

The

Chap. III. A Description of BATH.

THE joint Trade between the *Jews* and *Tyrians* seems to have fallen entirely into the Hands of the latter soon after the Death of *Solomon*; and those People seem then to have disguised the Situation of *Tarshish*, not only by bounding the World at the Straights of *Gibraltar*, to discourage Mariners from venturing into the *Atlantick* Sea; but by transporting the Tin from *Tarshish* to the Northern Shore of *Gaul*, and then conveying it over the Body of that Country to its Southern Shore, before they embarked it for the Ports of the *Mediterranean* Sea.

WE have the Testimony of *Isaiah* still on Record to convince us that the *Jews* understood *Tarshish* to be an Island; and the Trade with that Island having been of such vast Importance, and of such long Continuance, who would not have disguised it to the very utmost of their Power? And what Colony of People that wanted a Place of Settlement would not have gone through the greatest Perils to possess themselves of the Source of so much Wealth? The Object of *Brute*'s Views lay beyond the *Gallick* Bounds; and we find, by the *British* History, that neither Pirates nor Sea Monsters were any Obstruction to him in searching for it in the vast Ocean beyond the Limits which *Hercules* himself had given to the World, by the erection of his famous Pillars at the Mouth of the Sea that divides the Southern Coasts of *Europe*, from the Northern Coasts of *Africa*.

NOW as the great Transactions of the Eastern World, even so early as the Reign of King *Solomon*, could reach *Britain* within the Compass of two Years, nothing is more probable than that the News of *Cyrus*'s Decree for rebuilding the Temple of *Jerusalem*, with the Migration of the *Jews* from the Province of *Babylon*, was soon brought into the Island; and that those great Events were the real Causes of the Civil Dissention that broke out in the Kingdom towards the latter End of the Reign of King *Leil*: For the Minds of the *Britons* must have been vastly shocked to hear that the Gods of an Empire in the East, grown the greatest of the World, were stripped of their Divinity, and their Priests slain, in favour of the God of a captive set of People; and that God declared to be the only and true God in opposition to all others.

BUT when *Cambyses* killed the God *Apis* of the *Egyptians*, burnt all the Temples in that Kingdom, and drove the Priests to seek Refuge in all Corners of the Earth in the Year 526

before

before the Birth of Christ, and in the one and twentieth Year of the Reign of King *Leil*, the News of this reaching *Britain* also, must have brought the Discontent among the People into a Civil Dissention: And it was in this State of Disorder that a Prophet rose up in the Island, and predicted a great Change that would happen in the Government of it.

THIS Prophet we may very justly suppose to have been the Son of *Lud-Hudibras*, since he had a Name, implying an Eagle, given to him, no doubt from his transforming himself into the Shape of a Bird, as *Jupiter* himself is feigned to have done; and his other Name of *Bladud*, or a Name of the like import, might have arisen from his early Knowledge of the Motion of the Stars, signified by the Word *Blas*, and from his appearing as a meer Dudman while he was decked with Feathers to enable him to fly in the Air, as it is reported of *Dædalus*, and his Son *Icarus*; from whose last Flight the *Icarian* Sea received its Name: For the young Man's Wings failing him, on his soaring too near the Sun, *Icarus*, as *Diodorus Siculus* tells the Story, fell down into that Sea, and perished in the Water, which from thence forward bore his Name.

FROM the Names given to the *British* Prophet, and from the former especially, it seems reasonable to conclude that he began his Office with the outside Shew of Miracle, to enforce a Belief into the People of the Truth of his Predictions; and the better to qualify himself in the Arts and Sciences conducive to his Design of imposing upon the Understanding of Mankind, and the better to enable him to draw them into a new System of Religion, we find him not only taking a Journey to the South Eastern Part of *Europe*; but, as the Author of *The Bathes of the Bathes Ayde* informs us, spending eleven Years in his Studies abroad before he returned home.

THIS Journey falls in with the Age wherein *Zoroaster* flourished in *Persia*; wherein *Pythagoras* became eminent in *Greece* and in *Italy*; wherein *Zamolxis*, a Servant to the latter, turned Legislator in *Thrace*; and wherein a learned Sage from the *Hyperborean* Island became a Disciple, a Collegue, and even the Master of the *Samian* Philosopher himself.

TO this Northern Sage the *Grecians* gave the Names of AITHROBATES, and ABARIS; and *Eusebius* places his Journey to *Greece* in the fifty fourth Olympiad, or about the Year 560 before the Birth of Christ: *Suidas* declares ABARIS to have been the Master of *Pythagoras* before the *Samian* Philosopher went into *Egypt* in Pursuance of the last Advice of his other

Master

Master *Thales*, the *Milesian*, whose Death is placed in the Year 548 before our Lord's Nativity: But the Truth of these Things, in Point of Chronology, seems to have been best handed down to us by *Jamblicus* and *Porphyry*, those Writers telling us that the two Philosophers communicated their Knowledge to each other a little before the Death of *Phalaris*, which, according to *Dodwell*, happened in the last Year of the sixty eighth Olympiad, answering the Year 505 before the Birth of our Lord and Saviour Christ.

Now from the Identity of the *Hyperborean* Island of the Antients, and the *British* Promontory of *Belerium*; and from the perfect Agreement in respect to the Time wherein BLADUD and ABARIS lived, and took their Journey to *Greece*, the *British* Sage and *Hyperborean* Philosopher must have been one and the same Man. And therefore upon this Identity of Men and Country, I will rest the REALITY of King BLADUD; whose Existence was formerly so undoubted that Doctor *Jones*, when he wrote his *Bathes of Bathes Ayde*, found himself able to trace the Genealogy of several of our *British* Nobility up to him; " Howsoever the Injuries of Time, says the Doctor " in the Dedication of his Book to *Henry* Earl of *Pembroke*, " had then altered and obscured the same."

THE EMINENCE of King BLADUD will hereafter shine the more stronger by a short account of what chiefly relates to his Cotemporary Philosophers; one of which, the great *Pythagoras*, having been a Scholar of *Thales*, and travelling into *Egypt* for the Improvement of his Knowledge, was there received by the *Egyptian* Priests; among whom, as the Writers of his Life tell us, he continued no less than two and twenty Years; after which they acquaint us with his having spent twelve Years at *Babylon* under *Zoroaster*, perhaps at that Time Arch-Chaldean of the City, and Successor of the Prophet *Daniel* in that High Office: For *Zoroaster* seems to have been a Priest of one of the Orders which the *Chaldeans* were divided into during the Lifetime of *Daniel*, and in consequence thereof must have been a Disciple of the *Jewish* Prophet, as Doctor *Hyde* and others conjecture.

This learned Man having found by the sacred Writings of the *Jews*, and the Conversation of his Master, *Daniel*, that a great Prophet, described by *Baalim* under the Image of a Star, was to rise out of *Jacob*, pretended, after the Death of *Daniel*, to be that very Prophet; from thence the *Grecians* gave him the Name of *Zoroaster*, or the living Star; and all

his

his Studies tended, after the Destruction of *Bel*, and his College of seventy Priests, to the forming of a new System of Religion for the new *Persian* Empire.

It seems therefore to have been by the Means of *Zoroaster* that the disregard which *Cyrus* shewed to the Gods of the Pagan World, so increased with his Son *Cambyses*, as to cause this Monarch, when he invaded *Egypt* in the fourth Year of his Reign, to commit his sacrilegious Outrages in that Country, as above.

Pythagoras falling among the Captives taken by *Cambyses* in *Egypt*, was from thence sent Prisoner to *Babylon*; and his Captivity in that City was soon succeeded by a Fraud and Imposture in the *Persian* Empire which proved fatal to the Priests, and brought the Religion of the *Medes* and *Persians* into the highest Contempt: For *Herodotus* informs us in his third Book that *Cambyses* having appointed *Patizithes*, a *Median*, and one of the chief of the Sect in the East that worshiped God by Fire, Governor of his Houshold during his Absence on the *Egyptian* Expedition; this Man, on the Death of the King's Brother, usurped the Throne in favour of his own Brother *Smerdis*, another chief Priest of the Fire Worshipers, who, by personating the Deceased *Smerdis*, the Brother of *Cambyses*, held the Scepter of the *Persian* Empire during the first seven Months after the Death of the King before the Cheat was discovered: But no sooner was the Impostor detected than the Usurpers, and most of their Sect, were slain for their Imposition and Presumption; the rest had the contemptuous Name of *Mages*, or the *Cropt-Ear'd*, given them, from *Smerdis*, who had his Ears cut off in the Reign of *Cyrus*, for a Crime that deserved it; and the Religion of the whole Sect taking the Name of *Magianism*, was, from thence forward, held in the highest Disdain; *Darius Hystaspes*, on his Ascending the Throne, together with his whole Court, embracing Sabianism, or the Worship of God by Images; and none but the common People remaining prone to their old Religion of Magianism.

This Division gave *Zoroaster* an Opportunity of introducing into the World his own Impostures; for upon the Plan of Magianism he taught Doctrines which he pretended to have received from the Mouth of God, and performed it so effectually, that in a few Years his Tenets were established in *Media*; they were next received in *Bactria*; and then they were embraced at *Susa*, the Capital of all *Persia*; whereby by the greatest Empire of the World received, in its infant State, a new Religion; the Teachers of which still went under the Name of *Mages*, or *Magi*; and *Zoroaster* became the Archimagus, or chief of the whole Sect, with a Sovereignty in spiritual Matters equal to that of the King in temporal Affairs; and this he enjoyed from the Time that *Darius* and his Court embraced his Tenets till the last Year of that Monarch's Reign, when our Archimagus and his whole College of eighty Priests were killed by *Argasp*, King of the *Oriental Scythians*, for endeavouring to bring him into his System of Religion: A System which taught the Invocation of malevolent as well as benevolent Divinities; and to produce in Nature things seemingly above the power of Man, by the Assistance of the Gods, upon using certain Words and Ceremonies.

THE latter Part of this System was the whole Art of Magick, the Invention of which, says *Pliny*, l. 30. c. 1. was, by the unanimous Consent of most Writers, ascribed to *Zoroaster*, or, as our Author further observes, taught him by one whose Name was *Azonaces*: " It took its Rise by Physick, " under pretence of preserving Health and curing Diseases; " this was soon cloaked with Religion; and then to Medi- " cinal Receipts and religious Ceremonies the Skill of Astro- " logy was added to compleat the System, and bind the " Senses of Mankind with three of the surest Chains that " were ever contrived or invented."

NOTHING is more probable than that *Pythagoras* and his Master *Zoroaster* left *Babylon* at the same time, a Year or two after *Darius* had retaken it in the Year 515 before the Birth of Christ; the one to reform the Religion of the Eastern, the other that of the Western World: For *Pythagoras* holding the Magical Art of *Zoroaster* as a Divine Mystery, he highly praised it, and published it abroad to the utmost Bounds of the whole Earth, as *Pliny* most expressly writes.

WHILE these great Men were thus employ'd, ABARIS, or BLADUD, appears, by the Testimony of *Jamblicus* and *Porphyry*, to have been received in *Greece* as the known Priest of *Apollo*; a God whose chief Quality was Divination; whose Musick was the Harmony of the Spheres; and to whom the *Britons*, or *Hyperboreans* paid the highest Honours, as *Diodorus Siculus*, in speaking of the *Hyperborean* Island, informs us.

" THIS Island, according to that Historian, was the Birth " Place of *Latona*; and therefore, says our Author, the In-
" habitants

"habitants worship *Apollo* above all other Gods, ascribing "to him the highest Honours, daily saying Songs in his Praise, "and demeaning themselves as if they were his Priests. Here "*Apollo* has a stately Grove, with a renowned Temple, of "a round Form, beautified with many rich Gifts; and to "this God there is a City consecrated, whose Citizens are "most of them Harpers; and these playing upon the Harp, "chant sacred Hymns to *Apollo* in the Temple, setting forth "his glorious Acts."

"THESE *Hyperboreans* have had, of long and antient "Time, a particular Kindness for the *Grecians*, and more "especially for the *Athenians*, and the Inhabitants of *Delos*. "Some of the *Grecians* passed over to the *Hyperboreans*, "whose Temples they enriched with divers Presents, offered "to their Gods, and inscribed with *Greek* Characters; and, "on the other Hand, ABARIS formerly travelled thence into "*Greece*, and renewed the Antient League of Friendship "with the *Delians*."

"THE Moon in this Island seems as if it was near to the "Earth, and *Apollo* comes into it once in nineteen Years; "at which time he Plays upon the Harp, and Sings and "Dances all the Night from the Vernal Equinox to the "rising of the *Pleiades*. In this Period of nineteen Years "the Stars perform their Courses, and return to the same "Point; and therefore the *Greeks* call the Revolution of "nineteen Years, the Great Year."

THUS far *Diodorus Siculus* from *Hecateus* and other more antient Writers; to which he adds, "That the Sovereignty "of the City in the *Hyperborean* Island consecrated to *Apollo*, "and the Care of his Temple belonged to the Family of the "*Boreades*, who held the Principality by Descent, in a direct "Line from *Boreas* their common Ancestor."

THE Temple mentioned by our *Sicilian* Author, or some other antient Temple in the *Hyperborean* Island was, according to *Eratosthenes*, a wing'd Structure; that is a Temple composed of Pillars, or surrounded with such Ornaments, or with Porticoes composed of them: The City consecrated to *Apollo* must have been that which was built by King *Bladud*; as *Bath*, and a Temple in it, bore the Name of the Sun in the Times of Paganism: And the stately Grove of the same God was either the Grove now remaining near the hot Springs; or the Forest of *Kings Wood* lying Westward of them, as will be hereafter more particularly shewn.

THE

Chap. III. A Description of BATH.

The *Apollo* thus adored by the *Hyperboreans* having been the Son of *Latona*, and Brother of *Diana*, the God chose to hide the famous Arrow with which he slew the *Cyclops* in his Mother's native Country, rather than in the Island of *Delos*, his own; and to take upon him the Sirname of *Hyperborean* preferable to any other.

Mounted upon this sacred Arrow, Abaris, the Priest of the *Hyperborean* God, was reported, by the *Grecians*, to have flown in the Air over Rivers and Lakes, Forests and Mountains; from whence they called him Aithrobates, *i. e.* a Rider on the Winds: And in one of his Flights they pretended that he wafted himself from the *Hyperborean* Island to *Greece*, and therefore from that Flight they gave him the Name of Abaris, importing a Man that could cross the Seas without the help of a Ship.

With the same Arrow Abaris was enabled to go through all Parts of the World without eating, as *Herodotus* expresses it in his fourth Book; and after our famous Priest had visited every Part of *Greece*, built Temples in that Country, and there uttered those Oracles which *Apollonius* declared to have been still extant at the Time of his writing, he passed to *Crotona* in *Italy*, and, as *Jamblicus* informs us, presented the great *Pythagoras* with his sacred Arrow, the Possession of which gave the *Samian* Philosopher such a Spirit for Prognostication, that his Answers were looked upon to be as certain as those of *Apollo Pythius*; and therefore after the *Crotoniates* had, by his Advice, protected the five hundred chief Citizens of *Sybaris* that fled for Sanctuary to the Altars in the Forum of *Crotona*, and with one hundred thousand Men, headed by *Milo*, had defeated thrice the Number of *Sybarites*, they gave him the Name of *Pythagoras*, from the Sirname of the *Delphick Apollo*, and even believed him to be the *Hyperborean* God himself.

Among the Temples built by Abaris in *Greece* that of *Delphos*, or rather the Adytum of it, seems to have been the most eminent Work: For this famous Structure, enriched by *Crœsus* with inestimable Presents, having been burnt, by some unknown Accident, in the very Year that *Cyrus* vanquished the *Lydian* King; and the Amphyctions, or general Council of *Greece*, having assessed the *Delphians* with such a Sum towards rebuilding it, as drove them to the Necessity of Begging as far as the Court of *Amasis*, King of *Egypt*, and of recalling Exiles in Consideration of their Contributing towards

wards the Sum levied on them; the Temple, by these means, lay a considerable Time in its Ruins: And though *Spintharus*, an Architect of *Corinth*, rebuilt some of its Walls, yet the Adytum was not restored till BLADUD, or ABARIS, appeared in *Greece*, and circumscribed the oracular Cave of the *Pythian* God with a Row of Pillars that formed the Octostyle Monopterick Temple, fabled by the *Grecians* to have been erected by PTERAS with Wax and the Wings of the Bees *Apollo* had brought from the *Hyperborean* Regions.

THIS Monopterick Structure was soon adorned with a Present of immense Value, for the great Orator and Rhetorician, *Gorgias Leontinus*, having been desirous of immortalizing his Name, he first caused a solid Statue of pure Gold to be made of himself, and then set it up in the Temple about the seventieth Olympiad, answering the Year 497 before the Birth of Christ; *Pliny*, in the fourth Chapter of his three and thirtieth Book, making this Remark on the Image, that it demonstrated the prodigious Wealth accruing by teaching People in those Days the Art of speaking Well and Eloquently.

THIS Historian declaring that a Man would think the *Persians* first learned all their Magick of the *Britons*; and, at the same time, informing us that *Zoroaster*, the reputed Author of the Art, had one *Azonaces* for his Master, is it not highly reasonable to think that ABARIS, by some Means or other, communicated his knowledge in the Magical Art to the *Persian* Philosopher? Was not the Intercourse between *Persia* and the Western World free and open enough in the Age wherein *Zoroaster* and ABARIS, or BLADUD flourished, for one Philosopher to communicate what he knew to the other? And does not *Herodotus* tell us that the sacred Arrow of *Apollo* carried ABARIS, without eating, through all Parts of the World, and consequently reached *Zoroaster* by the Means of *Azonaces*?

THE Intercourse being granted, and the System of the Planetary World, which places the Sun in the Center of the Heavenly Bodies, and makes the rest revolve about it, appearing from *Diodorus Siculus* to have been so well understood in *Britain* as to have drawn *Apollo* himself into the Island to celebrate the Manifestation of the Discoveries by that System, makes it much more than probable that ABARIS communicated it to *Zoroaster* while he lived at *Babylon*; for the *Persian* Philosopher, and his Disciple, *Pythagoras*, after
leaving

Chap. III. A Description of BATH.

leaving that City, respectively retired to their Caves to study the glorious System; the first retiring to a Cave at *Xiz*, in *Media*, and therein representing it; and the second retiring to a Cave, in *Samos*, and doing the same.

THIS System was undoubtedly Part of the Knowledge concealed with the *Hyperboreans* under the Name of the Arrow of *Apollo*; and ABARIS presenting *Pythagoras* with that Arrow makes it highly probable that the *Samian* Philosopher was thereby perfected in his Studies touching the Planetary World; the System whereof he promulged in *Greece* and in *Italy*: But whether it took the Title of the *Pythagorean* System of the Planetary World from him, or from the Sirname of the *Pythian* God, is a Point which I shall now leave for further Examination.

THE Arrow which thus rendered ABARIS famous, and raised *Pythagoras* to the State of a God, was at last introduced into the Heavens as a Northern Constellation; and as the very next Constellation to it appears under the Figure of an Eagle, is it not highly probable that it was so represented in Honour of ABARIS himself? Who, by being one and the same Person with BLADUD, was consequently the *Aquila* mentioned in *Jeffrey* of *Monmouth*'s Translation of the *British* History, and so named from the Wings he made to fly with, and the Feathers with which he decked himself on those Occasions.

THUS by concurring Circumstances from Heaven and Earth, ABARIS and BLADUD appears to have been one and the same Man; for what Circumstance can amount to a stronger Proof of their Identity than the Art of Flying, and the Gift of Prophecy annexed to the Accounts of both? Besides the former is allowed to have been a Disciple of *Pythagoras*, and the latter appears manifestly to have been the same, since he was Cotemporary with the *Samian* Philosopher, went into *Greece* just after *Pythagoras* returned to *Samos* from *Persia*, followed him to *Crotona*, and compleated his eleven Years Absence from *Britain* in the very Year that *Pythagoras*, according to Dean *Prideaux*'s Chronology, was assaulted and slain in *Milo*'s House by the Hand of *Cylon*, one of his Scholars; and in the very Year that the *Samians* abandoned their native Country, fled to *Sicily*, and, as *Herodotus* writes in his sixth Book, seized on the City of *Zancle* for a new Place of Abode.

THE Person and Character of our *British* Philosopher, when he first appeared at *Athens*, may be conceived from what

the

the Orator *Himerius* writes of him, under the Name of ABARIS, in Words to the following Effect.

"THEY relate, says *Himerius*, that ABARIS the Sage, by Nation a *Hyperborean*, became a *Grecian* in Speech, and was a *Scythian* in his Habit and Appearance. Whenever he moved his Tongue, you would imagine him to be some one out of the midst of the Academy or very Lyceum. ABARIS came to *Athens* holding a Bow, having a Quiver hanging from his Shoulders, his Body wrapt up in a Chlamys, girt about his Loins with a gilded Belt, and wearing Trowzers reaching from his Waste to the Soles of his Feet. He was affable and pleasant in Conversation, in dispatching great Affairs secret and industrious, quick-sighted in present Exigencies, in preventing future Dangers circumspect, a Searcher after Wisdom, desirous of Friendship, trusting indeed little to Fortune, and having every thing trusted to him for his Prudence."

THIS great Philosopher had not long compleated the *Delphick* Temple before *Zoroaster* began to cover the Pyræia, or Pyrethus of the *Persians* to keep the Fires in them from being extinguished by the Inclemencies of the Weather; and this seems to have induced the *Grecians* to cover the Temple of the *Pythian* God at *Delphi*; which, as *Vitruvius* writes in the Preface to his seventh Book, had a Tholus, or spherical Roof, put on it by *Theodorus*, a famous *Phocean* Architect.

ABOUT five Years after the Time assigned for BLADUD's going into *Greece*, the *Ionians* in *Asia* revolted from the *Persians*, and those People having been joined by the *Athenians*, the confederate Army, in the Year 500 before the Birth of Christ, marched to *Sardis*, and burnt it, together with the Temple of *Cybele*; in Revenge for which *Darius* made a Vow, that he would burn all the Temples in *Greece*, which he in a great Measure did, before he died in the Year 486 before our Lord's Nativity; and the rest were, for the most Part, destroyed by *Xerxes* his Successor; who, after he had burnt *Athens*, set Fire to the Temple of *Babylon*, and, in short, burnt and destroyed all other Temples where Sabianism in the least prevailed: For the King was attended in his Expedition against *Greece*, by the *Magian* Priests, with *Osthanes* their High Priest; and these not only stirred up *Xerxes* to destroy all the Temples, wherever they went, that belonged to any Sect, save their own; but *Osthanes* himself endeavoured to bring every Body over to the *Magian* Religion; and for
that

that End was the firſt Perſon who, in the Opinion of *Pliny*, wrote upon the Excellency of Magick.

IN the midſt of this Deſtruction the *Delphick* Temple miraculouſly eſcaped, with all its Treaſures, notwithſtanding Part of the *Perſian* Army advanced within Sight of that Edifice with the King's Order to plunder it: For *Herodotus* informs us, that the City of *Delphi* having, upon the Approach of the *Perſians*, been deſerted by all its Inhabitants except ſixty Men, and the Prophet ACERATUS who preſided at the Temple; and that moſt of the *Delphians* flying to the Mountain *Parnaſſus*, the two Heads of that Hill immediately after broke from the Mountain with a prodigious Noiſe, and rolling down upon the *Perſians* killed many of them: And this, with ſeveral Prodigies that happened at the ſame time, ſo terrified the Army, that, as our Author concludes, they abandoned their Enterprize, and, betaking themſelves to Flight, ran into *Bœotia*, where they reported that they had been purſued, with a dreadful Slaughter, by two Perſons compleately armed, and of more than human Stature.

THE *Perſian* War with the *Grecians* ſeems to have been the Cauſe of *Pythagoras*'s leaving *Samos*, and BLADUD's following him to *Crotona* in his Way to *Britain*; and the additional Knowledge which the latter muſt have acquired abroad, during his eleven Years Abſence, enabled him, at his return to his native Country, to give his Father ſuch Advice as was neceſſary to quiet the Minds of the People; to put an End to the Civil Diſſention in the Kingdom; and to prepare the *Britons* for a new Syſtem of Religion and Government, which he, pretending to be endowed with the Gift of Prophecy, moſt undoubtedly foretold would happen while his Father was building the Wall of the Town of Mount *Paladur*: And therefore that Change, however applied to future times, BLADUD, in all Probability, began to make on his coming to the Throne; and ſoon after that to propagate a new Syſtem of Religion by the Aſſiſtance of the learned Men who fled from *Athens*, when that City, upon the Approach of the *Perſian* Army under *Mardonius*, was deſerted by its Inhabitants in the ſixth Year of the Reign of *Xerxes*, and in the Year 480 before the Birth of Chriſt.

IN this very Year BLADUD might begin the Works at *Bath* proper for his great Purpoſes; and their being recorded in the *Britiſh* Hiſtory of about the ſame Antiquity with *Elias*'s Prayer, might proceed from the Magi of *Perſia* affirming

firming that *Zoroaster* was a Disciple of *Elias*, that is of the Lord God, for such the *Hebrew* Name, *Elias*, imports; and *Zoroaster* himself pretended to have received the Doctrines he taught from the very Mouth of God.

It is enough therefore for our present Purpose to prove the REALITY and EMINENCE of King BLADUD, and at the same time solve the PROBLEMS touching the ANTIQUITY of BATH, that a Temple of *Jerusalem* was begun to be built in the Reign of King *Leil*: That *Haggai* was a Prophet in *Israel* when *Lud-Hudibras* governed *Britain*: That a Philosopher from an Island overagainst *Gaul*, situated as *Britain* is, was a Disciple, a Collegue, and even the Master of *Pythagoras*, and flew in the Air upon an Arrow, as King BLADUD is reported to have flown with Wings: That the Arrow of the former, and the Rebus of the latter, by his Name of *Aquila*, appears together in the Heavens, as Northern Constellations: That the *Hyperborean* Sage, like the *British* Philosopher, was endowed with the Gift of Prophecy: That the Inhabitants of *Athens* deserted that City in the Year 480 before the Birth of Christ: And that BLADUD sent to *Greece* for Necromancers to assist him in his Works about the Hot Springs of BATH, at the very Time that the learned Men of *Athens* wanted a Place of Safety to fly to.

This happened to them in the very Age. Mr. *Sammes* fixes for the *Greeks* first entering the *Britannick* Island, since our Author tells us in the seventh Chapter of his *Britannia*, that those People came here in the Time of *Pythagoras*, or a little after; and therefore the learned *Athenians* that assisted BLADUD were, most undoubtedly, the very Men mentioned by *Diodorus Siculus* to have passed over to the *Hyperboreans*, with Presents to enrich their Temples, after ABARIS had been in *Greece* renewing the antient League of Friendship with the *Delians*.

CHAP. IV.

Of the general MAGNITUDE *of* BATH *in its Antient, Middle, and Modern State.*

HISTORY and Tradition unanimously agree that the City of *Bath* had a more illustrious Beginning than such antient Cities, as from a small Group of Building, were so increased by Time as to render it necessary to transplant their Inhabitants into new Places till the Body of each City became

Chap. IV. A Description of BATH.

became invironed first with Towns, and then with Villages: For *Bath*, like *Alexandria*, was founded for the capital Seat of a famous King; and seems to have consisted, from the very first, of three principal Parts, whose Centers were widely detached from one another.

THE most material Part of the three lay immediately round about the hot Springs; the next in Degree stood eight computed Miles Westward from them, at a Place now called *Stantondrue*; and the third lay ten computed Miles South of the second, and fifteen of the same Miles Southward of the hot Fountains, at a Place now bearing the Name of *Okey*: So that the Centers of the three principal Parts of the City formed the Angles of a Triangle whose Base Line extended fifteen computed Miles in Length; its shorter Side eight of the same Miles; and its longer Side ten of the like Miles: And therefore the MAGNITUDE of this CITY, in its antient State, could not have been less, in respect to the Land of its whole Area, than that of *Babylon* when *Cyrus* took it.

NOW if the City had been originally surrounded with a Wall, *Bath*, in regard to her private Buildings, had appeared, at this day, what *Babylon* herself once was.

THIS extensive City seems to have been first reduced by the *Romans*, about the Year of Christ 81; and next by King *Alfred* the *Great*, when that famous Prince founded the *English* Monarchy, and divided the whole Kingdom into Shires; the Shires into Hundreds or Wapentakes, and the Hundreds into Tythings for the more ready and better supplying his Army with Men; and for the more speedy and effectual Administration of publick Justice in every Corner of his Dominions.

BY the first Reduction the City was brought to its chief principal Part; and by the second to a single Group of Building in the midst of such Demesne Lands as were just necessary for the immediate Subsistence of the Inhabitants: For King *Alfred* separated all the Villages that, in his Time, made the detach'd Parts of *Bath*, from the Body of the City and the Berton thereunto belonging; and forming them into a distinct Jurisdiction, made them subject to the Laws and Government prescribed for some larger Division of the County, or for the County itself.

THE Villages thus separated, constituted the Hundred of Bathforum in its original Size; and, with the Group of Building and its Demesne Lands in the Center, seem to have

extended

extended about twelve Miles in Length, and about ten Miles in Breadth: But the central Part of this Region, or that which constitutes the present City, with the Berton belonging to it, is but three quarters of a Mile in Length from North to South, and the Breadth from East to West is still less by an hundred Yards, or more.

The Group of Building that makes the Body of the City, thus reduced, was surrounded with a deep Ditch, and a thick Stone Wall by King *Alfred*, when he, about the Year of Christ 887, applied himself to the Reparation of such Cities as had been wasted by the *Danes*; as well as to the fortifying of the capital Places of his Kingdom against those People: And by that Work the City became a Place of vast Strength; so strong, that if it had been in a higher Situation, and not so overtopped with Hills as it is, it might have been made Tenable, even in the Time of the Civil Wars, as Captain *Henry Chapman*, the Author of *Thermæ Redivivæ*, assures us, in that small Treatise, the famous Admiral *Blake* declared when he had the Government of the City.

If King *Alfred* had extended his Fortification to the Bounds of *Bath*, in its middle State, the City had now appeared little inferior to any of the great Cities of Antiquity for Size; and perhaps to have exceeded them all for Strength, since no less than six large Intrenchments are yet to be seen in it within the compass of six Miles in Length from East to West, and five Miles in Breadth from North to South; each of which appears capable of containing a Body of Men equal to that of a Consular Army of the *Romans*, composed of two of their Legions.

These Intrenchments are the highest Demonstration of the Grandeur and vast Importance of *Bath* in the dark Times of our History; and they are manifest Proofs of the Valour and Eminence of the antient *Britons* in the Art of War: For unless they had known how to defend and preserve a Place of the greatest Consequence to them against the most violent Assaults of a potent Enemy to deprive them of it, the Marks of Hostility had never appeared in that Abundance as they do at present, within a Region little more than the eighth Part of that which the *Babylonians* inclosed with Walls and Ditches.

But if we extend that Region to a Figure containing upon it's Superficies two hundred and twenty five square Miles of Land, to answer the Superficies of *Babylon*, when *Cyrus* took it, it, and to comprehend all the Parts of *Bath* in its antient State and greateſt Splendor, the Intrenchments in it will then appear ſo numerous, and ſo ſtrong, that one would imagine the whole hoſtile World had here contended for the Empire of it.

Thus the City of *Bath* appears to have been a Place eminent for its Strength before the Invention of Guns; and, in its middle State, to have been of ſuch MAGNITUDE as to come in Competition with moſt of the great Cities of Antiquity, for Size: Even in its modern State it is equal to a *Roman* Camp, compoſed of a double Legion, and conſequently to a *Roman* City; a Camp and a City having been founded on one and the ſame Plan: And the Land of BATH-FORUM, in its original Size, anſwering the Land aſſigned to a *Roman* Camp for a conſular Army, is a Demonſtration that the CITY of BATH, in its middle State, was equal to a *Roman* City, extended to its utmoſt Bounds.

CHAP. V.

Of the various NAMES of BATH.

BY what Mr. *Sammes* and ſeveral other Authors write concerning the Original of *Bath*, the City appears to have been firſt dignified with the Title of CAERBRAN, or CAERBREN; a *Britiſh* Name compounded of CAER, a CITY, and BREN a KING: The Name likewiſe imports the King's Throne or Palace; his Temple compoſed of Pillars, or a Place of Addreſs to the Gods; and his Oracle: So that CAERBREN was a Title vaſtly comprehenſive; and ſeems to point out to us, that the City, in it's antient State, was famous for an Oracle, for a Temple, for a Palace, and for a Tribunal, or great Court of Juſtice.

THE Name of CAERBREN is now in a Manner loſt at *Bath*; but nevertheleſs it is preſerved in *Somerſetſhire* in the Names of two of its Hundreds, to wit in BRENT Hundred, a divided Region ſituate on the weſt Side of the upper Part of the County; and in CAERHAMPTON hundred lying Southweſt of the former, and making the extreme Corner, Weſtward, of the whole County: For as the Word *Caerhampton* is partly *Britiſh*, partly *Saxon*, ſo if we take what is *Britiſh*, *viz.* CAER, and add it to BRENT, the Name of the other Hundred, we ſhall have CAERBRENT, or rather CAER-

G 2   BREN,

BREN, the original NAME of the CITY of BATH without the least Corruption.

BRENT Hundred is bounded Southward by a large Stream of Water, bearing the Royal Title of BRENT or the King's River; towards the Source of which, and at the Distance of about eighteen Miles Southward of BATH, the Town of BRUTON is situated; the Name of which seems to indicate that it was BRUTUS's TOWN, founded by himself, or by some other Person in honour of him.

CAERBREN was undoubtedly the City in the *Hyperborean* Island mentioned by *Diodorus Siculus* to have been consecrated to the God *Apollo*; and therefore the Final of the Name was applicable to the Heavenly, as well as Earthly King of the Times when *Bath* was founded: For *Apollo* was then, as well as in all other Ages of Paganism, esteemed as the King of the Celestial Bodies, and bore the Name of *Bel*, with different Terminations, to imply it, as well as his glorious Attribute of illuminating the whole World by the Rays of Light issuing from him. Monf. *Banier* derives *Belenus* from *Belos*, an Arrow, and tells us the Arrows of *Apollo* were the Rays or Beams of the Sun; we may add that they implied most of the other Qualities attributed to the God.

THE Name, *Bel*, still remains in all the extreme Parts of the City of *Bath*, in its antient State; a Tree, a Street, and a Meadow retaining it in the north Part near the hot Springs; the Land of a whole Farm preserving it in the south Part near *Okey*; and a Tything of the Parish of *Stantondrue* bearing it in the western Part.

CUNO, as an Initial to *Bel*, imported a Son; and that Name was borne by many of the antient *British* Princes who pretended themselves to be the Sons of *Bel*: On the other Hand *Cad*, as a Final to *Bel*, imported Unity or One; and that Name was applied to such Things as were consecrated to the Sun, as the Supreme, and only God. *Cad* alone, and joined with *Bel*, still remains in *Somersetshire*; and as *Apollo* had a stately Grove with a renowned Temple, of a round Form, in the *Hyperborean* Island, so that very Grove, and that very Temple, were Part of the Works of *Bath* in it's antient State, as will be hereafter shewn; and are expressed in the original NAME of the CITY.

THAT NAME, according to Doctor *Jones*, was not CAERBREN, but KAYER-BLAIDIN, so denominated, says he, from the Name of BLADUD: Now that BLADUD built Cities,

and

and called them after his own Name, may be very true; but the City of *Bath* does not appear to have been one of them: The Places bearing the Name of the King were probably Frontier Towns, or Fortresses to his Kingdom, and CAER-BLADON, now the Town of *Malmsbury* in *Wiltshire*, whose Situation was formerly described to be upon, or by the Side of the River *Bladon*, was probably one of them; and BLEYDON, a Place lying upon the North Side of the River *Ax*, in *Somersetshire*, within three Miles, or thereabouts, of the *Severn* Sea, seems to have been another.

So the KAERBADUS of *Jeffrey* of *Monmouth* was not the CITY, but the FORTRESS of BATH; and therefore that Name must have been applied to some Outwork raised for the immediate Defence of the Place.

THE principal Part of the City, in its antient State, lying round the hot Springs, the *Britons* called it, or rather the Central Part of it, by the Name of CAER-ENNAINT, importing the City of Ointment: They likewise called it CAER YR NAINT TWYMIN, that is the City in the warm Vale: And they also gave it the Names of CAER PALLADDUR and CAER BADON, or BADUN, the former implying the City of *Pallas*'s Water; the latter the City of *Bath*.

THUS from a King presiding in Heaven or Earth; from his Temple, his Oracle, his Palace, and his Tribunal; from the healing Virtues of the hot Waters; from their Situation; from the Waters themselves consecrated to a Divinity; and from the Cisterns at the Heads of the Springs, the antient *Britons* denominated the City, and particularly the chief Part of it.

IN like Manner the *Romans* from the hot Waters in respect to their Heat or Consecration; and from the Cisterns made to receive them: And the *Saxons* from the same Reservoirs; from the Heat of the Waters; and from the vast Number of Druids, or Priests of the Oak, who had their Abode about those Waters, denominated the City; the AQUÆ CALIDÆ, AQUÆ SOLIS, THERMÆ, and BALNEA of the former importing hot Waters, Waters of the Sun, and Cisterns to receive them; and the Initials of the BATHANCESTER, HATBAHAN, and ACKMANCHESTER of the latter signifying Baths, hot Baths, and Oak Men.

FROM hence the City in it's Antient, in it's Middle, and in it's Modern State appears to have borne the NAME of BATH; and it was so denominated from the Baths which

BLADUD,

BLADUD, according to the *British* History, made in it for the Use of the Publick.

BATH is a Word literally importing a Daughter, as well as a House: A Daughter when applied to an inferior Measure of Capacity; and a House when considered as a Thing capable of holding liquid or dry Substances. *Verstegan* tells us the Word was antiently wrote *Bade*; and that *d* was of our Ancestors used in Composition as *th*.

THE principal publick Work of *Bath*, so far back as the Reign of King *Alfred*, having been that which the *Grecians* called an AGORA, and the *Romans* a FORUM; from that Work all the Region round about the City in its Modern State, and within the Limits of it in its Middle State, was then denominated the HUNDRED of BATHFORUM; and notwithstanding that Region has been since reduced and divided, the greatest Part of it still goes by the Name of *Bathforum* Division, while the principal Part of that Division retains its original Name; the rest bearing the Names of *Wellow* Hundred, and the Liberties of *Hamton* and *Claverton*.

BY the Name FORUM we are to understand those spacious open Areas in antient Cities, to which the People resorted on publick Occasions; and that Name seems to have been derived from the *Greek* Word *Fero*, to Bear, or Carry, and implying the flat Roofs over the Porticoes of the *Grecian* AGORAS, for People to stand and walk upon. Accordingly we find that as often as the open Areas of the *Romans* were surrounded with Porticoes covered with a flat Floor for the Use of the Publick, they were called FORUMS; but when those open Areas had no such elevated Floors for People to stand or walk upon, they went by the Name of Atriums, from the Word *Aithrios*, expressing the real Nature of them, as Places that were open and exposed to the Air.

OF the *Roman* Atriums some were publick, some private; some had Porticoes round them, some had none; and these kind of Courts were common in other Nations; for the *Grecians*, the *Persians*, and the *Jews* had them in great Abundance, and in great Perfection.

THE *Jews* called their Atriums by the Name of *Chatzar*; and from those *Chatzars* they denominated several of their Towns and Cities, such as have *Hazar* for their Initial, or rather proper Name; as *Hazar-Gaddi*, signifying a Court of Goats, *Hazar-Shual*, a Court of Foxes, and *Hazar-Susim* a Court of Horses; the Finals or Sirnames to which Places

arose,

arose, perhaps, from the Inhabitants of those Places carrying on some sort of Traffick with the Beasts they denote: And therefore from *Hazar-Shual* it seems probable that *Samson* got the three hundred Foxes which sacred History declares him to have first coupled together, and then to have turned into the Fields of the *Philistines* with Firebrands fixed between their Tails to burn their Corn, then ready for reaping, their Vines, and their Olives, in revenge for an Affront he conceived to have been put upon him by those People, in general; though executed by his Father-in-Law, as his own private Act.

As it was by these sort of Courts that the Antients entered the chief Parts of a City, or the chief Parts of the supreme Structures of it, whether Sacred or Prophane; so the People, from the remotest Ages, adorn'd them with the Statues of their Ancestors; and in them they kept their publick Entertainments; for which Reasons no Expence was wanting to make them grand and beautiful.

We read in the first Chapter of the Book of *Esther*, that the Floor of the Atrium in the City of *Shushan*, or *Susa*, in *Persia*, was paved with Marble of four Colours, Red, Blue, White, and Black; and that it was of such an enormous Size, as to enable *Ahasuerus* to entertain all the Princes and Nobility of *Persia*, of *Media*, and of the Provinces under his Dominion in it! The King, on that Occasion, first screening such Part of the Court from the Weather as was necessary to contain the Company with beautiful Hangings of three Colours, White, Green, and Blue, fastened to Marble Pillars with Rings of Silver, and Cords of white and purple Thread; and then causing curious Beds of Gold and Silver to be placed under them for the Princes and Nobility to recline themselves upon during the Time of the grand Repast.

The Forums were still more magnificent; for *Diodorus Siculus* assures us in the third Chapter of his sixteenth Book, that *Dion* encamped his Army, consisting of fifty thousand Men, in the Forum of *Syracuse*; the Porticoes whereof, as our Author further declares in the seventh Chapter of his fourteenth Book, served the Tyrant *Dionysius*, the Elder, some Years before, as the chief Workshops for the Multitudes of Artificers employed by him in his military Preparations against the *Carthaginians*.

This Forum was surrounded with Houses inhabited by the principal Citizens of *Syracuse*; and they were so well secured against the Danger of a general Conflagration, that
though

though the Soldiers of the Tyrant *Dionyſius*, the Younger, ſet every Houſe on Fire after they had plundered them; yet *Dion*, forcing his Way into the City, deprived the Plunderers of their Prey, ſlew above four thouſand of them, and got time enough to the Forum to quench the Flames ſo as to preſerve the Buildings that made the Splendour of the City: An Exploit ſo glorious that the *Syracuſians* unanimouſly elected *Dion* their ſupreme Governor, and conferr'd on him the Honours due to a Demi-God.

As for the *Roman* Forums we cannot form too great an Idea of them when we conſider that the very Floor of that which was built by *Julius Cæſar* coſt him, as *Suetonius* and *Pliny* atteſt, one hundred Millions of Seſterces; which, according to Doctor *Arbuthnot*'s Calculation, amounts to eight hundred and ſeven thouſand two hundred and ninety one Pounds thirteen Shillings and four Pence of our Money, and exceeds the whole Expence of building and finiſhing the two capital Structures of the Metropolis of *Great Britain*; namely the *Royal-Exchange*, and *St. Paul*'s Cathedral in the City of *London*.

The Antients applied their Forums to the moſt noble Purpoſes; for in them they convened the People, held their ſolemn Aſſemblies, ſacrificed to their Gods, delivered their Orations, and proclaimed their Kings. I have already mentioned the five hundred *Sybarites* that flew for Refuge to the Altars erected in the Forum of *Crotona*; and *Diodorus Siculus* tells us in the fourth Chapter of his ſeventeenth Book, that after *Alexander* the *Great* had taken the famous City of *Tyre*, he complimented *Hepheſtion* with the Power and Liberty of beſtowing the Kingdom upon which of his Friends he pleaſed: *Hepheſtion* accordingly offered the Crown of *Tyre* to one of the Citizens that had courteouſly entertained him; but he refuſing it, becauſe he was not of the Lineage of the Kings, *Hepheſtion* thereupon paid him the ſame Compliment, which he himſelf had received from *Alexander*; and one *Ballonymus*, a prudent good Man of the Royal Blood, though extremely poor, having been named, *Hepheſtion* accepted of him; and from the ſervile Employ of drawing Water in an Orchard for his Hire, inſtantly advanced him to the Throne; ſending the proper Officer for inaugurating the new Monarch, to ſtrip him of his Rags, cloath him with the Royal Robes, introduce him forthwith into the Forum, and there to declare him King of *Tyre*; which was accordingly done, to the great Joy and

Satisfaction of the *Tyrians*; *Ballonymus*, as *Diodorus* concludes, bearing his wonderful Change of Condition so well, as to become an Example to all that are unacquainted with the sudden and various Turns of Fortune in the World in which we live.

THE Forum, or rather Forums of *Bath* were undoubtedly applied to as noble Purposes as any of the Forums of the Antients; and when we reflect that *Agricola* the *Roman* Governor, and High Priest in *Britain*, under the Emperor *Vespasian*, privately exhorted, and even publickly assisted the *Britons* to erect such sort of Structures, we may conclude the last Forums of *Bath* to have been built in his Time; and to have been most stupendous, and most beautiful Works: For *Vitruvius* informs us in the first Chapter of his fifth Book, that the Romans surrounded their Forums with a second Order of Columns, sustained by the first, whereby the Walks over the Porticoes were skreened from the Weather, and became Colonades of such Use that the Profits arising from them vastly increased the publick Revenues of the Empire.

ONE of the Forums of *Bath*, graced the North End of the Region that formed the City in its antient State; and the other adorned the South End: So that the Country for some Miles round about the first took the Name of *Bathforum*, and the Country for some Miles round about the Second took the Name of *Wellsforum* when King *Alfred* reduced the City from its Middle to its Modern State.

CHAP. VI.

Of the SITUATION of BATH; of its VALES; and of its HILLS.

BATH considered in its Middle State as a single Group of Building encompassed with a Stone Wall, and that surrounded first with Towns, and then with Villages, each having a proper Berton about it for raising Necessaries for the immediate Subsistence of its Inhabitants, is situated in the midst of a rich Tract of Land, spreading itself into three different Counties, and extending at least fifty Miles in Length, by twenty Miles in Breadth.

THIS great Region of Country appears low in respect to the Lands about it, but nevertheless its Surface is vastly irregular, and composed of nothing but Hills and Vales, naturally abounding with Rivers as well as rich Meadow and Pasture

Grounds: It is bounded on one Side by the open and extensive Plains of *Wiltshire* and *Dorsetshire*; and on the other by the second River of *England*, the River *Severn*, increased into a Sea upon its uniting with the River *Wye*, within Sight from the Summit of one of the Hills of *Bath*; and within the Distance of about fifteen Miles of the hot Springs of the City.

THE City thus situated makes the North-East Corner of the County of *Somerset*: And Geographers place the central Part of it in the Latitude of fifty one Degrees twenty Minutes North, and in the Longitude of two Degrees thirty two Minutes West from *London*, the capital City of the *British* Empire.

THE Surface of the Land within the antient Limits of *Bathforum*, is divided into great variety of Vales and Hills; and the Buildings now constituting the Body of the City that contained that Forum stand upon an Isthmus of declining Ground, at the Foot of the South-East Corner of one of the chief Hills; commanding, at the same Time, the principal and most pleasant Vale of the whole Hundred for more than two Miles to the North-East, and for about two Miles to the North-West, with the *Avon*, a common Name in the *British* Tongue to all Rivers, winding thro' it.

THIS River forms the Out-Line of a parabolical Figure about the south-eastern Part of the Buildings in the Body of the City, as well as the Berton belonging to them; and by that curving Line of the *Avon*, a Man would imagine that the cold Waters of the River were destined by Divine Providence to pay Homage to the hot Mineral Fountains as they glide by them; for in the central Part of the Body of the City the hot Springs boil up.

THE principal Vale of *Bath*, by the *British* Name of NANT-BADON, appears by the Writings of the learned Author of the *Britannia*, to have extended to such a considerable Length all along the River *Avon*, as to comprehend *Caèr Oder*, now the City of *Bristol*: So that the *Britons* describing the Situation of that City to be in *Nant-Badon*, shews the Antiquity of *Bath* to be greater than that of *Bristol*; or the former to have been a more eminent City than the latter in antient Times.

THE meandring Form of this Vale seems to have induced the *Britons* to call that Part of it which lay near the hot Springs of the City, by the Name of TROY-NOVANT, *i. e.* the turning Valley: And the same Part of *Nant-Badon* being

skreened

Chap. VI. A Description of BATH.

skreened by Hills whose Sides are broke into several Cliffs, and sunk into many Dents or Combs, covered for the most Part with Wood, was undoubtedly the Reason why the same People gave it the Appellation also of NANT TWYMIN, or the warm Vale.

THE Cliffs and Combs of the Hills that skreen the quick turning Part of *Nant-Badon* are Beauties in Nature, so exceeding great, that the Author of *Palæ Albion* declares the Vale wherein the hot Springs of *Bath* boil up a finer Seat for *Apollo* and the Muses, than they could have had even about *Parnassus* itself!

THE antient *Britons*, well satisfied of this apparent Truth, seem to have given *Apollo* a Summer Seat in it; a Meadow about half a Mile to the Westward of the hot Springs still bearing the Title of *Bel*; and some of the Pasture grounds that make the ascent from thence to the Summit of the next adjoining Hill, are, to this Hour, called the Hays; no doubt from the *British* Custom of dancing the Hay, or in Circles, on those rising Fields, at the Festivals that were celebrated by the antient *Britons* in honour of the King of the Heavenly Bodies; and more particularly on their *May* Day Festivals, which Time nor Circumstance hath not yet eradicated in any Part of the Island that I have seen.

THE other Vales of *Bath*, all branching from *Troy Nevant*, and of the very same Kind with it, seem to have been Seats for the other Gods of our Pagan Ancestors; for three Miles and a half North of the hot Springs of the City there is a Place in the bottom of a Valley called TATWICK; a Name implying the Mansion of *Tutates*, or *Mercury*; two Miles South of the same Springs there is a hollow Dent against the Back of a Hill, corruptly called HORSE COMB, a Name importing the small Vale of *Hesus*, or *Mars*; and not far to the West of this Dent we have another COMB bearing the *British* Name of the Sun, or rather of the Image by which that Luminary was represented, called, and worshipped.

THIS Name was HAUL, HAYL, HEIL, or HEOL; it implies a Circle; and the Sun still goes by it, in *Cornwall* and in *Wales*.

THE particular Spot of Ground where the hot Springs boil up, is so advantageously situated, in respect to Altitude, that from the Surface of the hot Water in the Cistern at the Head of the chief Spring, to the Surface of the cold Water of that Part of the *Avon* that makes the Out-Line of the parabolical

Figure above mentioned, is seventeen Feet five Inches; which is a Fall sufficient to guard the hot Baths against the highest Floods; and to keep the Land between the hot and cold Waters perfectly dry, as the distance between them does not exceed a Quarter of a Mile in the broadest Part.

The Land about the hot Springs, and upon this gentle Declivity, extends, at least, a Mile and a half in Length from East to West; and is in Breadth from North to South, three Quarters of a Mile or more: So that if the City in the middle of it was ten times as large as it is at present, it would not be so confined but that the Company would have Room to converse out of the Smell of their own Excrements, without ascending any of the Hills about it; contrary to the MALICIOUS INSINUATIONS of the first Compilers of the *Tour through Great Britain*.

The gentle declining Land about the hot Springs is surrounded with venerable and stupendous Hills of a much quicker Ascent to the South and to the East, than to the West and to the North; and the Surface of the River that runs thro' it, is at least thirty Feet above the extraordinary Flow of the *Severn* Sea.

NINETY Feet seems to be the medium Breadth of this River; and the Rapidity of the constant Stream is entirely taken off by several Wears that Traverse it in oblique Lines; and at the same time that they form so many Cascades, or great Falls for some Part of the Water to beautify the Country, they conduct the rest to Mills of various Kinds for the Use and Advantage of the Inhabitants.

The South Side of the Area wherein the hot Springs boil up, is bounded by a steep Mount branching from a Hill behind it, and, from the Body of the City, looking like a vast Heap of Earth whose Northern Side had been undermined so as to slip down, and leave a stupendous Cliff above in the Shape of a large Cressant, now covered with Wood, and called Beaching Cliff; from a narrow Beach between the Foot of the Hill and the River *Avon*.

The original Name of this Mount appears to have been BLAKE-LEIGH, and to have been so denominated from its Fertility in a naked and exposed Situation: The Crown of it still retains its antient Name; and there is a gentle Ascent to it from the West: It is backed by the curving Hill from which it branches; and that Hill formerly bore the Name of CAMALODUNUM; most undoubtedly from *Camalos*, or *Camulus*,

one

Chap. VI.   A Description of BATH.

one of the Names of the *British* God of War, and *Dunum* a Hill: For to this Hour part of it retains his most antient Name of *Odin*, since it is called OD-DOWN; and lies between the Group of Building now constituting the Body of *Bath* and the Village of *Camerton*, a Name compounded of *Camalos*, and *Tun*, the *Saxon* Name for a small Town or Village.

THE Name of *Odin* being thus retained in the North Part of *Somersetshire*, if we go to the South Part of the same County we shall likewise find it preserved in a Place called *Odcomb*, the paternal Habitation of the famous *Tom Coryat*; the Bishop of *London* tells us in the *Britannia* p. 747, that *Odin* or *Odyn* is a common Name of Places in *Wales*, but more particularly in one Part of *Caermarthenshire*; and Monsi. *Banier* takes notice that the Person acknowledged by the *Thracians* as the *Hyperborean* Mars bore the Name of *Odin*, was King of *Thrace*, and became their God of War: *Verstegan* informs us, that the God of Battle of our *Saxon* Ancestors was stiled *Woden*, a Name signifying fierce or furious; and Mr. *Sammes* tells us, that the *Gothick* Nations called this God sometimes *Voden*, and sometimes *Oden*.

OD-DOWN, or rather *Camalodunum*, curves so as to bound the Area in which the hot Springs of *Bath* boil up both to the West, and to the East; increasing in its Altitude as it advances towards the rising Sun, and at the North-East it yields for a Passage to the *Avon*; but rising immediately again it forms a more stupendous Hill on the North Side of our gentle declining Area, than on any of the other Sides.

MONS BADONCA, as Mr. *Sammes* writes it, and LANSDOWN are the common Names of this Hill; and *Badonca* seems to have been a Name compounded of the Word *Bath*, and *Onca*, the *Phœnician* as well as *Egyptian* Name of *Minerva*.

ONCA, is a Name importing a young Maid, and as such it appears to have been made use of by the Antients to express the new Moon; but *Minerva* signifying one whose Business was to warn, the Pagans seem to have made Choice of that Name to express the Moon in her several Phases: So that the first Appearance of that Luminary, after a Change, was in all Probability watch'd for on *Lansdown*; and the Neomenia was most undoubtedly celebrated in the Heart of the City, to cause the Moon, worshipped at *Bath*, to have been expressed under her most youthful Name; and this Hill to have been denominated from her in that Character.

THE

THE Initial of the other Name of this Mountain imports a Temple or sacred Place; from whence one would naturally conclude that *Lansdown* was so denominated from some sacred Structure once upon it, and *Dunum*, a Hill, if there was no remains of a pagan Temple or Christian Church to be seen on its Summit; but as there are both, we may from them very fairly derive the Initial in the Name of this Mountain.

As *Camalodunum* backs *Blake-Leigh*, so FAR-LEIGH, a most stupendous Hill, whose western Side is partly Forest, partly Rock, and whose northern End bears the Title of KINGS-DOWN, backs the eastern Part of *Camalodunum*; and if we pursue the Curve of that Hill, after its yielding twice for a Passage to a Couple of Brooks perpetually discharging themselves into the *Avon* about two Miles and a half to the North-East of the hot Springs, we shall find a Hill backing *Mons Badonca*, which, in antient Times, bore the Name of the Sun; for the principal Part of that Hill still retains his *British* Title of HAUL; while another Part preserves his *Roman* Name of SOL, but with the *Saxon* Termination of BURY to it, to denote the Use to which this Part of the Mountain was appropriated: Bury importing an Intrenchment, or fortified Place, and Solsbury still carrying the Marks of such a Place of Defence of more than ordinary Strength.

THE Hill that first preserves the Curve Line of *Far-Leigh*, or rather the *Kings-Down*, is commonly called BANNAR-DOWN; but *Bannar* seems to be a Corruption of *Banno*, or *Bannagh*, a Name importing a Region that was sacred, blessed, or holy.

Now the Hills of *Bath* being four in Number, and bearing the Names of *Camalodunum*, *Mons Badonca*, *Kings-Down*, *Bannagh-Down*, and *Haul Down*; and these Names implying *Mars*'s Hill, the Moon's Hill, the Sun's Hill, the King's Hill, and the Holy Hill, what can be a greater Demonstration of their antient Eminence?

THE Elevation of these Hills is such, that their Summits command a Country so exceeding beautiful, and of such vast Extent, that the Eye that views it, and the Mind that considers it with Attention, can never be enough satisfied: Nor is the Air upon them to be less admired for its Salubrity; upon *Mons Badonca* especially; where we could lately see an Inhabitant in every House, so very old, that their Ages, upon an Avarage, amounted to upwards of ninety Years.

SPRINGS

Chap. VI. A Defcription of BATH.

SPRINGS of foft, fweet, cryftal Water iffue out of the Ground, at the very Tops of the Hills of *Bath*; and when united in the Combs, funk into their Sides, they form little Rills, which, in their Defcent to the larger Vales below, are increafed by frefh Springs to Brooks of no inconfiderable Size in fome Places; in others they greatly augment fuch Rivulets as were formed before from other Sources. And at the fame time that Nature plentifully fupplies the Hills and Vales of the City with cold Water, it inftantly carries off all manner of Superfluity arifing from the Fluid Element: Even after Rains and Inundations no ftanding Pools or Sloughs are to be found in any Part of the Hundred of *Bathforum*, the Surface of the Ground within its moft antient Limits declining every where to the *Avon*, and thereby naturally draining itfelf fo as inftantly to difcharge its furplus Water into that River, which yields her Super-abundance to the *Severn* Sea within a Day or two after the hardeft Rains.

IN the Formation of the Hills that furround the hot Springs, Nature feems to have had a Spiral Motion, fo as to form a Kind of Volute; tho' the Contour is often broke to admit of a Paffage for the *Avon*, as well as for the Brooks perpetually difcharging themfelves into that River; and the Probability of this Thought is not a little enhanced by the Spiral Motion manifefting itfelf by Whirlwinds, and Whirlpools; and by the Spiral Figures which I fhall hereafter fhew to be peculiar to the Soil of *Bath*; and perhaps no where elfe to be met with in fuch great Abundance, and in fuch infinite Variety, as in the Ground near the hot Fountains of the City; to the Weftward of them efpecially.

THE Hills that firft furround the gentle declining Area in which the hot Springs boil up, are not fo near it as to intercept the good Effects of the Sun from any Part of it; and the Spiral Form of thofe Hills hath this good Confequence attending it, that it fkreens the whole City in its prefent State, together with all the low Land about it from every principal Wind; admitting, at the fame time, the collateral Streams of the agitated Air to refrefh and purify the fame Land and City by their more gentle Breezes, as well as the Beams of the rifing Sun to diffipate and dry up the Damps of the Morning Fluid in which we breathe, and give fuch a Relaxation to the Element, after its Compreffion by the Moifture of the Night, as is neceffary to difpel the Caufes of Sleep, and awaken the whole Animal World.

How

How pernicious to the Health of the Inhabitants the Termination of some of the principal Winds upon any City are, may be conceived from what the great *Hippocrates* delivered in the following Words, or to that Effect, an Age or two after the City of *Bath* was founded.

"The Inhabitants, says he, of the City that is exposed to the southerly Winds, and at the same Time defended from the northerly Winds, are short Lived, and subject to many Diseases: The Men to Dysenteries, Diarrhœa's, chilly cold Fevers, long Winter Fevers, many Pustules of that Sort which break out in the Night, and to the Piles; the Women are sickly, and subject to Fluxes, apt to miscarry, and many prove Childless; and the Children are liable to Convulsions, as well as to Asthma's."

Again, "The Inhabitants of the City that is exposed to the northerly Winds, and at the same Time defended from the southerly Winds, are longer Lived than the former, but subject to more Diseases: The Men to Pleurisies, and other acute Diseases, to Pus, to Ophthalmies, to Hæmorrhages, and to Epilepsies; the Women to hard Deliveries, to Consumptions, and to a Dryness which quenches and dries up their Milk, and renders them unable to suckle their Children; and the Children themselves are not only restrained in their Growth, but are apt to have Dropsies in their private Parts."

In the last place, "The Inhabitants of the City that is exposed to the westerly Winds, and at the same Time covered from the easterly Winds, are more sickly than any; and the Situation of such a Place RESEMBLES the AUTUMN: But those Cities, adds our Author, that face the East, and are sheltered from the westerly Winds, RESEMBLE the SPRING; they are more healthy than the Cities exposed to the North, or to the South; the Inhabitants have good Complexions; and the Women, besides being very fruitful, have easy Times."

From hence it is evident, that *Hippocrates* was of Opinion, that no City on which the southerly, northerly, or westerly Winds terminated could be healthy; and therefore he judged that City which faces the East, and at the same Time is sheltered from the westerly Winds, the best situated, and most healthy Place of Habitation.

Now the Body of the City of *Bath*, with the Berton belonging to it, by being sheltered from the westerly Winds, and

Chap. VI. A Description of BATH.

and at the same Time receiving the Beams of the rising Sun, may be very justly said to be in a SITUATION that RESEMBLES the SPRING; ever Youthful, ever Gay: And that SITUATION is manifestly attended with all the good Consequences *Hippocrates* has enumerated as peculiar to a City perfectly healthy, without subjecting the Inhabitants to any Diseases: Even at the Time

" When Fevers bore an Epidemic Sway,
" Unpeopled Towns, swept Villages away;
" While Death abroad dealt Terror, and Despair,
" The Plague but gently touch'd within our Sphere,"

as the late Mrs. *Chandler* very truly observes in her Poetical Description of *Bath*: And if we examine into the Nature of the Inhabitants, we shall find that they have good Complexions; that the Women, besides being very fruitful, have easy Times; and that the Longevity of the People in general hath been always remarkable: The late Doctor *Oliver* could not avoid taking particular Notice of a Circumstance so very material; for in the twelfth Chapter of his *Practical Dissertation on Bath Waters*, first published in the Year 1707, he declares that he had BEHELD more old healthy People in *Bath*, and the neighbouring Villages, than he had ever HEARD of any where else.

THE antient *Britons*, as a stronger Testimony of this Truth, made *Bath* the Seat of the very God whom they imagined to have had a Power of curing their Diseases; and the Names preserved in the Hills and Vales of the City seem to indicate that the same People placed all their other Idols about the hot Fountains, so as to make the City appear as the grand Place of Assembly for the Gods of the Pagan World.

CHAP. VII.

Of the SOIL of BATH, and the FOSSILS peculiar to it.

EXPERIENCE hath sufficiently demonstrated, that the Body of the City of *Bath* stands upon a hard Clay and Marl, of a bluish Colour, with Stratas of Rock, as well as Veins of Marcasite, of several Kinds, intermixed: In some Places there are also Beds of Gravel, in others small Veins of Coal: But there is no Appearance of a Quagmire in the Heart, or in any other Part of the City, as it was generally reported

reported and believed an Age or two back; and particularly when Mr. *Glanville* compofed the Letter printed in the Tranfactions of the *Royal Society*, as above.

THIS Letter bears Date the fixteenth of *June* in the Year 1669; and the Author, after mentioning therein the common Report that the Town, for the moſt Part, is built on a Quagmire, endeavours to confirm it by telling the learned Society, to whom he wrote, that fome Workmen, who had been employed in digging, found a Mire in one Place at ten Feet in Depth; in another at feven; and that even in the Queen's Bath a yielding Mud was difcovered fo deep, that a Pike thruſt into it could not reach the Bottom.

THESE Inſtances, to prove a Quagmire under the greateſt Part of the Body of the City, were again offered to the Publick by Doctor *Guidott*, to fupport his *Hypothefis*, of a Bog near the Baths made beneath fome Yards in Depth of Gravel by the Confluence of Waters thither: And the above-mentioned Doctor *Oliver*, believing the Town to ſtand on a Quag, further promulged the Inſtances recited by Doctor *Guidott* to prove it: Inſtances which can amount to no more than this, that the Workmen, from whom Mr. *Glanville* firſt had the Information, accidentally dug into Places that had been before penetrated on fome Occafion or other, and then filled up again.

THE Soil of the Vale of *Bath*, to the North-Weſt of the hot Springs, hardens as we go weſtward; fo that the Stratas of Rock intermixed with the Clay and Marl foon become a kind of Marble, called Lyas; fome of a white Colour, and fome of a grey Colour. Thefe Rocks increaſe in their Progreſs weſtward; and the Beds of Gravel, as well as the Veins of Coal, increaſe likewife; the latter to fuch a high Degree, that large Quantities are now raifed and fold within three Miles of the hot Fountains in the Heart of the City.

THESE Coal-Works are the Property of Mr. *Harrington* of *Cofton*, a Defcendant of the famous Sir *John Harrington*, who flouriſhed in the Reign of Queen *Elizabeth*; and they are fituated on each Side the chief Road leading from *Bath* to *Briſtol*.

THE Hovel for working one of the Pits is exceeding remarkable, as it lately reprefented a covered Monopterick Temple, with a Porticoe before it. The former ſhelters the Windlaſs, the latter ſheltered the Mouth of the Pit; and one was raifed upon a Quadrangular Bafis, while the other appears

elevated

Chap. VII.   A Defcription of BATH.   59

elevated upon a circular Foundation; a Figure naturally defcribed by the Revolution of the Windlafs.

The Diameter of this Figure is juft four and thirty Feet, and the Periphery is compofed of fix and twenty infulate Pofts, of about feven Feet fix Inches high, fuftaining a Conical Roof terminating in a Point and covered with Thatch: Mere Accident produced the whole Structure; and if the Convenience for which it was built was of a more eminent Kind, the Edifice would moft undoubtedly excite the Curiofity of Multitudes to go to the Place where it ftands to view and admire it, as a perfect Copy of one of *Zoroafter*'s Fire Temples; as a Structure of the fame Kind with the *Delphick* Temple after it was covered with a fpherical Roof by *Theodorus*, the *Phocean* Architect; and as a Structure of the fame Kind with the Temple of *Minerva* wherein BLADUD kept his perpetual Fires.

The Stratas of Rock in that part of the Vale of *Bath* which extends North-Eaftward of the hot Springs, are neither fo large, nor fo hard as thofe under the Body of the City; fo that it may be very juftly faid, that the Soil of this Part of the Vale foftens as we go Eaftward; the Beds of Gravel increafing, at the fame time, fo exceedingly, that, in fome Places, the Soil of many large Fields confifts of nothing but a loomy Kind of Gravel to a very great Depth from the Surface of the Land.

If we afcend the Hills on the North, Eaft and South Sides of the hot Springs, we fhall find them incrufted with Freeftone Rocks, lying juft under their Surfaces in fome Places, in others at feveral Feet in Depth: Thefe Rocks are much harder towards the Weft, than towards the Eaft; and I take it that the Freeftone Rocks in general are not above thirty Feet thick; beneath which we come to a hard Clay and Marl, as under the Body of the City: And if we defcend again into the Vale between thofe Hills, we fhall find the Meadow Land on each Side the River *Avon* with an acquired loomy Surface, by frequent Inundations, of about nine Feet thick, in fome Places; under which the natural Soil begins, and is the very fame with that under the Body of the City.

The fame Soil will likewife appear if we penetrate the Ground below the hard Lyas Rocks to the Weftward of the hot Springs; and according to the late Mr. *Strachey*'s Obfervations on the Coal-Works a few Miles farther Weftward than Mr. *Harrington*'s, it begins on the higher Lands, or Hills, at sixteen Feet in Depth from the Surface of the Ground: But the harder the Stratas of Rock are, the softer and richer the Clay and Marl under them appears to be.

THE natural SOIL of the whole Region about the hot Springs of *Bath* may therefore be looked upon to be a hard CLAY and MARL, intermixed with Veins of MARCASITE and COAL, with Beds of GRAVEL, but, principally, with Stratas of ROCK, which, for the most part, lie horizontally; but there are others that lie perpendicularly, and are known among Miners by the Name of Ridges, tho' pronounced by some Rudges, by others Roaches.

THESE Ridges have been often found by digging in several Parts of the City; they generally run from East to West; they are from ten to fifty Feet in Depth, and of various Thicknesses; they, in the Miners Phrase, trap the Stratas of natural Soil downward, as the Surface of the Ground declines; and they have been observed to abound in almost all kinds of Stone, though in a less Degree of Depth, than in Clay, Marl, or Coal.

THE Ridges in the old Coal-Works, beginning about seven Miles Westward from the Heart of *Bath*, will appear by Mr. *Strachey*'s Observations on those Works, printed among the *Philosophical Transactions*, and making a Part of N° 360, and N° 391, to be partings of Clay, Stone, or Rubble; as if the Veins were disjointed and broken by some violent Shock, so as to let in Rubble, Stone, or Clay between them: And by that Gentleman's Calculation, the Traps together, in four Miles in Length, amount to a Mile and a half in Depth; but he don't mention how much one of those Traps falls short of the Ridge that makes it; which was a great Omission in a Man of his reputed Accuracy.

SUCH is the Nature of the SOIL about the hot Springs of *Bath*; and the Land, in general, appears not only richly cloathed, but exceeding fertile; even to the Summits of the highest Hills! The Herbage too is sweet to Admiration; so sweet, that the Mutton from the tops of the Hills, and the Butter from the lower Grounds, have been always celebrated by Strangers frequenting the City, for a peculiar Goodness.

THE natural SOIL of *Bath*, is the very Manure made use of elsewhere to enrich barren Ground; and a Man who considers it maturely, can't well avoid concluding, that its Effluvia forces its Way up, or is attracted through every
Incrustation

Chap. VII.   A Defcription of BATH.   61

Incruftation upon it to fweeten and enrich the Surface of the whole Land.

This Soil, and almoft every thing peculiar to it, will, as Doctor *Guidott* informs us, ferment on the Affufion of any Acid; and the fame Soil, with its Mixtures and Incruftations, abounds with Fossils of various Kinds; but moftly with fuch as are of a Spiral Figure; and fuch as our Naturalifts believe to have been formed in Nautili Shells.

The Rocks at *Twiverton*, a Village lying about a Mile and a half to the Weft of the hot Springs, and fo on Weftward to *Cainfham*, produce Stones ribb'd and coil'd up like an Adder, which the credulous, as Mr. *Camden* takes notice, formerly believed to have been real Serpents turned into Stones by an imaginary devout Virgin, that bore the Name of *Keina*: I myfelf have found the like Stones in feveral Beds of Gravel under the Body of the City; the outfide Scale of fuch fpiral Foffils abound in the marly Soil about two or three hundred Yards to the Eaftward of the hot Springs, but in a kind of Ore that looks like Silver; and in the very Freeftone Rocks of the Hills on the North, Eaft and South Sides of thofe Springs, I have often feen the Moulds of Serpentine Stones, but covered with little Stalactites, or fparry Ificles, of divers Shapes, as though Water congealed had made the Vacuum.

Multitudes of Conical Stones, with Elliptical Bafes, are found in almoft all the Stratas of Clay and Marl, within the whole Region of *Bath*; they are commonly called Thunderbolts, from a firm Belief that fome of them fall down from the Clouds every Clap of Thunder, and are of a hard Confiftence, of a dark Colour, and when broken parallel to the Bafe, the Surfaces appear like tranfparent Subftances with an infinite Number of bright Rays iffuing from the Center, or radiating Point of each Stone, to the Circumference of it; while the outfide of fome of them appear like Brafs as bright as new coin'd Gold; and thefe have been found in that very Part of the marly Soil, to the Eaftward of the hot Springs, which produce fpiral Figures incrufted with an Oar that looks like Silver.

These Stones are undoubtedly the very fame with that which the *Phœnicians*, according to *Herodian*, imagined to have fallen from Heaven, and believed to have been the real Image of the Sun: And from thefe kind of Foffils it feems extremely reafonable to believe, that the *Grecians* took the

Idea

Idea of reprefenting their Deities by Blocks of Stone, terminating in a Point; the *Venus* of *Paphos* efpecially; whofe Image, as *Tacitus* defcribes it in the fecond Book of his Hiftory, exactly anfwers the Figure of one of our Thunderbolts.

This Image, and the Temple that contained it, was reported to ftand on the very Spot of Ground, whereon the Goddefs herfelf landed, carried thither by the Sea, from whence fhe had been juft generated: But *Tacitus* declares, that the Reafon why *Venus* was fo reprefented was unknown to the Age wherein he lived; and if her Image was not taken from the Conical Foffils in the Bowels of the Earth, it is highly probable that the Rays over the Sea, when the Sun is faid to draw Water, produced it.

From the Top of *Mons Badonca* we often fee this Effect of Nature over the Arm of the Sea, that makes the upper End of the *Briftol* Channel; and the Scene is generally fo beautiful at thofe Times, that one would imagine Heaven and Earth, combined together, could not exceed it. We then fee the Sea, by the Intervention of the irregular Land next its Coafts, divided into vaft Bodies of Water brightened by the declining Sun into extenfive fmooth Surfaces carrying the Appearance of Fire; from which arife dark Conical Rays, intermixed with Beams of Light, promifcuoufly croffed with curling Clouds highly fhadowed below, and edged with refplendent Light above: And this Phænomena being partly backed with, and furmounted by a fhining Sky, like burnifhed Gold before a luminous Body, rifes between the high Mountains of South *Wales* and the rich Vale of *Somerfetfhire* and *Gloucefterfhire*; both prefenting the Eye with thoufands of fine Objects, whofe Receffes, by being penetrated with the Light of the Sun, render the Objects themfelves vifible, diftinct, and truly picturefque in the midft of an univerfal Glow, as if the Earth, thus richly decked, blufhed at the fuperior Beauties of the other Elements.

The Beds of Gravel about the hot Springs abound with thin Round Fossils, generally convex on one Side, and concave on the other; and the convex Sides are always adorned with Lines iffuing from a radiating Point in the middle, to the Periphery of the Foffil.

Shells are infinite in Number, as well as Shapes; and I have preferved the flat Shell of an Oyster, full four Inches and a half broad, which was cut out of the Body of a Block of Free Stone raifed from one of the Quarries on that Part of
Camalodunum

Chap. VII.   A Defcription of BATH.   63

Camalodunum where the folid Rocks don't begin till fifteen or fixteen Feet in Depth from the Surface of the Land.

MANY other little MIRACLES of Nature abound in the SOIL of BATH to excite a Man's Curiofity to examine into them; and an Age may be fpent in a Purfuit of this Kind; fo abundant are the FOSSILS wherever the Ground is penetrated for Foundations for Buildings, for Wells, or for any other Purpofe.

Now if a rich, hard, and firm SOIL, abounding with foft fweet Springs of the fluid Element, and yet naturally drained of its fuperfluous Water, of every Kind, be proper for a City to be built upon; and if a SITUATION fheltered from all obnoxious Winds; open to the Beams of the Winter and Summer Sun; purified and cooled with the gentle Breezes of the collateral Winds; and yielding Longevity, good Complexions, Fruitfulnefs and eafy Child-bearing to its Inhabitants, be proper to place the Body of a City in, then the SOIL and SITUATION of the CITY of BATH may be looked upon to be as perfect, as tho' both had been made by human Art; and as though the latter had been contrived to guard againft all the Defects pointed out by a Man who, for his fupreme Knowledge, was ftiled by fome the Prince of Phyficians; while others adored him as a God: I mean the great *Hippocrates*.

CHAP. VIII.

Of the MINERAL WATERS of BATH.

THE Mineral Waters of *Bath* rife out of the Ground in many Places, and in great Abundance; of which fome Springs are hot, fome cold. The HOT SPRINGS to which the City owes its ORIGIN, its CONTINUANCE, and its FAME, boil up in three different Places; and though their Heat is probably owing to the fame Caufe, yet they are differently impregnated; and the Heat of every Spring, as well as the daily Produce, is likewife different.

THE Spring that rifes up the neareft to the Eaft is the largeft and the hotteft of all the warm Fountains; for the Water, upon its iffuing out of the Ground, will blifter the Skin of a Man; and when the Cifterns at the Head of the Fountain are filled by the whole Spring, the Water in one of them is often too hot to be endured by the Bathers: The very contrary may be faid of the Spring that rifes to the Weft of the

3   former:

former: But the Spring that breaks out of the Earth to the South of the smallest warm Fountain, is of a medium between the other two Springs for its Heat; since the Water, upon its rising out of the Ground, is sufferable, and never so hot in the Cistern that receives the whole Spring, but it may be very well endured.

THO' the Heat of these Springs is probably owing to the same Cause, yet it is evident they cannot come from one and the same Source, because they don't rise in the present Cisterns to one and the same Level; neither does the keeping the Cistern at the Head of any one Spring empty, prevent the Cistern at the Head of either of the other Springs from filling in its usual Time; notwithstanding all the Springs break out of the Ground within so small a Compass as the Limits of half an Acre of Land lying in the Form of a Triangle, whose Base, as it was lately measured by some accurate Workmen, extends about four hundred and fifteen Feet, its longer Side about three hundred and eighty Feet, and its shorter Side about one hundred and ten Feet.

WHEREVER the Sources of these Springs may be, this is very certain, that they are considerably higher than the Tops of the Bodies of Water formed at present by them on their rising up from the Bowels of the Earth: For the Ebullition of the Springs, and of the chief Spring especially, appear on the Surfaces of those Bodies of Water with a Force and Vehemence equal to that of boiling Water, in a large Furnace, heated by a moderate Fire.

THAT the hot Springs rise from a very great Depth, and in a perpendicular Manner, through a firm and solid Soil before they burst out of the Earth, is undeniable from their still remaining uninterrupted in their Course by the Penetrations that have been made in almost every square Perch of Ground round about them, to the Distance of five hundred Feet, or more, from the Fountains for Foundations for Buildings, for Wells, and for divers other Purposes incident to a compact and close built City of more than two thousand two hundred Years standing: And more particularly by their not being affected by the grand Penetration made by King *Alfred* round all the lesser sunk before and since his Time within the Walls of the City.

Of the lesser Penetrations that have been made since that Monarch's Reign, a Common Sewer traversing the central Part of the Body of the City from North to South, was the chief.

Chap. VIII. A Description of BATH.

chief. This Sewer was made at the Expence of the Chamber of the City in the Year 1727, and the Drain passing between the hot Springs, is many Feet below the bottom of the Baths.

The Success attending this Work encouraged the late Duke of *Chandos*, the Year after, to make a Sewer for the Use of his Buildings; and this Sewer passing on the West Side of the smallest hot Springs, is many Feet below the bottom of the Baths filled by those Fountains: And the same Year the late Mr. *Thayer* of *London* sunk a Canal of seven hundred Feet in Length in a Garden belonging to him on the East Side of the Body of the City; the Bed of which, answering one Part of the Bed of the River, was more than twenty Feet below the Beds of the Baths; it was lower than the Bed of King *Alfred*'s Ditch; and it was of a Depth sufficient to drain every Penetration above the Level of the Surface of the *Avon*, and, at the same time, fill such as were below it with the Water of that River.

But all these Penetrations do not amount to such a strong Proof of the Point in Question, as the great Antiquity of the Springs, and the regular Heat and Quantity of the Water; neither the one nor the other varying the least, let the Season be what it will: And the boiling up of the Water is not only the highest Demonstration of the vast Antiquity of the Springs; but, as *Pliny* remarks in the third Chapter of his one and thirtieth Book, a sure Indication of their Perpetuity.

The great Depth from which the hot Water, by all outward Appearances, springs up, and the vast Quantities of cold Water breaking out of the Sides of every Hill round about the hot Fountains, must entirely destroy an Hypothesis formerly advanced by Doctor *Guidott*, and a few Years ago repeated by some Anonymous Physician in the *Tour thro' Great Britain*, that the Source of the hot Springs is upon the Top of one Hill, on the North Side, and upon the Summit of another Hill on the South Side of the Vale wherein those Springs rise up.

The Produce of the hot Springs in the Cisterns that now receive them, seems to have been abated within these fifty Years last past, by some imperceivable Leaks between the Surface of the Water, when the Cisterns are full, and the Surface of the natural Ground under them. In the Year 1693 Mr. *Joseph Gilmore*, a Teacher of the Mathematicks in *Bristol*, having measured the several Baths, and taken the Gauge of the Water in every Cistern, from his Account it

K appears,

appears, that the Cisterns at the Head of the chief Spring contained, upon a full Bath, four hundred and twenty seven Tons and fifty Gallons; that the Cistern at the Head of the smallest Spring contained, upon a full Bath, fifty two Tons three Hogsheads and sixteen Gallons; and that the Cistern at the Head of the Spring rising South of the former contained, upon a full Bath, fifty three Tons two Hogsheads and eleven Gallons.

THE Cisterns at the Head of the chief hot Spring, the principal distinguished by the Name of the King's Bath, would, according to the best Observations of the Bath Guides in Mr. *Gilmore*'s Time, fill with the Water of that Spring in nine Hours and forty Minutes; the Cistern at the Head of the smallest hot Spring, long since denominated the Cross Bath, distant from the King's Bath about three hundred and eighty Feet, would fill with the Water of that Spring in about eleven Hours and a half; and the Cistern at the Head of the hot Spring rising South of the former, now called the Hot Bath, but antiently the Common Bath, distant from the Cross Bath about one hundred and ten Feet, from the King's Bath about four hundred and fifteen Feet, would fill with the Water of that Spring in about eleven Hours and thirty Minutes: So that in the Space of four and twenty Hours, the Spring in the King's Bath produced about one thousand and sixty Tons of Water, and, when *Leland* wrote the second Volume of his *Itinerary*, it turned a Mill; in the same Space of Time the Spring in the Cross Bath produced about one hundred and ten Tons; and in the like Space of Time the Spring in the Hot Bath produced about one hundred and twelve Tons.

THUS the Produce of all the Hot Springs appears each natural Day, to have been about one thousand two hundred and eighty two Tons of Water, exclusive of what was pumped up, and ran to waste through the Sluices.

OF the one thousand and sixty Tons of Water daily produced by the chief hot Spring, no more than seven hundred and thirty two Tons commonly found its way into the Bath, at the Head of it; for the Spring, from the remotest Times, was, and is now covered with a small inverted Cistern, fixed below the bottom of the Bath; from which Cistern the rest of the Water is conveyed, by a Pipe, into a Drain that conducts it to the River; and by this Contrivance the King's Bath becomes more temperate than the Hot Bath to the Ba-
-thers;

Chap. VIII. A Description of BATH. 67

thers; which gave rise to the Error many have run into, that the Water of the King's Bath, is colder than the Water of the Hot Bath.

THE Cistern that antiently covered the Spring in the King's Bath having been broke up in the Year 1664, the very instant that the Water had its Liberty of flowing, by some dextrous Contrivance it threw up Nuts; some whereof were black and rotten, others were fresh, and had Kernels in them, and some had Shales very green about them; from whence the Inhabitants of the City concluded that the hot Springs were fed by the cold Water of some open Spring near a Copice, or Wood's Side; and this Conjecture was made use of by Doctor *Guidott*, to serve his *Hypothesis* touching the Source of the hot Fountains; though he accounts for the Admission of the Nuts into the Cistern in another Manner, and in his *De Thermis Britannicis*, p. 180, supposes them to have been drawn into it from the Bath itself.

NOTHING can appear more ridiculous than the common Story, still prevailing, touching these Nuts, when we consider the Probability of their being drawn in, and continuing a single Hour, much less Years, under a Cistern that daily confined one thousand and sixty Tons of Water, and, while seven hundred and thirty two Tons of it was forcing its Way through every little Crevice into the Bath, three hundred and twenty eight Tons had an easy Vent through a Pipe to a Drain that conducted it to the River: Besides, was it true that the hot Springs are fed by Water, that in any Place run above Ground, would not the Baths be discoloured, made colder, or have a greater flux of Water in the wet Winter Weather than in the dry Summer Season?

SOME of these Consequences commonly attend the Fountains of *Okey Hole* in *Somersetshire*, and *Holy Well* in *Flintshire*, both supposed to be fed by Waters soaking into the adjoining old Mines: But not one of them do ever happen in either of the Baths of *Bath*; nor do the hot Springs, in fact, throw up any thing but Scum, and an extreme fine Sand, which, according to some Experiments made by Doctor *Guidott*, and others since him, the Load Stone attracts, and the Fire kindles into the same Flame as it does Sulphur, attended with the like Smell while burning, demonstrating thereby, that the Sand is principally composed of Steel and Sulphur.

AFTER all, the Wells of cold Water about the Baths are the strongest Proofs that the hot Springs not only rise from

K 2 a great

a great Depth; but that they are fortified with Ridges against the cold Springs: For such Springs, like the Veins in the human Body, so fill the Bowels of the Earth, that upon digging almost where you will in the Heart of the City, you may meet with one of them at no great Depth from the Surface of the Land.

No less than five Springs of cold Water have issued out of the Ground, in the Memory of Man, within five hundred Yards of the hot Baths; and it is well known that the Bowels of the Earth contain cold Water within fifty Feet, or less, of the hot Springs.

We have an Account in the *Philosophical Transactions*, N° 8, p. 133. of warm and cold Water issuing out of the Ground within the Compass of half a Yard; one of the hot Springs at *Buda*, in *Turkey*, rises in an open Pond of cold Water; and our own Country produced a Spring of hot Water and another cold at *Buxton* in *Derbyshire*, so near one another, that you might, as some have wrote, at once, put the Finger and Thumb of the same Hand, one into hot Water, and the other into cold; tho' now they are blended together, as we read in the *Philosophical Transactions*, N° 407, p. 22: So that, as *Pliny* long since observed, in the second Chapter of his thirty first Book, hot and cold Water rising so near together is a common thing; and there seems to be no doubt, but that the Springs producing such opposite Waters, run within the Bowels of the Earth between different Stratas of Soil, 'till they are stopped in their Course by Ridges lying very near one another, and so as to cause them to break out of the Ground in or near the same Place.

Of the cold Springs of Water that run within the Bowels of the Earth, near the Places where the hot Springs of *Bath* break out of the Ground, several have been intercepted by digging, and found to be of a strong Mineral Quality; and particularly the Springs that feed some of the Wells, that have been sunk since the Year 1728, about a Quarter of a Mile to the North-Westward of the hot Baths; in the digging of which Wells the Workmen met with several Veins of Marcasite, with Beds of Gravel, and, in the sinking of one Well in particular, with a small Vein of Coal lying about fifteen Feet under the Surface of the Earth.

On the other Hand divers Springs of cold Mineral Water issue out of the Ground all round the hot Fountains, as if the whole Earth was of a strong Mineral Quality; and the

nearest

Chap. VIII. A Description of BATH.

neareſt Spring of this Kind, by the Name of FROGS WELL, breaks out of the Ground about ſeven hundred Feet to the Northward of the principal hot Spring.

MONS BADONCA or *Lanſdown* ſends forth a Brook from its South Side, which formerly turned a Mill; it now bounds the Berton of *Bath*, to the Weſtward, by the Name of Muddle Brook; and the Source of this Brook is made partly by a Spring of Water, which, for ſome Mineral Quality, was, in former times, dedicated to *St. Winifred*; the Fountain ſtill bearing the Name of WINIFRED'S WELL; and it is much frequented in the Spring of the Year by People who drink the Water, ſome with Sugar and ſome without.

MUDDLE Brook is augmented by a ſecond SPRING of Mineral Water breaking out of the Ground on its eaſtern Bank, about two hundred and forty Yards from the River *Avon*: About half a Mile to the Weſt of this Spring, there is another which now bears the Title of the LIME KILN SPAW, from the Water riſing juſt by a Lime Kiln: And about two Miles and a half further Weſtward, SPRINGS of Mineral Water break out of the Ground in the middle of the common Road that leads from *Bath* to *Briſtol* on the North Side of the *Avon*.

THE Eaſt end of *Mons Badonca* yields a remarkable Spring of Water, which is conveyed into an Alcove built by the Side of the great Road leading from *Bath* towards *London* for the Uſe of the Publick, and, from the remoteſt Times, it hath borne the Name of the CARN-WELL; the Water of which was always looked upon as impregnated with ſome fine Mineral, and therefore ſo highly eſteemed, that People from far and near were uſed to flock to the Fountain to fill their Bottles and Pitchers at it.

THE North-Eaſt Part of the Vale of *Bath* produces a Spring of Mineral Water now bearing the Name of BATH-FORD SPAW, from the Water riſing in the Pariſh of *Bathford* about three Miles from the hot Springs; and it iſſues out of the South-Eaſtern Bank of a large Brook, mixing itſelf in a few Paces with the Water of that Brook, about half a Mile before it diſcharges itſelf into the *Avon*.

THIS Brook receives two other Springs of Mineral Water, one breaking out of the Ground on its Northern Side about a Mile to the North-Eaſtward of *Bathford* Spaw, and the other iſſuing out of its Southern Side about a Mile and a half ſtill further from the ſame Spaw: The remoteſt of theſe

Fountains

Fountains being situated in the middle of the Village of *Box*, is well known by the Name of FROGS WELL; and the other lying at a Place called *Shockerwick*, formerly bore the Name of ST. ANTHONY'S WELL.

THE East end of *Blake-Leigh* is remarkable for a SPRING of Mineral Water issuing out of it; and this, like the Water of *Carnwell*, hath filled the Bottles and Pitchers of many that have frequented the Fountain: But the Vale at the Back of the same Hill is yet more remarkable for another Spring of Mineral Water rising up in it; and bearing the Title of LYNCOMB SPAW, from the Name of the Village in which the Spaw is situated.

THIS Spring breaks out of the Ground about a Mile to the South of the hot Fountains of *Bath*; and there are other SPRINGS at the Foot of the East End of *Blake-Leigh*, which, to all outward Appearance, are of the same Kind with that of the Grand Spaw above them.

THE known Mineral Waters of *Bath*, and such as are now commonly made use of, rise up in nine different Places, of which three Springs are hot, and the other six are cold: The cold Springs break out of higher Ground than those which are hot, tho' with much less Affluence, and the higher the Situation of the Spring, the weaker the Mineral Quality of the Water appears to be.

DOCTOR *Guidott* having examined the cold Water of *Frogswell* in the Parish of *Box*, found it to contain the same Salts as the hot Waters of *Bath*, as he himself hath informed us, in his *De Thermis Britannicis*, p. 154.

THE hot Waters once exposed to the Air, and thereby growing cold, lose a very material Quality, which is that of receiving a Purple Tincture when mixed with Galls; a Quality supposed to be owing to the Gas, or an exalted Vitriolick Steel, which by Taste and Smell manifests itself to be in them: And this Acid being likewise supposed to be that which corrodes all the Iron Work in and about the Baths; the same corroding Quality appears in some of the cold Mineral Waters of the Wells about a Quarter of a Mile to the North-Westward of the hot Springs.

BUT if the hot Waters are kept from the Air, and pumped up directly from the Spring, they will preserve their tincturing Quality, whether the Pump applied to any one Spring discharges the Water just over the Fountain Head, or at a considerable Distance from it; from which Circumstance it seems

more

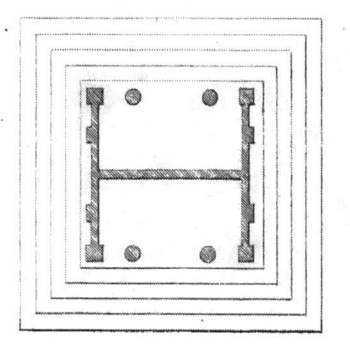

The PLAN and ELEVATION of
a Square Pavilion for Bathford Spaw
begun to be Executed A.D. 1746.

P. Fourdrinier Sculp.

Chap. VIII. A Description of BATH.

more than probable, that the hot Waters will retain all their Ingredients, wherever they are conducted tolerably warm, and well secured in their Passage from any external Air.

As for the HEAT of those Waters, it can neither be a WORK of ART, nor the EFFECT of PIETY, as the Heathens and Monks in antient Times pretended; and, in their Turns, made Mankind believe: It is really a SECRET of NATURE far beyond the Researches of Man, from any thing that yet appears; and therefore a further Enquiry into it would be spending Time to no other End, than that of exposing ones Weakness to satisfy an impertinent Curiosity.

CHAP. IX.

Of the first DISCOVERY of the MINERAL WATERS of BATH, and their having MEDICINAL VIRTUES.

CHANCE being the common Source of such Discoveries as bring Mineral Fountains, and the healing Virtues of the Waters to the Knowledge of Mankind, we shall find it manifesting itself in a very high Degree at *Bath*; and, in the most eminent Case leading a most ingenious young Prince to one of the greatest Secrets of Nature, for the Cure of a loathsome Disease which he laboured under.

THE Story touching this Prince having been solemnly handed down to the Elders of the present Age, as they received it I will here repeat the Substance of it.

"WHILE *Bladud*, the only Son of *Lud Hudibras*, the
" eighth King of the *Britons* from *Brute*, was a young
" Man, he, by some Accident or other, got the Leprosy;
" and lest he should infect the Nobility and Gentry, that at-
" tended his Father's Levy, with that Distemper, they all
" joined in an humble Petition to the King, that the Prince
" might be BANISHED the *British* Court. *Lud Hudibras*
" finding himself under a Necessity of complying with the
" Petition of his principal Subjects, ordered *Bladud* to depart
" his Palace; and the Queen, upon parting with her only
" Son, presented him with a Ring, as a Token, by which
" she should know him again, if he should ever get cured of
" his loathsome Disease."

"THE young Prince was not long upon his Exile, nor
" had he travelled far, before he met with a poor Shepherd
" feeding his Flocks upon the Downs, with whom, after a
" little

"little Discourse, about the Time of the Day, and the Va-
"riations of the Weather, he exchanged his Apparel, and
"then endeavoured for Employ, in the same Way. Fortune
"so far favoured *Bladud*'s Designs, that he soon obtained
"from a Swineherd, who lived near the Place where *Cainsham*
"now stands, the Care of a Drove of Pigs, which he in a
"short time infected with the Leprosy; and to keep the
"Disaster as long as possible from his Master's Knowledge,
"proposed to drive the Pigs under his Care to the other
"Side of the *Avon*, to fatten them with the Acorns of the
"Woods that covered the Sides of the neighbouring Hills."

"BLADUD had behaved himself so well in his Service,
"and had appeared so honest in every thing he did, that his
"Proposal was readily complied with; and the very next
"Day was appointed for putting it in Execution: So that
"the Prince, providing himself with every thing that was
"necessary, set out with his Herd early in the Morning;
"and soon meeting with a shallow Part of the *Avon*, cross'd
"it with his Pigs, in token whereof, he called that Place by
"the Name of *Swineford*."

"HERE the rising Sun, breaking through the Clouds,
"first saluted the Royal Herdsman with his comfortable
"Beams; and while he was addressing himself to the glorious
"Luminary, and praying that the wrath of Heaven, against
"him, might be averted, the whole Drove of Pigs, as if
"seized with a Phrenzy, ran away; pursuing their Course
"up the Valley by the Side of the River, till they reached
"the Spot of Ground where the hot Springs of *Bath*
"boil up."

"THE Scum which the Water naturally emits mixing
"with Leaves of Trees, and decayed Weeds, had then
"made the Land about the Springs, almost all over-run with
"Brambles, like a Bog; into which the Pigs directly im-
"merged themselves; and so delighted were they in wallow-
"ing in their warm ouzy Bed, that *Bladud* was unable to
"get them away, till excessive Hunger made them glad to
"follow the Prince for Food: Then by a Sachel of Acorns
"shook, and slightly strewed before them, *Bladud* drew his
"Herd to a convenient Place to wash and feed them by Day,
"as well as to secure them by Night; and there he made
"distinct Crues for the Swine to lie in; the Prince conclud-
"ing, that by keeping the Pigs clean and separate, the In-
"fection would soon be over among the whole Herd: And
"in

Chap. IX. A Description of BATH. 73

"in this Pursuit he was much encouraged when, upon wash-
"ing them clean of the Filth with which they were covered,
"he observed some of the Pigs to have shed their hoary
"Marks."

"BLADUD had not been settled many Days at this Place,
"which from the Number of Crues took the Name of *Swines-*
"*wick*, before he, by driving his Herd into the Woods
"for Food, lost one of his best Sows; nor could he find
"her during a whole Week's diligent Search: But at last
"accidentally passing by the hot Springs, he observed the
"strayed Animal wallowing in the Mire about the Waters;
"and on washing her, she appeared perfectly cured of the
"Leprosy."

"THE Prince struck with Astonishment at this, and
"considering with himself, that if the Cure of the Sow was
"owing to her wallowing in the Mud and Waters, why he
"should not receive the same Benefit, by the same Means,
"instantly resolved to try the Experiment; and thereupon
"stripping himself naked, plunged himself into the Sedge
"and Waters; wallowing in them as the Sow, and his other
"Pigs had done; and repeating it every Morning before
"he turned out his Herd to feed, and every Night after
"crueing them up: So that in a few Days his white Scales
"began to fall off; and then *Bladud* was convinced that
"the hot Waters had Virtues of the greatest Efficacy for
"his Disorder."

"THE Prince therefore, with the strongest Hopes of ob-
"taining a perfect Cure for himself and Pigs, came daily
"from *Swinefwick* to the hot Springs, bringing Part of his
"Herd with him, and bathing in the Mud and Waters alter-
"nately, till they had all received the Cure he hoped and
"prayed for: After which *Bladud* drove his Swine home,
"and not only told his Master who he was; but gave him a
"particular Account of his late Disorder, and that he, by a
"Miracle of Heaven, was restored again to his Health:
"The Prince, at the same Time, assuring the Swineherd,
"that as soon as he should come to the Crown he would
"make him a Gentleman, and give him an Estate suitable to
"his Dignity.

"THE Swineherd listened with great Attention to what
"his Servant said; and notwithstanding he saw a wonderful
"Change in his Countenance to what he had observed before,
"yet he could not avoid looking upon him as a Madman,

L "and

"and more especially for saying he was the King's only Son:
"But *Bladud*, by the Uniformity of his Behaviour, and the
"Politeness of his Conversation, so far removed his Master's
"Suspicion, that at last he gave such Credit to what he said,
"as made him resolve upon conducting him to Court, to be
"satisfied of the Truth of it."

"As soon as Matters were prepared for the Journey, the
"Prince and his Master set out for the Palace of *Lud Hudi-*
"*bras*; and after their Arrival there, it was not long before
"*Bladud* found an Opportunity, while the King and Queen
"were Dining in Publick, of putting the Ring his Mother
"had given him into a Glass of Wine that was presented to
"her; which the Queen, after drinking the Liquor, no
"sooner perceived at the bottom of the Glass, than she knew
"it to be the Token she had given her Son; and with Rap-
"tures cried out, where is *Bladud* my Child?"

"At these Words an universal Consternation overspread
"the whole Assembly; and while the People were looking
"at one another with Surprize and Amazement, the Prince
"made his Way thro' the Crowd; and prostrating himself
"before the King and Queen, he was thereupon, to the
"great Astonishment and Satisfaction of his Master, received
"by them, and all the Nobles present, tho' in his Shepherd's
"Cloaths, with the utmost Transports of Joy, as the Heir
"Apparent to the *British* Crown; but could not be pre-
"vailed upon to tell where, or how he got his Cure.

Thus the hot Waters of *Bath*, as well as their having
Medicinal Virtues in them, are reported to have been first
Discovered; and the Author of *The Bathes of Bathes Ayde*
firmly believing the Reality of King *Bladud*, hath traced his
Genealogy up to *Adam*; making him the thirtieth Person, in
a direct Line, from that common Parent of all Mankind.

But be that as it will, Tradition goes on with informing
us, that "when the Rejoicings were over on the happy Event
"of *Bladud*'s Return from Exile, and the young Prince
"had sent his Master home, loaded with Presents, he began
"to sollicit his Father for leave to take a Journey into foreign
"Parts, not only to improve himself in the Knowledge
"of Things; but to be out of the Way of those that had
"been the Cause of his Banishment from Court, the better
"to stifle his Resentment for such cruel Usage; and the
"King approving of his Son's Designs and Reasons, resolved
"upon sending him to *Greece*, as he was a Youth of an ex-
"traordinary

Chap. IX. A Defcription of BATH.

" traordinary Genius, to be inftructed in the Learning which
" the *Grecians* were then eminent all over the World for."

" EMBASSADORS were therefore immediately appointed
" to go to thofe learned People and notify to them the
" King's Intention; *Lud Hudibras*, at the fame time, order-
" ing a numerous Retinue, arrayed in the moft fplendid
" Manner, to attend his Son: But *Bladud* befeeched his
" Father to omit all this, and inftead of fending him abroad
" as the Heir Apparent of the *Britifh* Crown, to permit him
" to fet out on his Travels as a private Perfon, dreffed in
" the Habit of a Student defirous of nothing but the Attain-
" ment of Knowledge."

" THE King, after many perfuafive Arguments, com-
" plied with his Son's Defire; and *Bladud* fet out for *Greece*,
" chufing *Athens* for his chief Place of Abode, and continuing
" eleven Years abroad learning Philofophy, Mathematicks,
" and Necromancy: So that at his return to *Britain*, he was
" of great Service to his Father in the Management of the
" Government; whereby he learned the Art of Ruling fo
" well, that when *Lud Hudibras* died, and *Bladud* fucceeded
" him, no Monarch could be more capable of governing a
" Nation than he was."

" BLADUD had no fooner afcended the *Britifh* Throne,
" than he went to the hot Springs where he had got his
" miraculous Cure, when in Exile, and made Cifterns about
" them; built himfelf a Palace near thofe Cifterns, with
" Houfes for the chief of his Subjects; and then removed,
" with his whole Court, to the Palace and Houfes he had
" erected; which from thenceforward went under the Title of
" *Caerbren*, and became the capital Seat of the *Britifh* Kings."

" AFTER this *Bladud* fent for his old Mafter, and gave
" him a handfome Eftate near the Place where he lived;
" which he fettled upon him and his Heirs for ever; building
" thereon a Manfion Houfe for him, Habitations for his Fa-
" mily and Servants, and proper Crues for his Herds of
" Swine: Thefe together made a Town, divided into two
" Parts, the North Town and the South Town, to which
" the Swineherd affixed the Name of thofe Animals that had
" been the Caufe of his good Fortune; and, to this Day,
" the North Part of the Town is called *Hogs-Norton*; but
" by fome *Norton-Small Reward*, from a Tradition that the
" King's Bounty was looked upon, by the Swineherd, but
" as a fmall Reward for what he had done for him."

" WHEN

"When these Works were compleated *Bladud* applied
"himself to nothing but ingenious Studies, which he pursued
"with so much Assiduity, that at last he invented and made
"himself Wings to fly with; but in one of his Flights he
"unfortunately fell down upon *Solsbury* Church, and, to the
"great Grief of all his Subjects, broke his Neck, after a
"Reign of twenty Years."

THUS far Tradition; to which such Credit was formerly given by the Natives of *Bath*, that almost every Body believed the whole Story for Truth; celebrated it in their Songs; and instructed their Children in their very Infancy in it, telling them many other Particulars, which, for the Sake of Brevity, I have omitted.

BUT soon after the Restoration of King *Charles* the Second, the Zeal for *Bladud* began to cease; for the famous *John* Earl of *Rochester* coming to *Bath*, the Story of *Bladud* and his Pigs became a Subject for his Wit, and this proved the Cause of striking it out of the Inscription placed against one of the Walls of the King's Bath: And in the next Age, one *Powell*, mentioned with no small Applause in the *Spectator*, N° 14, 31, and 40, having introduced the *British* Prince upon his Stage in *Bath*; and every thing reported of him becoming Matter for that little *Æsop*'s Ridicule; it made the Aboriginal Inhabitants of the City extremely cautious of repeating afterwards what had been so solemnly handed down to them: So that the Tradition is now in a Manner lost at *Bath*.

HOWEVER to be a Town's Born Child of the Place, descended from a Parent whose Origin in the City is beyond any Memorial, is still reckoned, by some, as the greatest Honour an Inhabitant can enjoy; and formerly such a Birth-Right set a Person upon a Level with almost any Body that entered within the Gates of the City: The same Birth-Right made the People exceedingly tenacious of admitting Aliens amongst them, even by Marriage; and some of the old Families of the last Age could ascend their Pedigrees as many Generations back, as the *Welsh* themselves, and, if possible, with more Circumstances attending every Descent, as well as the Branches from it.

THERE is certainly nothing impossible nor very improbable in the Story touching King *Bladud*'s DISCOVERY of the HOT WATERS, and their HEALING VIRTUES; his making the Baths; or his building the City: "All which, says Doctor
"*Peirce*

Chap. IX. A Description of BATH.

" *Peirce* in his *Bath Memoirs*, page 175, is every Jot as likely
" as that *Charles* the *Great* should find the Baths at *Aix-la-*
" *Chapelle* by the Tread of his Horse, when he was riding a
" Hunting, as Monsieur *Blondell* relates: And it may be,
" adds the Doctor, the Pigs had a Share also in discovering
" the neighbouring Baths at *Borcett*, since they are called, as
" the same *Blondell* also relates, *Thermæ Porcetanæ*, from the
" wild Pigs frequently coming down from the neighbouring
" Mountains; perhaps, concludes the Doctor, to warm them-
" selves, or rather to wallow in the hot Waters of *Borcett*, as
" *Bladud*'s Pigs had done in those of *Bath*."

It is likewise as likely that a Herd of Swine, and particularly a Sow, should lead *Bladud*, by Chance, in his Exile to the Place where he built a City, as that a Sow should lead *Æneas*, by Chance, in his Exile to the Spot of Ground whereon he erected a City: The Story of the *Trojan* Hero stands recorded in the *Roman* Histories by *Dionysius* of *Halicarnassus*, and *Titus Livius*, by whom we are told, that when *Æneas* fled from *Troy*, and embarked in quest of a new Place of Settlement, he no sooner landed in *Italy*, than a white Sow, that he was about to offer as a Sacrifice to know his future Destiny, escaped the Sacrificer's Hands, ran away, and led the Hero to the Place destined for him; and there he built the famous City of *Lavinium*, so denominated from the Name of his *Italian* Wife.

AFTER all, whether the particular Circumstances of these Stories are derived from one another, or whether they are not, the Tradition relating to *Bladud* seems nevertheless probable; and by its fixing the Antiquity of *Bath* in the beginning of that Prince's Reign, it gives us such a Period as was sufficient for doing every thing which *Bladud* is reported to have done between his Exile and Inauguration.

THE Distance between *Swineford*, or the shallow Part of the *Avon*, where the young Prince is said to have crossed that River with his Herd of Swine, and the hot Springs of *Bath*, is about four measured Miles and a half; but following the Course of the River about two Miles more; and the Distance between *Swineswick* and the hot Springs is about two measured Miles and a half.

SWINEFORD lies North-West and by West of *Bath*; *Swineswick* North North-East; and while the former Place is remarkable for its bounding to the Westward, that part of the County of *Somerset*, as well as that part of the Hundred of *Bathforum*

which

which lies on the North Side of the River *Avon*; the latter is as remarkable for a House which still goes by the Name of King *Bladud*'s Palace.

The antient Way from *Bath* to *Cainsham* crossed the River at *Swineford*; Queen *Anne*, with her Royal Consort, the Prince of *Denmark*, passed and repassed that shallow Part of the *Avon* in their Way to and from *Bristol* on the first of *September* in the Year 1702; and the Agreement between the Tradition concerning *Bladud*, and all these Places proves, at least, the Antiquity of that Story to be very great; adding, at the same time, all the Probability to it which a thing so immersed in Darkness, and extreme Age, is capable of receiving.

From the Hot we now come to the Cold Mineral Waters of *Bath*, and such as have been most famed for their medicinal Virtues; the first of which being the Spring that supplies the *Carn Well*, and that which issues out of the Ground at the East End of *Blake-Leigh*, the first Discovery of them, and also of their Virtues, was undoubtedly owing to the Situation of the Fountain Heads; for *Hippocrates* writes, that of all Waters, those which break out of the Ground direct East are the purest: People therefore seeking after these Waters for their Purity, and, when found, applying them to such Purposes as the purest of cold Water was esteemed to be good for, at length Discovered them to be proper for Disorders in the Eyes; and as such they have been made use of, from Times immemorial; the Water of *Carn Well* especially.

This Water was found, upon Examination by Doctor *Guidott*, to be of an acid Kind, and to curdle Milk; which Qualities appeared likewise in the Water of *Frogs Well*, near the Heart of the City, and in the Water of the Well at *Shockerwick*; and according to our Author all these Waters were esteemed chiefly for their Efficacy in the Cure of Inflammations and Rheums in the Eyes.

The first Discovery of *Frogs Well* may be carried up to the first Discovery of the hot Springs, but the Virtues of the Water, and also of the Water of *Shockerwick*, came to the Knowledge of the World in some uncertain Period beyond any Memorial, which was not the Case with our modern Spaws.

For the first Discovery of the *Lime-Kiln Spaw*, and the medicinal Virtues of the Water, was no earlier than about the Year 1729; in which Year, or near it, one *James Hellier*, a Carpenter of *Bath*, having been troubled with a Diabetes,

Diabetes, he was directed to drink the *Bristol* Water for its Softness; but the Cost of that Water prevented him from doing it, and set him upon enquiring for a soft Water nearer home. He was not long before he met with the Spring now called the *Lime-Kiln-Spaw*; of which Water he no sooner began to drink, than he found great Relief in his Disease. Mr. *John George*, an Inn Keeper of *Bath*, having had the same Disorder at that time, he drank of the same Water, and it had the like Effect upon him: So that the Cases of these two Persons DISCOVERING a medicinal Virtue in the Water of our *Lime-Kiln-Spaw*, several People began to drink of it for other Complaints, and thus that Spring, as well as the Virtues of the Water, were first rescued from Oblivion.

THE Proprietor of the Fountain, Mr. *John Hobbs*, a Merchant of *Bristol*, conceiving great Advantages from the Water, made a Cistern about the Head of the Spring, together with proper Conveniencies for drinking the Water and bathing in it; erecting, at the same time, a dwelling House near it: But all this was scarce done before an Attempt was made to draw down the Spring into lower Land belonging to the late Sir *Philip Parker Long*; and the Experiment so far succeeded, that part of the Water of this Spaw rose up in a slip of Meadow Land belonging to that Gentleman, who thereupon caused a small Porticoe to be erected, wherein People that came to drink of the Fountain might shelter themselves: And thus the *Lime-Kiln-Spaw* was divided in its Infancy into the upper and lower Wells; and a Spring that began to stand in Competition with Saint *Vincent*'s Well near *Bristol* was reduced to little or nothing.

THE DISCOVERY of the *Lyncomb-Spaw*, and the medicinal Virtues of the Water was owing to the following Accident: Mr. *Charles Milsom*, a Cooper of *Bath*, commonly called Doctor *Milsom*, having, in Partnership with four other People, rented an old Fish-Pond at *Lyncomb*, for twenty Shillings a Year; and there having been Leaks in the Pond, Mr. *Milsom*, about the latter end of *June* in the Year 1737, searched the Ground under the Head of it, then over-ran with Briars, Willows, &c. in order to discover and stop the Chinks; at which Time he perceived a void Piece of Ground, of about six Feet long, and three Feet broad, which, as he approached it, shook, and looked much like the Spawn of Toads: This, upon Examination, he found to be of a glutinous Substance; to have a strong sulphurous Smell; and to be of the Colour of Oaker.

THIS

This Slime, as it was not above fifteen Inches thick, Mr. *Milsom* soon removed with a Shovel; and then perceiving several little Springs to boil up, and emit a black Sand, like the filings of Steel or Iron, he dug a small Hole to collect all the Springs together: The Soil he threw out was partly a petrified Earth, in Lumps, which at first resembled Cinders; but when those black Lumps of Earth were exposed to the Air, and dried, they turned grey, and grew less, like pieces of Spunge taken out of Water, squeezed and dried. The other part of the Soil was a white Earth, like Chalk, so soft that he could thrust his Cane, horizontally, up to the Head in it; but this Strata of white Earth was not above four or five Inches thick; it was about nine Inches under the Surface of the solid Ground; and the Water that run thro' it was of the Colour of White-wash, made with Lime and Water.

These things, and the Taste of the Water, made Mr. *Milsom* conclude it to be a strong Mineral; and the Doctor having asked Mr. *Palmer*, a Surgeon, several Questions relating to the Methods of trying Mineral Waters, and borrowing a Book of him on that Subject, he began to try the Water of the Spring he had thus opened, by putting a drop of it into a Glass of Brandy, which tinged and made it of a purple Hue; and three or four Drops more turned the Brandy as black as Ink. The Doctor tried other Experiments to confirm him in his Opinion; and as he was very much troubled with the Gravel, so he resolved to try the Water in his own Case; he drank of it, and soon found great Benefit by it, which induced him to recommend it to others, who also drank of it; so that in a short time the Water was known to have medicinal Virtues, of great Efficacy, in several Cases.

But that which made this Water most talked of, in the Year 1737, was the Doctor's making Punch with it, at an Entertainment made by him at the Fish-Pond, just above the Spring, for several of the chief Tradesmen of *Bath*, and their Wives; for he knowing the Effect the Water mixed with Brandy would produce, resolved to surprize his Friends with it: Proper Ingredients for a Bowl of Punch were therefore put upon the Table, and, separately, approved of by the Company; after which the Doctor put them together in the Sight of every Body present; when, to their great Surprize, the Punch instantly turned of a blackish purple Colour, and no one dared to taste it:—However, after some merry things

had

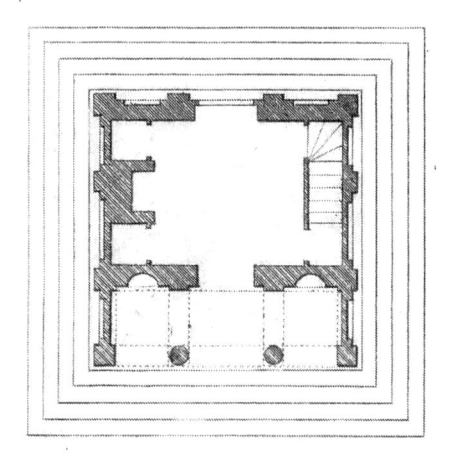

The PLAN and ELEVATION of
the Lime Kiln Spaw Porticoe, with the
House of the lower Well, near Bath.
As it was first Designed.

Arch.

P. Fourdrinier Sculp

Chap. IX.   A Description of BATH.   81

had passed, the Doctor, to save the Liquor, explained the Reason of its Colour; and proving the Truth of what he had said at the Fountain Head, the Punch was then drank with no little Mirth and Jollity.

This being rumoured abroad it occasioned Doctor *Hillary*, the next Year, to make a more particular Enquiry into the Nature of the Water; and on his finding it to be a strong Mineral abounding with medicinal Virtues not much unlike those of the *Geronstere* in *Germany*, he first possessed himself of part of the Property of the Spring, with the Land about it; and then brought the original Proprietor into an Agreement to raise, at their joint Expence, a lofty Edifice over the Fountain to resemble, in some Measure, the Building by the Well of *Geronstere*.

But alas! to make a proper Foundation for the Building, the Spring was in effect ruined: For the Ground about it being weak, and unable to bear a great Weight, part of it was piled, at least eight Feet deep, to sustain the Burthen of the Edifice; which was no sooner finished, at the Expence of about fifteen hundred Pounds, than the following Inscription was placed over the Fountain.

The Medicinal Virtues of
this Water were
First Discovered by
William Hillary. M. D.
A. D. 1738.

If Doctor *Hillary* had not taken upon him more of the Architect than the Physician in this Work, and had been contented to copy the Works at *Geronstere* as we find them inserted in the first Volume of the *Gallantries of the Spaw*, p. 168 and 173, without adding to the Magnificence of the Design; *Lyncomb-Spaw* had undoubtedly remained a fructile Spring to the great Advantage of the Proprietors, and of Mankind in general.

About a Year or two after the Discovery of *Lyncomb-Spaw*, one *Arnold Townsend*, a Miller of *Bathford*, began to clear a certain Piece of Ground, part of a small Estate purchased by him in that Parish, of an Ash Bed which grew upon it: And one Mr. *Hull* of *Berfield*, near *Bradford*, having been at that Time at *Bathford*, as he was amusing himself with seeing the Wood cut down, he observed a Spring of Water in the midst of it, which discoloured every thing it

M   ran

ran over, and made him conclude that it was strongly impregnated with some sort of Minerals.

In this Opinion he was more and more confirmed on trying a few Experiments with the Water; and this encouraged him to persuade the Miller to send some of it to *Oxford* and other Places, to have it examined by Persons of greater Skill, which was accordingly done: And the Water appearing what Mr. *Hull* conjectured it to be, the People in the whole Neighbourhood of *Bathford* began to try it in all manner of Cases; and its first medicinal Virtue was, by such Trials, Discovered in the Cure of several Wounds and running Sores.

Then the Spring was dignified with the Title of a *Spaw* and the Miller selling his Estate to one of the *Bath* Physicians the Spaw received some small Improvements by building but rather for the Doctor's own Amusement and private Use than for the Convenience of the Publick.

The Efficacy of this and all the other Mineral Fountains of *Bath* have, from the Times of the first Discovery of their having medicinal Virtues in them, been experienced in such Variety of Cases, that there are few Diseases incident to Mankind but one or the other of them is now well known to be good for

CHAP. X.

Of the Physical Plants of Bath.

WHERE Mineral Waters of different Kinds rise out of the Earth in so many Places, and with such vast Affluence, as they do at *Bath*, it seems to be no more than a natural Consequence for the Soil of the whole Region to produce great Variety of Physical Plants; and accordingly among the Traditions of the Place, there is one informing us that the back part of *Blake-Leigh* was antiently nothing but a natural Physick Garden, while the other Parts of the Hills and Vale of the City abounded with Plants of the same Kind with those that grew in that Garden.

Doctor *Johnson*'s *Mercurius Botanicus*, printed in the Year 1634, is a Demonstration that the learned World knew of more Physical Plants at that Time peculiar to the Soil of *Bath*, than to any other Region of *Britain*:—And it was formerly a common Observation that Nature produced in the Fields, the Hedges, and the Woods round about the hot
Springs,

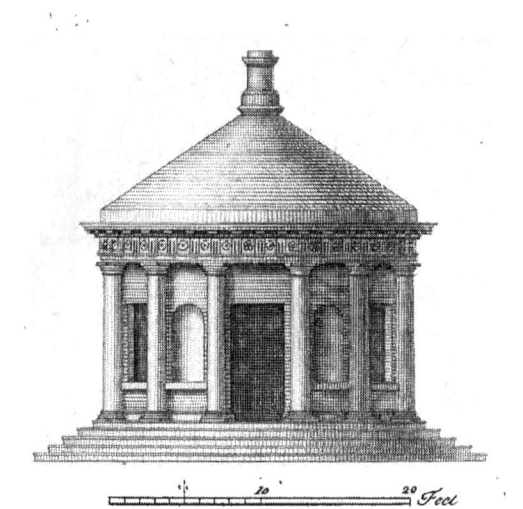

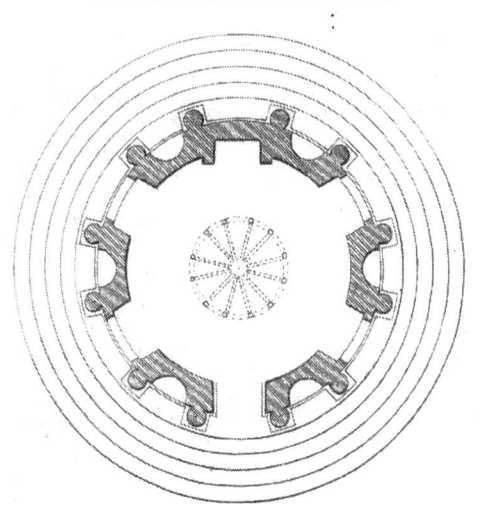

The Plan and Elevation of
a Duodecastyle Edifice for preserving the Casa Rotella of
Doctor Milsom at Lyncomb Spaw near Bath
Designed A.D. 1737.

Arch.   P. Fourdrinier Sculp.

Springs, almoſt every Shrub, Plant, or Flower that could be met with in the choiceſt of Gardens.

By the Catalogue of Plants in the above-mentioned Tract it appears that the Rocks and Walls of *Bath* produce Wall-Rue, or Tentworte; Rock Creſſes, or dwarf dayſe leaved Lady Smock, wild White Hellebore; and Navillwort, or Kidneywort: That the Hills yield Horſe Shoe; Fly Satyrion; Onion Aſphodill; and Onion Green Starflower: That from ſome of the arable Grounds Hedgehogge Parſley ſpring up: That the low Paſture Fields produce Meadow Saffron: That the Woods yield the wild Cherry Tree; Quackſalvers Turbith, or Water Spurge; and great Wood Vetch, or Fetch: And that the Ditch Sides, the Rills, and the moiſt Places which are ſometimes made by the Acceſſion of decayed Weeds, or ſuch other things as generally obſtruct the common Water Courſes, are productive of Impatient Cukowflower, or Lady-Smock; ſmall Water Saxifrage; round leaved Water Pimpernell; and Horſe Tail Coralline.

It would be almoſt endleſs to enumerate the other Plants naturally growing in the Places with thoſe I have named; and therefore I ſhall conclude this Chapter with obſerving that ſeveral People maintain themſelves by collecting, for the Apothecaries, ſuch Phyſical Plants as the Region round about the hot Springs are abundantly enriched with.

CHAP. XI.

Of the general Form and Size of the Body of the City of Bath.

THE Group of Building that now conſtitutes the Body of *Bath*, ſtands upon a piece of Ground, of an Hexagonal Form, encompaſſed with a Stone Wall; the Sides of which Figure are curved and unequal, the longeſt and the ſtraiteſt of them fronts the North; and the publick Ways traverſing the central Part of the *Polygon*, from North to South, as well as from Eaſt to Weſt, forms the Hieroglyphical Figure of the Antients that repreſented the Principle of all Evil, and their Deliverance from it.

This was a Figure compoſed of the Letter *T*, ſuſpended by the Link of a Chain; and, as the Author of the Hiſtory of the Heaven obſerves, the *Egyptians* hung it round the Neck of their Children, and ſick People; they placed it near to those to whom they wished Life and Health; and they applied it to the Fillets with which they wrapped up their Mummies.

It is therefore credible, says Monsieur *Pluche*, the Author of the History above-mentioned, "That the T of the Figure, "thus made use of by the *Egyptians*, appeared to them as the "Beginning and Abbreviation of *Typhon*, the Name of the "Symbol, which those People not only made the Principle "of all kind of Disorder; but the Author of every Physical "Evil they could not avoid, as well as every Moral Evil they "did not care to lay to their own Charge; and that the "Chain that confined it seemed to them the Mark of an "assistant Power, intent upon diverting all manner of Evil "from them: This Custom, adds our Author, of bridling "the Powers of the Enemy, and of hanging a Captive *Typhon* "about the Neck of Children, of sick Persons, and of the "Dead, appeared so beneficial, and so important to the "*Egyptians*, that, as he concludes, it was adopted by other "Nations."

Now to see a Captive *Typhon* represented in the Body of the City of *Bath*, is no more than what we may expect; especially since it so well expresses the real Nature of a Place, blessed with the Means of restraining the Diseases of Mankind; and diverting the Evil from them in almost all Cases that afflict the human Body.

The Size of the irregular *Polygon* into which the Body of the City is formed, appears from a Survey taken of it in the Year 1725, by Mr. *Reynolds*, for his Grace the Duke of *Kingston*, to be about twelve hundred Feet in Length, between its East and West Angles; by about eleven hundred and fifty Feet in Breadth, between its North and South Sides: And as a View of the City was taken in the Reign of Queen *Elizabeth*, to illustrate *The Bathes of Bathes Ayde*, so the reprinting that View will explain, and perhaps better confirm what hath been said touching the Body of it, than any of the more modern Draughts: I have therefore copied it, as in the following Print; and therein the Reader will find the North Side of the Hexagonal Figure I have been describing, marked with the Letters h and i; the Streets forming the Letter T, denoted by the Letters I. N. and T; and the publick Ways representing a Link of a Chain suspending the Letter T, distinguished by the Letters O and P, and by the Figures 6 and 9.

THIS

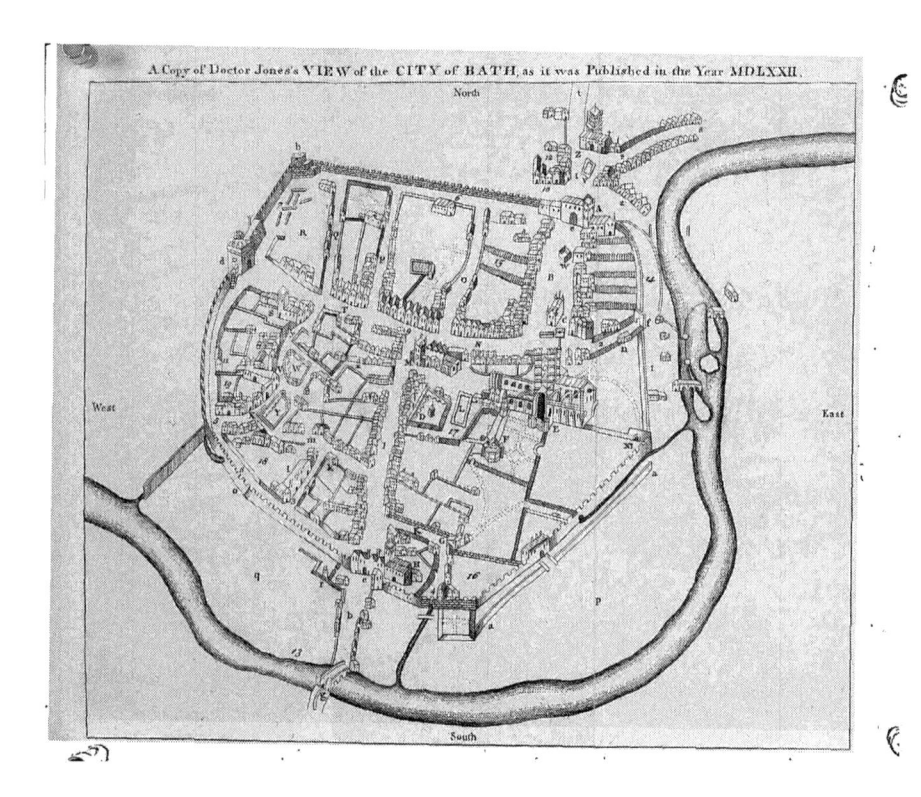

A Copy of Doctor Jones's VIEW of the CITY of BATH, as it was Published in the Year MDLXXII.

Chap. XI. A Description of BATH.

THIS Captive *Typhon* was sometimes represented as detained by a Hand; the Body of *Bath* considered therefore as a Hand, the Thumb will appear in the publick Way marked with the Letter B, the Fingers in the other publick Ways, marked with the Letters O, P, and Q. and with the Figure 7; and there are many other Conformities between the Symbolical Figure of the evil Principle of the Antients chained up, and the Hexagonal Figure of *Bath*, which I shall purposely omit in this Essay, where Brevity is only intended.

THE re-printing Doctor *Jones*'s View of the City may be the Means of informing Posterity of several things already grown obsolete; it will demonstrate the State of *Bath* soon after the Reformation; and it will shew many People now living how inconsiderable it was so far back as their own Memory will carry them; since, by this View, the Body of the City, with the Suburbs without the North and South Gates, must appear to them to have received little or no Addition, by building, between the Time it was taken, and the beginning of the present Century.

AT the same time that Mr. *Joseph Gilmore*, of *Bristol*, measured the Baths, and gauged the Water in the several Cisterns, he took a Plan of the City; and the Year after he published a new View of *Bath*; in which the Suburbs appear small, and the Body of the City but very thinly covered with Buildings, few more than in Doctor *Jones*'s View; and those so mean, and of so little Value, that the second best House within the Walls having not long before been the Property of the then Lord *Lexington*, he assigned it over to one Mrs. *Savil*, in lieu of a Legacy, of one hundred Pounds, which he was to pay her; and that House, commonly called *Skrines* lower House, because it became the Property of Mr. *William Skrine*, an Apothecary, on his marrying Mrs. *Savil*, not only made the Habitation of her Royal Highness the Princess *Caroline*, in the Spring Season of the Year 1746; but of the same Princess, and her Sister, the Princess of *Hesse*, in the Autumn Season of the same Year.

THIS House stands by the Figure 5 in Doctor *Jones*'s View of the City; some of the parts of which View he thus described:

A. The Church of Saint *Mary* by the North Gate.
B. *High* Street.
C. The Market House.
D. The *King*'s Bath.
E. The Church of Saint *Peter the Apostle*.
F. The Abbey.

G.

G. *Abbey* Gate.
H. The Church of Saint *James the Great*, by the South Gate.
I. *Stall* Street.
K. *Abbey* Lane.
L. The Tennis Court.
M. *Stall's* Church.
N. *Cheap* Street.
O. *Locks* Lane.
P. *Vicarage* Lane.
Q. *Spurriers* Lane.
R. The *Timber Green*.
S. The Church of St. *Michael*.
T. *West-Gate-Street*.
V. Saint *John's* Hospital.
W. *Cross* Bath.
X. *Lepers* Bath.
Y. Hot Bath.

STALL's Church was probably dedicated to Saint *Paul*, and belonged to a Parish of that Name in the Center of the Body of the City; the Parts of which City that were neither named nor referred to by Doctor *Jones* were as followeth.

Z. Saint *Michael's* Church belonging to the Parish of that Name lying without the North Gate of the City.

a. a. Part of a Ditch on the outside of the Wall that surrounded the Body of the City, long since filled up, and perhaps mistaken for a Bog by such as dug into it in Mr. *Glanville's* time.

b. *Horse* Street in the Berton of *Bath*; which Berton appeared to *Leland* in the Year 1542 as Meadow Land home to the Street.

c. *South* Gate, just without which, the remains of a Draw Bridge were found within our own Memory.

d. West Gate.
e. North Gate.
f. East Gate.
g. Saint *Laurence's* Gate, to the South of which *Leland* describes a long Street that subsisted in the Year 1542, and extended against the North Side of *Blake-Leigh* as a Suburb to *Bath*.

h. *Gascoyn's* Tower.
i. *Counter's* Tower, but hid by the adjoining Church.
l. St. *Catharine's* Hospital.
m. *Bell Tree* Lane.
n. The Grove.
o. That part of the City Wall where a growing Rock is shewn.
p. A large Meadow called the *Ham*, and making one part of the Berton of *Bath*.
q. A small Meadow called the *Ambrey*, another part of the Berton of *Bath*.
r. The *Ambrey* House.
s. s. *Waldcot* Street.
t. Z *Old* Street.
Z. t. *Broad* Street.
u. St. *Michael's* Conduit.
w. St. *Mary's* Conduit.
x. *Cross Bath* Lane.
y. Saint *Michael's* Street, or rather Lane.
z. *Fish Cross* Lane.
1. *Lot* Lane.

Chap. XI.   A Description of BATH.   87

2. *Boat-stall* Lane.
3. *Bynebury* Lane.
4. St. *James's* Street.
5. *No where* Lane.
6. St. *Mary's* Rampire.
7. *Gascoyn's*, or rather St. *Michael's* Rampire.
8. St. *James's* Rampire.
10. *Berton* Lane, the antient Way to *Berton* House, or the Farm House of the Berton of *Bath*.

THE common Sports of *Shrove* Tuesday, or the Day whereon our Ancestors used to confess their Sins for the religious Observation of *Lent*, were carried on in the *Ham* 'till within our own Memory; one of which being throwing at Cocks, that barbarous and unmanly Custom seems to have taken its Rise from the Modern *Jewish* Custom of sacrificing those Birds on their great Day of Expiation, when the Master of every Family taking a Cock in his Hand, strikes it thrice on the Head, and then the rest of the Family join in killing it. This Meadow contains about five and twenty *English* Acres of Land; and upon opening the middle of the Ditch a. a. in the Year 1740, we found a Rocky Foundation, out of which a fine cold Spring rose up, and, in all probability, it filled that part of the Ditch with pure Water.

ABOUT the middle of the South End of the *Ham* there is a hard shallow Place in the *Avon*, and according to a Tradition now subsisting, the great Road leading from *Bath* to the western Part of the Kingdom, crossed the River there before the Bridge just below it was built; the Way to that Ford turning from *Stall* Street, and passing thro' Abbey Lane and St. *James's Street* to it.

THE natural Ground by Saint *Mary's* Church, is at least forty Feet above the Surface of the Water of the *Avon*; the Torrent of which, and a great one it is after heavy Rains, coming in a Line for more than two Miles in Length from the North East, and directing itself full against the hot Springs, had long since washed them away, if they had not risen out of a firm Soil: But such was the Kindness of Providence, that tho' the Water of the River softened the Foundation of the lofty part of the Hill, at the Foot of which the Body of the City is situated, so as to cause the Eastward Side of it to slip down, even to the End of *Waldcot* Street, yet there the Land became so firm as to resist the Force of the Stream, and turn the threatning Torrent.

FROM the middle of *Lot* Lane, marked with the Figure 1, round by the South to West Gate, or near to those Points, the Wall that furrounds the Body of the City is upon one Level, and I take it for granted that the Foot of *Mons Badonca*, or *Lanfdown*, extended fo far; or rather that the common Floods of the *Avon* reached the curving Line which this part of the Wall defcribes: The Ditch without it was, in moſt places that I have examined, about fourteen Feet in Depth; and if the Land within the Body of the City had not been naturally hard and firm, the Wall that environs it could not have furvived the day of its firſt Erection: So that every thing contributes to prove the Solidity of the Soil of *Bath*, and difprove the vulgar Opinion that the City is built upon a Bog; through which it has been imagined, for I know not what Reafon, that the Walls of the Cifterns about the hot Springs have been raifed to their prefent Levels.

IT has likewife been imagined that the Beds of the bathing Cifterns were raifed from the Bottom of the fame Bog to their prefent Altitudes; and that this, as well as the Building of the Walls of thofe Cifterns, was done by the confummate Art, and indefatigable Induftry of the *Romans*; Mr. *Glanville* acquanting the *Royal Society* with the very Ingredients in the Mortar for the Work; and telling them, in the Letter above quoted, that the Cement was made of Tallow, Clay, Lime, and beaten Bricks.

THAT the Bed of the whole City has been raifed confiderably, and, with it, the Beds of the *Baths*, is very evident; but this will be fhewn hereafter to have been from the Viciffitudes of the Place, no City whatever fuffering more than this has done.

THE Superficial Content of the Ground on which the Group of Building now conftituting the Body of the City ſtands, amounts to about five and twenty *Englifh* Acres; the Wall that furrounds it is about three thoufand eight hundred Feet in compafs; and the irregular Polygon which this part of the City makes, is, by the Streets forming the Letter T within it, divided into three principal Parts, like the Divifion of the Human Face into Forehead and Cheeks. The Monks of *Bath*, fo far back as *Edward* the *Confeffor*'s time, poffeffed the Eaftward Part of the City thus divided; the Poor feeking Relief from the hot Waters poffeffed the Weftward Part; and the King's Burgeffes, with others of a lower Denomination, occupied the Northward Part.

How the Body of *Bath* came to receive its prefent general Form and Size will be hereafter fhewn in treating of the

Works

Chap. XI.   A Defcription of BATH.   89

Works that firft conftituted the City; together with fuch as were, from time to time, performed by thofe that re-edified or adorned it, after it had fuffered Defolation, and other dreadful Effects of War in the Time of the *Romans, Saxons, Danes, Normans* and their Succeffors.

CHAP. XII.

Of the SHAPE of the detached PARTS of BATH; with their SITUATIONS, BEARINGS, and DISTANCES from the hot Springs of the City.

THE City of *Bath*, or rather the principal Part of it, don't appear to have had fuch a fmall beginning as the Cities in general in the early Ages of the World; but from its firft Foundation to have confifted of a large Body, with the hot Springs in the Center, and feveral detach'd Parts immediately furrounding it; fuch as *Haulway, Waldcot, Charlcomb, Bathwick, Hamton, Claverton, Farleywick, Limplyftoke, Iford, Telsford, Southftoke, Duncarnton, Cofton, Solford, Northftoke, Langridge, Tatwick, Wolley,* and *Swinefwick*.

As the City, or any of its original Parts, increafed fo as to make it neceffary to tranfplant fome of the Inhabitants to their utmoft Borders, the People that were, from time to time, removed feem to have feated themfelves firft at the Feet, and in the Combs of the internal Sides of the Hills that firft furrounded the Area in which the hot Springs boil up; and next in the Valleys at the Feet, and in the Combs of the external Sides of the fame Hills; as well as in the warm and fertile Places of the next adjoining Hills and Vales.

BY thefe means the Body of the City feems to have been firft environed with *Wefton, Widcomb, Lyncomb,* and *Twiverton:* And fecondly with *Kelfton, Eafton, Bathford, Frefhford, Henton, Wellow, Inglefcomb, Stanton Prior,* and *Newton*.

ON the other Hand, fuch as were tranfplanted from the original detached Parts of the City, feem to have thus feated themfelves: The People from *Claverton* feem to have removed to *Comb*; from *Southftoke* to *Combhay*; from *Duncarnton* to *Carnecot, Priefton, Welmarfton* and *Camerton*; from *Iford* to *Farleigh*; from *Telsford* to *Norton*; and from *Swinefwick* to *Catharine*.

ALL thefe Places becoming new detach'd Parts of the City, there is no doubt but that the Names of them were
significant

significant and expreffive of the very Places themfelves, or of the Inhabitants that refided in them; and as fuch I fhall endeavour to explain thofe Names.

HAULWAY, the firft original detach'd Part of *Bath*, was formerly a Village of itfelf lying partly on a Beach at the Foot of *Blake-Leigh*, and partly againft the North Side of that Hill, fo as to form the two fhorter Sides of a plain Triangle: It ftands about the third Part of a Mile South from the hot Springs; and the Initial of its Name imports the Sun. This Village, with thofe of *Widcomb* and *Lyncomb*, were united together in the Reign of Queen *Elizabeth*; and at the time of that Union they were made part of the Rectory of *Bath*.

WALDCOT, another original detach'd part of *Bath*, is a *Saxon* Name fignifying Cottages belonging to a Grove; and the Village thus named being of the Shape of the Letter Y inverted, bears North and by Eaft half eafterly from the hot Springs, at the Diftance of about three Quarters of a Mile from them: It ftands upon the great *Roman* Fofs Road; and it begins juft before that Road divides itfelf into two Branches, the firft running Southward through the County of *Somerfet*, and the fecond running Weftward to the antient Trajectus, by which People croffed the *Severn* to *Venta Silurum*.

THE Buildings of *Waldcot* have an eaftern Afpect, and the River *Avon* runs juft below them, while a ftupendous Cliff of Stone, whofe Summit is now called *Beacon* Hill, backs the whole Village.

THIS Hill rifes up on a declining Branch of *Mons Badonca*; its antient Name was *Carnhill*, fo denominated from the Fires lighted upon it in the Times of Paganifm; and it is remarkable for the Defeat of thofe *Saxons* upon it, who, in Breach of publick Faith, had befieged *Bath* in the Reign of King *Arthur*, in or about the Year of Chrift 520.

FOUR Miles Southweftward of this *Carnhill* there is a fecond of the fame Kind, but much more ftupendous, and much more confpicuous: It goes by the Name of *Duncarn*, and it is a vaft natural Mount upon a declining Branch of *Camalodunum*. From this *Carnhill* a Village juft below it was denominated *Duncarnton*; and this Village having been one of the original detach'd Parts of *Bath*, and forming a North and South Line, terminated at the South End with the Parifh Church, is fituated at the Bottom of a Valley; bears South Weft and by South, three Quarters wefterly from the hot Springs;

Chap. XII. A Description of BATH.

Springs; is about four Miles distant from them; and lies by the Side of the same *Roman* Road that *Waldcot* is built upon.

CHARLCOMB is a Village situated in a great Dent of *Mons Badonca* at the East End of that Mountain; and its Shape answers that of the two shorter Sides of a plain Triangle. The Village lies direct North of the hot Springs, at the Distance of about a Mile and a half from them; and it seems to have had its Name from the Largeness of the Comb in which it is built.

BATHWICK, or, as the *Britons* called it, *Kaerbadus*, being another original detach'd Part of *Bath*, its Name seems to indicate it to have been the Fortress of the City: It is situated just overagainst *Waldcot*, and the Buildings traversing the Bottom of *Nant Badon*, form a Line at the Foot of the internal Side of *Camalodunum*, terminated to the Westward by the Church, and divided to the Eastward into two small Branches: This Village bears North East from the hot Springs; it lies about two thirds of a Mile from them; and the Lands belonging to it extending from the River to the Top of *Mars*'s Hill, makes one entire and compact Lordship on the East Side of the Body of the City: It was formerly the Property of the late Earl of *Essex*, but now it belongs to the Earl of *Bath*; and as many of the Citizens of *Bath* have already beautified the Village by their little Places of Retirement in it, so nothing is more probable than that the higher Lands of the whole Lordship will soon be inriched with nobler Villas, and the lower Grounds be covered with such Structures as will augment the Body of the City, and become the chief Beauty of *Bath* in respect to her Works of Architecture.

HAMTON bears North East and by East, three quarters Easterly from the central Part of *Bath*, and lies at the Foot of the North End of *Camalodunum*, at the Distance of about two Miles from the hot Springs. The Name of this Village, in effect, demonstrates it to have been a Town belonging to the *Ham* in the Berton of the City; as such we may very reasonably suppose it one of the original detach'd Parts of it; and its general Shape is like that of *Bathwick*.

THE River *Avon* forms the out Line of a parabolical Figure before the End of *Hamton*; and the extreme Banks at the Head of that Figure are adorned with two Villages, which, with that of *Hamton*, answer the Angles of an Equilateral Triangle, whose Sides are every one about three quarters of a Mile in Length.

CLAVERTON,

CLAVERTON, another original detach'd Part of *Bath*, is situated almost at the bottom of the external Side of *Camalodunum*, at the Distance of about two Miles and a half East South East from the hot Springs. The Name is compounded of the *Roman Clavis* a Key, and the *Saxon Tun* a Town; and the Buildings of the Village having an Eastern Aspect, they, at the same time, form a single Line just below the Parish Church. The Mansion House is a venerable Structure; it was formerly the Seat of Sir *William Basset*; and in the time of the Civil Wars a Canon, placed on the Hill overagainst the Village, was so well directed against the East Front of the House, that, when discharged, the Ball, piercing thro' the outer Wall of the Hall, passed over the Table at which Sir *William*, Sir *Edward Hungerford*, and several other Gentlemen were then sitting at Dinner, and lodged itself in the Breast Wall of the Chimney, without hurting any one Person in the Room.

FARLEYWICK is situated on the top of the Hill from which the above-mentioned Canon was discharged; it bears East and by South, half Southerly from the hot Springs, and is about three Miles and a half from them: The Houses are few in Number, but such as are there form a long Line; and the Name indicates it to have been the chief Place of Habitation belonging to the whole Hill; the modern Name of which being *Far-Leigh*, it implies the furthest Piece of high Pasture Land, lying in common, from the Body of the City Eastward: On the other Hand its ancient Name of *King's-Down*, seems to have been so denominated from *Bel*, as King of the heavenly Bodies, and *Dunum*, a Hill; since a great Dent in the South End of it still goes by the Name of *Belcomb*; and since other Names applicable to the Sun, are yet preserved in the Names of some of the Places on the Top of the Mountain.

BELCOMB is inriched with the House and Work-Houses of a very eminent Clothier; and a small Pavilion in his Garden may be looked upon as a Model of the Octostyle Monopterick Temple of *Delphos*, after it was covered with a Tholus, by *Theodorus*, the *Phocæan* Architect.

LIMPLEYSTOKE, for the chief part, forms a Line in the Bottom of *Nant Badon* on the West Side of the River *Avon*, and is rendered venerable by the quick Rise of *Strouthill* to the West, and *King's-Down* to the East: The Village spreads itself against the Side of the former, and the Church being built on the Summit of the Mountain at a considerable Distance from the Houses, the People, to account for its Situation, tell

us,

Chap. XII.   A Description of BATH.   93

us, that the sacred Pile was intended to be erected in the Valley; but some invisible Spirits pulled down by Night, whatever was set up by Day, and carried the Materials to the Place where the Church now stands.

THIS Village bears South East and by South, a third Southerly from the hot Springs; it is about three Miles and a Quarter from them; and in former Times it was severed from the Hundred of *Bathforum* and made part of the County of *Wilts*. Its Name seems to imply the Grove of *Diana*, since the *Saxon Stocce* imported the hollow Stem of a Tree, or a Grove; and since *Limnatis* was a Sirname of the Goddess: So that nothing seems more probable than that the Festival called *Limnatidia* was here celebrated; and as *Strouthill* is parted from the North End from *Camalodunum* by nothing but a narrow Valley, who can doubt of its having been dedicated to *Strenua*, the Goddess that was held to inspire Mankind with Courage and Vigilence?

IFORD consists of two Capital Houses, and a few others, lying very near one another on the Eastern Bank of the River *Fraw*, or *Frome*, about a Mile from its Confluence with the River *Avon*: It bears South East and by South from the hot Springs; is five Miles from them; and stands in two different Counties, and in three different Parishes, one of which makes part of the Hundred of *Elstube* and *Everlye*, a Region of Country lying between the antient Works of *Stonehenge* on *Salisbury* Plain, and those of *Abury* on *Marlborough Downs*: And as *Iford* is backed by a stupendous Hill, there are many Reasons for inducing me to believe that Hill to have been dedicated to *Jupiter*, under his *Celtick* Name of *Jou*; and this Place to have been denominated from the same Hill, and a shallow Part of the River, at the Foot of it, that was fordable before the present Bridge was built.

TELSFORD is situated by the side of the same River *Frome*, at the Distance of about a Mile and a half from *Iford*; it bears South East and by South from the hot Springs; and the Name of this Village seems to arise partly from a shallow Place in the River that runs by it, and partly from those Idols of the Pagan World called *Talismans*, as well as from those Priests that bore the Name of *Telchines*, on the Score of their Sorceries and other Acts, to make Mankind believe them capable of revealing the hidden Secrets of Futurity.

SOUTHSTOKE seems to have been so named from its Southern Situation before the hot Springs, and from the

Saxon

Saxon Stocce.—It is a small compact Village lying in a Square Form; and was undoubtedly one of the original detach'd Parts of *Bath*: It stands in a high Situation against the external Side of *Camalodunum*; and it is distant from the hot Springs about two Miles and a Quarter, bearing almost South and by West from them.

NORTHSTOKE, another original detach'd Part of *Bath*, being of a square Form, is situated against the North West End of *Mons Badonca*, at the Distance of about four Miles from the hot Springs; and bearing North West, a third Northerly from them. The *Roman* Road branching Westward from *Waldcot* passes through this little Village; and its Name must have arose from its Northern Situation from the Body of the City, and from the *Saxon* Name of the Trunk of a Tree.

COSTON lies in the Shape of the Letter T; it is situated on rising Ground bearing West and by North from the hot Springs, at the Distance of about three Miles and a half from them; and the Name of the Village seems to arise from the Name of that kind of Divination which was performed by a Sieve, and called Coscinomancy; and from the *Saxon* Name of a small Town. This Name bespeaks the Village an original detach'd Part of *Bath*; and a Tree at the North End of the Head of the Figure it forms, claims the Goddess *Trivia*, or *Diana* for its Patron; while a capital Building at the South End of the same Line makes the Seat of the abovementioned Mr. *Harrington*.

BUT *Solford* lying about a Mile to the Northward of *Coston*, and about four Miles and a Quarter from the hot Springs, in a West North West, and one third northerly Line, was a Village sacred to *Apollo* or the Sun; from which Luminary and a shallow Part of the River *Avon* it manifestly received its Name; and the Village lying against the Side of a Hill, called *Pardies* Hill, *i. e.* the Hill of Swearing, forms one compleat Line opening at the Bottom like the Fork of the Letter Y.

LANGRIDGE is situated on a declining Branch of *Mons Badonca*; it bears North and by West from the hot Springs; and is about three Miles from them. This Village forms a small Line; and its Name arises from some sacred Structure on the Top of the Mountain, and the narrow Branch of the Hill it stands upon.

TATWICK lies at the Bottom of a Valley between the
Foot

Chap. XII. A Defcription of BATH.

Foot of the North Eaft Corner of *Mons Badonca*, and the Foot of the North Weft Corner of *Haul Down*, and the Houfes forming a fmall Line, that Line bears North from the hot Springs, and it is about three Miles and a half from them. The Name imports the Manfion or Fortrefs of *Tutates*, or *Mercury*; and as the Pagans made this God an Affiftant or Coadjutor to the King and Queen of Heaven, where could the antient *Britons* have feated him fo properly as between the Mountains confecrated to thofe Deities?

DIAMETRICALLY South of *Tatwick* we find another Manfion of *Mercury* fituated in the Bottom of a Valley, at the Diftance of about four Miles and three Quarters of a Mile South from the hot Springs; and this Place retains more of the Name of the God, than the former, it being called *Taites*.

WOLLEY, an original detach'd Part of *Bath*, is a little Village compofed of a few Houfes that form a Figure like the Letter T. It is fituated in the Valley between *Mons Badonca* and *Haul Down*; bears North, a Quarter eafterly from the hot Springs; and is diftant from them about two Miles, and the third Part of a Mile. All the Side of *Mons Badonca* above this Village was formerly nothing but Wood; and no lefs than fifty Acres of it, by the Names of *Lypwell*'s Wood and *Middle* Wood, together with *Lybwell*'s Copice, were granted by *Edmond Colthurft*, Efq; to Sir *George Snigge*, by Deeds bearing Date the twenty ninth Day of *September*, A. D. 1591: In thefe Woods it is probable that *Miffeltoe* naturally grew, or was cultivated by Art; and *Pliny* telling us that the *Britons* called it by a Name which, in their Language, imported All-heal; and that Name appearing from what Mr. *Toland* writes in his Hiftory of the *Druids*, p. 74. to have been *Ol-hiach*; from thence we may fairly derive the Name of the Village, fince by leaving out the Termination *ach*, *Ol-hi* comes nearer to the Name, as it is commonly pronounced, than *Wolley*.

SWINESWICK is fituated in the fame Valley with *Wolley*, ftands half a Mile Eaftward from it, and bears North North Eaft from the hot Springs, at the Diftance of two Miles and a half from them. I have already accounted for the Name of this Village; nothing therefore remains to be faid touching the original detach'd Parts of *Bath*, but that the publick Ways of *Swinefwick* form one principal Line in the Middle of the Village, and two fmall Lines iffuing from each Side of it.

WESTON, the firft new Place of Abode for such as were obliged to migrate from the City, lies upon the *Roman* Road; branching

branching Weſtward from *Waldcot*; and the Village begins at the Diſtance of a Mile and a half in a North Weſt Line from the hot Springs. This Village ſtands at the Bottom of *Chelſcomb*, a great beautiful Dent in the South Side of *Mons Badonca*; it forms one long Street with a Brook running down the Middle of it; its Name ariſes from its Weſtern Situation, and the *Saxon* Name of a ſmall Town; and the Lady of the late Sir *Philip Parker Long*, Bart. has now a capital Houſe in it, which Sir *Philip* once intended to improve, and make a handſome Seat, ſuch as ſhould be ſuitable for a Gentleman of his great Fortune.

WIDCOMB, ſo named from the great Breadth of the Dent wherein it ſtands, in Compariſon of another juſt by it, called *Smallcomb*, from its Narrowneſs, is a Village beginning upon a high Nap of Ground on the Side of the Dent, not unjuſtly ſtiled *Mount Pleaſant*.

SOME of the Citizens of *Bath* have here their little Villas, while a more conſiderable Seat adorns the extreme End of the Village at ſomething leſs than a Mile from the hot Springs: This Seat is now in the Occupation of My Lord *Anne Hamilton*; and the Village bearing South Eaſt half eaſterly from *Bath*, forms a Line divided into two ſmall Branches to the Eaſtward, with the Pariſh Church lying between them.

THE Comb in which this Village is ſituated, ſinking into the North Side of *Camalodunum*, extends almoſt to the Summit of that Hill, and terminates itſelf in the Shape of the Head of a vaſt Niche, with natural Terraſſes riſing above one another, like the Stages between the Seats of a *Roman* Theatre; and on one of thoſe Terraſſes Mr. *Allen*, one of the Citizens of *Bath*, hath lately built himſelf a Seat, conſiſting of a Manſion Houſe in the Center, two Pavilions, and two Wings of Offices: All theſe are united by low Buildings; and while the chief Part of the whole Line fronts the Body of the City, the reſt faces the Summit of *Mars*'s Hill.

BY the following Print the general Plan of this Seat, as it was firſt intended, may be conceived; the Houſe being marked with the Letter A, the Pavilions with the Letters B, C, and the Wings of Offices with the Letters F, G : H is a Baſon of Water; and the Extent of the Seat from F to G was propoſed to anſwer that of three Sides of a Duodecagon, inſcribed within a Circle of a Quarter of a Mile Diameter: But in the Execution the Wing of Offices, marked with the Letter D, was joined on to the Pavilion B.

THE

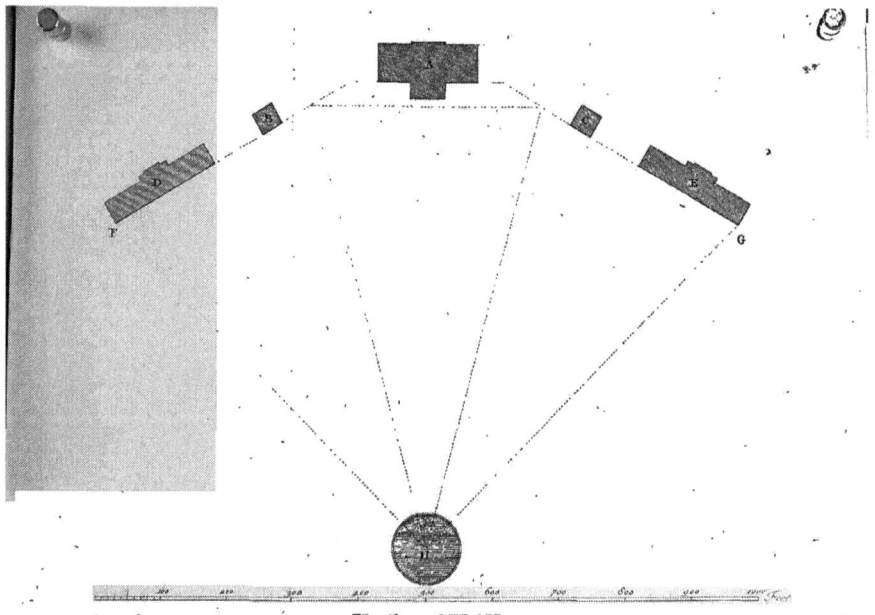

The General PLAN
Of Mr Allen's House and Offices, in the Widcomb of Camalodunum, near Bath;
as it was first Designed.

I Wood Arch.

P Fourdrinier Sculp

Chap. XII. A Description of BATH.

THE Village of *Lyncomb* was antiently situated at the Bottom of the Dent of that Name; and *Lyn* signifying Water, the Name itself imports the Water or watery Valley. Few of the Houses of this Village are now remaining, but those that do exist are about a Mile from the hot Springs, and bear South and by East from them.

TWIVERTON in the Shape of a long Curve Line, branched into two Parts at the extreme End, seems to have been so named from *Tun* a Town, and a couple of shallow Places in the *Avon* that were fordable there before the Wears were built across the River. The Village stands about a Mile and a half from the hot Springs; bears West from them; and seems to have been the last Place of abode for such as migrated from the City upon its being first environed with new Villages to accommodate the Increase of her Inhabitants.

KELSTON, on the other hand, seems to have been the first Place of abode for such as were obliged to migrate from the City upon its being surrounded a second time with Villages to receive the Increase of the Inhabitants; and the general Shape of the Place answers that of the Letter T, supposing it to have a Curve Line for its Head. The Name of the Village is compounded of the *British Kelhe*, signifying a Wood, and the *Saxon Tun*, importing a Town; it stands in an elevated Situation, bearing West North West, three Quarters Northerly from the hot Springs; and it is three Miles and a half from those Fountains.

THIS Village, and the Lands about it, make one entire and compleat Lordship; and for its Size may be looked upon as the Flower of all the Manors within the Limits of the City of *Bath* in its antient State: It was the Seat of the above-mentioned Sir *John Harrington*; and the Mansion House was erected by him after a Draught of the celebrated Architect, *James Barozzi*, of *Vignola*.

EASTON, so named from its Eastern Situation from the Body of the City, and *Tun* a Town, is a Village in the Shape of the Letter Y, and stands, for the most part, on the *Roman* Foss Road, at the Distance of about two Miles and a half from the hot Springs; from which it bears North East, two Thirds Easterly.

THIS Village seems to have received its first Inhabitants not only from the Body of the City, but some of its original detached Parts; for it is composed of three Districts, *Easton*, *Amrill*, and *Catharine*; and *Easton* being divided, *Amrill* is

annexed

annexed to one half, *Catharine* to the other: But, at the fan time, *Amrill* is an Appendage to *Hampton* and *Claverton*; a *Catharine* seems to have been the same to *Swinefwick*.

CATHARINE is lately become a Village of itself; beari North East and by North from the hot Springs, at the Distan of almost four Miles from them; and this Place having be only an Arm of *Easton*, it makes a long Curve Line in t Valley at the East End of *Haul Down*.

BATHFORD, almost in the Shape of the Letter Y, with long Line for its Base, is situated on high Ground towar the Foot of the North West Corner of *Far-Leigh*, or t *King's Down*; it bears East North East, half Easterly fro the hot Springs; and it is two Miles and a half from ther The Name arises from a shallow Part of the *Avon* which a mits of a Passage over the River just beneath the Village, a from *Bath* itself as the only Place to which the Road thro' t River at this Village originally led.

FRESHFORD, the last on the River *Frome*, and so nam from the Modern Date of its Original, in respect to *Iford* a *Telsford*, is a Village whose chief Parts are in the Shape the Letter T; while the rest form three small Lines risi up from the Head of it. It is for the most part situated on t Summit of a small Hill; bears South East and by South fro the hot Springs; is four Miles distant from those Fountain and the Buildings of it appear to such as view them from t South West End of the *King's Down* like a Collection little Palaces!

HENTON implies the old or antient Town, and bearing Sou and by East from the hot Springs, is situated on the Top of Hill four Miles and a half from the warm Fountains: T Village is divided into two Parts widely detach'd from o another; and each Part appearing in the Shape of an L, Capital Building stands between them, and makes one the principal Seats within the Limits of *Bath*, in its midc State.

WELLOW or *Welewe*, is a Village in the Shape of a Crof and lying in a low Situation, it bears South and by West, Third Westerly from the hot Springs, at the Distance of abo four Miles and a Quarter from them. The Name seems have arose from some remarkable Well in it set apart for religio Purposes; or used for watering Sheep; and a Hill rising on the North Side of the Village backs one part of *Cama dunum* to the South, the same as *King's Down* backs it to t
Eaf

Chap. XII. A Description of BATH.

East; continuing, at the same time, the Curve Line of the North End of *Strouthill*, and carrying some Marks of a Dedication to the Twin Brothers, *Castor* and *Pollux*; Heroes worshipped in *Gaul*, as Monsieur *Banier* concludes from their Bas-reliefs dug up in the Choir of the Cathedral at *Paris* on the 16th of *March*, A. D. 1711.

INGLESCOMB seems to have been so denominated from the angular Feet of the Hills whereon the Village is situated, and the small Vales that meet in angular Points before them. This Village bears South West and by West, half westerly from the hot Springs; and lying at the Distance of about two Miles and a Third from the Fountains, it forms one principal Line, with several others of a less Size branching from each Side of it. We may divide it into two Parts, the Antient and the Modern; both Parts are near upon the same Level; and both Parts stand so far back from the angular Feet of the Hills whereon they are situated, as to appear high in respect to the Vales beneath them.

THE Manor of *Inglescomb* is the Property of his Royal Highness the Prince of *Wales*, as Duke of *Cornwall*; and the angular Foot of the Hill, from which the Village was principally denominated, is adorned with a Work vulgarly called the Castle; this is sever'd from the Land above it by a deep Trench; and that Land taking the Name of the Plain of the Breach, terminates itself with a large natural Grove extending to the Brow of *Camalodunum* under the Name of *Breach* Wood: This Castle appears to be a Work of the remotest Antiquity; the neighbouring Inhabitants speak of a remarkable Well in it; and therefore it may be looked upon as one of the original detach'd Parts of *Bath*, notwithstanding I have ranked the more modern Part of the Village among those Places to which the People migrated when the City was invironing, a second time, with Villages to receive the Increase of her Inhabitants.

THIS Castle appearing on a declining Branch of *Camalodunum*, makes it probable that the Well in it bore the Name of the God of War; and as such it must have made part of the first Works that were executed on the Hill sacred to that God.

PRIORS STANTON, or *Stanton Prior*, a Name implying the Stone Town belonging to the chief of a Religious Order of Men, is in a low Situation four Miles and a half from the hot Springs; and bearing West and by South from them, its general Shape answers that of an L, with one small Line

branching

branching from the angular Point of it, and another dropping from its Base.

NEWTON, so named from its having been the last detach'd Part of *Bath* to which the People removed on their Increase, is situated on the Top of a Hill; it bears West, half Westerly from the hot Springs; and lying two Miles and three Quarters from them, it forms several Lines that may be all comprised within the Limits of a Quadrangular Figure whose Length is to its Breadth as 5 is to 2.

This Village bears the Sirname of *Saint Lo*, from one of the chief Seats of the Lord *Saint Lo*, that was situated about half a Mile to the Westward of it. *Leland* takes Notice of this Building in the 7th Volume of his Itinerary, and tells us that the last Lord *Saint Lo* dying without Heirs Male, his Lands descended to the Lords *Hungerford* and *Botreaux*; our Author adding that the Castle-like Seat at *Newton* was, at the time of his writing, in the Possession of Lord *Hastings*, Earl of *Huntington*.

This Nobleman was Baron *Hungerford* of *Heitsbury*, *Botreaux*, *Molines*, and *Moels*, in right of his Mother, *Mary*, the Daughter of Sir *Thomas Hungerford*, and Niece of *Robert* Lord *Hungerford*, who, by being descended from the Heiresses of those Families, came to the Possession of Lord *Saint Lo*'s Seat at *Newton*; and thereby to a Place of Habitation which still appears not only with a Dignity suitable to that of the antient Nobility of the *British* Nation; but with a Strength sufficient for detaining King *John* a Prisoner; for in one of the Towers of this Castle-like Seat that Monarch, as Tradition informs us, was confined.

Now touching such as removed from the original detach'd Parts of the City, the first Migration of this Kind seems to have been from *Claverton* to *Comb*, a Village lying against the back Side of *Camalodunum* in the Shape of an L; bearing South East and by South from the hot Springs, at the Distance of about two Miles and a Quarter from them; and taking its Name from the small Valley wherein it stands.

COMBHAY, forming a double Line, bearing South South West from the hot Springs, and lying about three Miles and a Quarter from them in a high Situation against a declining Branch of *Camalodunum*, seems to have been a Village that received the Increase of People from *Southstoke*; and to have taken its Name from the narrow Vale below it, and the apparent Figure of the Sun: It is adorned with a Capital House

that

that makes no inconsiderable Seat; and the Side of the Hill that bounds the Vale beneath the Building yields a Concave Recess before the Front of it, the Theatrical Form of which makes a Beauty in Nature capable of charming the most curious Eye.

THE Bottom of this Vale is marked with a Meandring Brook which seems to have been dedicated to *Camalos*; for it takes its Rise near a Place called *Camely*, and after running all along the Back of *Camalodunum*, it discharges itself into the *Avon*, by the Name of *Camber* Brook.

THE Migration from *Duncarnton* to *Carnecot* in the same Valley with it, was but small, as the Name seems to indicate; but to *Prieston* it must have been very considerable: This Village lies in a Valley separated from that wherein *Duncarnton* is situated, by a declining Branch of *Camalodunum*; and being in the form of the Letter Y, upon a Curve Base Line, it stands about four Miles and a half from the hot Springs; bearing South West and by West from them.

WELMARSTON bearing South South West, half Westerly from the hot Springs, and lying at the Distance of about three Miles and three Quarters from them, in the Shape of a small Quadrangle; and *Camerton* lying about two Miles further in the same bearing, being Towns, the first denominated from the Well of *Mars*, the second from *Mars* himself; it must necessarily follow that the People from *Mars*'s Hill migrated to them when *Duncarnton*, *Carnecot*, and *Prieston*, were filled with Inhabitants: Or the Town of *Mars*'s Well might have been founded as early as the Well in the Castle of *Inglescomb*; and by receiving its Name from that sacred Pit, might thereby become an Original detach'd Part of *Bath*.

WHEN the Inhabitants of *Iford* grew too numerous for the Place, some of them undoubtedly removed to the Top of the opposite Hill and founded the Village of *Far-Leigh*, so named from *Leigh*, a Piece of high Pasture Land, and its remote Situation from the Body of the City, Southward, in respect to the other common Pasture Ground belonging to it: And in like manner when the Inhabitants of *Telsford* grew too numerous for the Place, some of them, by removing Northward from their old Abodes, might found *Norton*, or the North Town.

CARNECOT stands in a high Situation on the South Side of the Vale that is watered by *Camalos*'s Brook; and the Buildings fronting two publick Ways, crossing each other, the

Point

Point of Interſection bears the Name of the Croſs, and is marked with a Tree which preſerves, to this Hour, the Object of Adoration that, in Pagan Times, muſt have grown on the ſame Spot of Ground.

This Place is a computed Mile from *Duncarnton*; and a computed Mile further on, againſt the Side of the ſame Hill, *Camerton* is ſituated at the Bottom of a ſmall Dent or Comb; wherein it forms a long Line beginning with the Pariſh Church, and a Manſion Houſe that may be placed in the firſt Rank of Capital Houſes within the antient Limits of the Hundred of *Bathforum*.

The Buildings of *Far-Leigh* are widely detach'd from one another, and ſtanding in a high Situation, they front two publick Roads. Here we ſee a Capital Seat that yields to few within the Limits of *Bath*, in its middle State: And here we likewiſe ſee the Ruins of a Caſtle that formerly made one of the moſt ſtately Seats in the Kingdom; it was the Habitation of one of the wealthieſt Families; and *Leland* tells us, in the ſecond Volume of his *Itinerary*, that one of the *Hungerfords* built the Grand Apartment in the Inner Court, conſiſting of a Hall and three Chambers, by the Prey of the Duke of *Orleaunce* whom he had taken Priſoner.

This Caſtle made a large Quadrangular Pile of Building, with a ſpacious Court in the middle of it; a round Tower adorned every Corner of the Structure; and another was placed on each Side the Entrance into it: This was in the Weſt Front; before which there was an outward Court, with a Gate at each End of it: Stupendous Offices extended all along the Weſt Side of this external Court; and a Chapel adorned the South Eaſt Corner of it: The ſacred Edifice ſtill continues a lamentable Proof of the Inſtability of Fortune; for it exhibits the Marks of a Family that ſunk, from the Wealth and Grandeur of a Sovereign Prince, to errant Beggary, within the compaſs of half an Age! But how much longer it will remain a Teſtimony of ſuch Magnificence muſt be determined by the Rain, the Wind, and every other Inclemency of the Weather that now beats thro' the Roof, and daily brings the Building towards that State in which we ſee the Ruins of the Caſtle itſelf.

Norton is a large Market Town lying againſt the Side of a Hill; and the chief Part conſiſting of a long Street, croſſed by one that is much ſhorter, the Interſection is adorned with a Monument riſing up from an Octangular Baſis. The Manor

Chap. II.   A Defcription of BATH.   103

of *Norton*, like that of *Inglefcomb*, is the Property of his Royal Highnefs the Prince of *Wales*; and the Town bearing the Sirname of *St. Philips*, is thereby known from the other *Nortons* near the hot Springs of *Bath*.

Such were the detach'd Parts of *Bath*, exclufive of all their little Hamlets, when reduced to its middle State; and the *Britifh, Grecian, Roman, Saxon*, and other Names of them, however corrupted or blended, is a fufficient Proof that they were, for the moft Part, facred to the Idols of the Pagan World: On the other Hand the general Name of *Achmanchefter*, given to the City by the *Saxons*, is a Demonftration that they found it a City of Priefts; as fuch, when Chriftianity began to triumph over Paganifm, the Monks poffeffed themfelves of the facred Works of the Priefts of the Oak; Confecrating to Chrift, and divers Saints, what had been before Dedicated to Idols; and placing Images of the Crofs of the Meffiah, where thofe of the Idols ftood, for everlafting Marks of the Converfions made by them.

These Marks of Converfion were alfo Marks of Expiation, and feem to have derived their Original from the Law made by *Theodofius*, the Younger, for the Deftruction of Paganifm: For about one hundred and fifty Years after the time of that Emperor, *Gregory* the *Great*, as *Bede* affures us, gave *Auguftin* the Monk Inftructions to convert all the well built Temples in *Britain* from the Worfhip of Devils to the Service of the true God by a folemn Confecration, fealed with an Image of the Crofs of Chrift, as the *Theodofian* Law directed.

The Crofs that was fet up for a Token of converting the hot Waters from the Patronage of the Sun, to that of Chrift, was maintained in the *Crofs* Bath till the beginning of *November*, in the Year 1745; and when Saint *Auguftin*, or his Followers, deftroyed fuch things on *Camalodunum* as belonged to *Mars*, they erected a Crofs on the Middle of the Summit of that Mountain, where it is ftill maintained by the Name of *Gregory*'s Crofs.

These Croffes were, by the *Saxons*, called *Rodes*; and from thofe Marks of devoting to the Service of the true God what had been before applied to that of Idols, and of making Atonement for the former Ufes of the Works converted, many of our Towns and Villages received their Names; of which *Rodeftoke, Rode*, and *Rodeafhton* now lying near the Southern Bounds of the City of *Bath*, in its modern State, are undeniable Proofs.

Again,

AGAIN, the Festival Day for celebrating the Invention of the Cross took the Name of *Rudmas* Day from the *Saxon* Name of the Instrument at that time honoured; and from the Form of the Prayer then made use of for the solemn Dismission of the People: And the Festival Day for celebrating the Exaltation of the Cross took the Name of *Holy Rood* Day from the *Saxon* Names of the same Instrument; and from its consecrated Nature.

THESE Festivals were antiently celebrated on the third of *May*, and the 14th of *September*; but now they are both observed on *Holy Thursday*: And as this Day answers the third of *May*, when the sixth Day of the Moon's Age makes the Day of the Vernal Equinox, or the Commencement of the old *British* Accounts of Time; so it seems much more than probable that *Augustin*, and his Followers, opposed the Pagan Priests while they were honouring the Sun at their *May Day* Festivals; and thereby converted the *English*, in Multitudes, to Christianity.

The End of the FIRST PART.

AN ESSAY TOWARDS A DESCRIPTION of BATH.

PART the SECOND.

WHEREIN

The Gods, Places of Worship, Religion, and Learning of the antient Britons are occasionally considered; and the British Works of Bath, and in its Neighbourhood; the Grecian Ornaments with which those antient Works were adorned; and the Devastations as well as Restorations of the City in the Days of the Romans, Saxons, Danes and Normans; together with its Additional Buildings down to the Year MDCCXXVII.

Are respectively Treated of.

CHAP. I.

The Introduction.

CÆSAR's Commentaries will be an everlasting Testimony that the *Britons* in his Time were People of consummate Knowledge in the Art of War; that they were great Philosophers and Astronomers; and that they were the most learned Divines: The same Commentaries will likewise bear Witness that the Inhabitants of the *Britannick* Island were not only infinite in Number when *Cæsar* first arrived in it, but that they had Buildings in great Abundance to answer all their Occasions: And tho' the common People, at that time, appear by the Words of our illustrious Author to have led a Pastoral Life, seldom troubling themselves with Agriculture, yet the *Trinobantes* raised so much Corn as enabled them to supply the *Roman* Conqueror with what was necessary for his Army: We may suppose them, on this Occasion, to have opened

opened their subterranean Magazines; for *Diodorus Siculus* tells us in the second Chapter of his fifth Book, that the aboriginal *Britons*, in reaping their Corn, cut off the Ears from the Stalk, and then housed them up in Repositories under Ground.

CÆSAR's first Expedition into *Britain*, according to his own account, was to revenge the Injuries he had received during his Wars in *Gaul*, by the *Britons* furnishing his Enemies with considerable Supplies: But according to what *Suetonius* writes, he was allured to that Expedition by the Hopes of obtaining a great Prize of Pearls; we may add of Gold, Silver, and other Metals also; and nothing is more probable than that he attained his Ends, since *Pliny* tells us in the thirty fifth Chapter of his ninth Book, that *Cæsar* having had a curious Breast Plate made of *British* Pearls, the *Roman* High Priest dedicated the same to the Mother of *Venus* within her Temple; and *Tacitus* declares in the Life of *Agricola*, that the Gold, Silver, and other Metals which *Britain* yielded, proved the Prize and Reward of her Conquerors.

THE Eminence of the *Britannick* Island at the time of *Cæsar's* first entering into it, carries us beyond that Period which hath been generally assigned for civilizing the *Britons*, and bringing an imaginary Wild and Dispersed People, from Habitations in Woods and Caverns, to dwell together in handsome Houses made by Art: It carries us into the obscure Period of our History: But it demonstrates what the People were in that dark time of our Records; they were then the Masters of the *Gallick* Druids; and tho' *Cæsar* celebrates those famous Priests of the Continent for their Knowledge of the Stars and their Motion; of the Nature of Things; of the Magnitude of Heaven and Earth; and of the Power and Majesty of the immortal Gods; yet he absolutely gives us to understand that they were but mere Smatterers in their Profession, and then tells us, that such as desired to be perfect Masters of it went into *Britain* to learn it.

THE great Learning of the *Britons* is spoken of more than two hundred Years before *Cæsar's* coming into the Island by *Berosus*, a *Chaldean* Priest of *Belus*, so eminent for his Knowledge in Astrology that the *Athenians* caused his Statue, with a Golden Tongue, to be erected in the publick School of their University, as *Pliny* assures us in the seven and thirtieth Chapter of his seventh Book: And this Priest carries the Commencement of the Astronomical and other

Learning

Learning of the firſt Inhabitants of the Iſland up to the Year 152 after the Deluge; *Beroſus* beginning a Monarchy at that Time, with a Perſon who bore the Name of *Samothes*; or had that Name applied to him.

THIS Monarchy, according to Mr. *Sammes*'s Account, continued 945 Years, and ended at the Time of *Brute*'s firſt Entrance into our Iſland: So that from hence we may place the Inauguration of *Samothes*, or the King ſignified by that Name, about the Year 1653 before the Birth of Chriſt; and ſuppoſe a real Monarchy to have commenced in *Britain* about the Time of the Commencement of the *Egyptian* Bondage, which began on the Death of the Patriarch *Joſeph* in the Year 1635 before our Lord's Nativity.

THE *Britiſh* Prieſthood having been annexed to the Royalty, and the *Perſians* learning all their Magick from the *Britons*, it can remain no Matter for Wonder that the Hiſtory of the earlieſt Times of the latter ſhould be communicated to a Prieſt of the former, and, by him, be recorded in Writing; ſince the Liberty of the Pen was allowed to the *Perſian* Magi, but reſtrained from the *Britiſh* Druids in every thing that related to their Religion and Learning: Neither can it remain a Matter for Wonder, that a Hiſtory wrote by a *Chaldean* Prieſt ſhould, after the Courſe of more than ſeventeen hundred Years, fall into the Hands of a learned Fryar advanced to the high Office of Maſter of the ſacred Palace.

IT is therefore much more probable that the Hiſtory bearing the Name of *Beroſus*, and publiſhed about two hundred and fifty Years ago by the great Antiquary, *John Nannius*, commonly called *Annius* of *Viterbo*, ſhould have been a genuine Account, than thruſt into the World as the Forgery of the Dominican Fryar: And it is alſo much more than probable that *Beroſus* carried the Learning of the *Britiſh Druids* up to the Æra of the firſt *Celtick* Kings, to advance the Antiquity of his own Sect, as the *Perſian* Magi were ſuppoſed to have learned all their Magick of the *Britiſh* Prieſts of the Oak.

THE *Germans*, in *Cæſar*'s time, had not ſo much as heard of any of the other Gods of Paganiſm, than *Sol*, or the Sun; *Vulcan*, or the Fire; and *Luna*, or the Moon; all viſible to them, and whoſe Influence they were apparently obliged to: But the *Gauls* had then their inviſible Gods, and entertained ſuch Notions of them as the People of other Countries; making *Mercury* their Tutelar Deity, and believing

lieving him to have had a particular Influence over Merchandize, and all manner of Gain.

APOLLO was the God next in esteem to *Mercury*; *Mars* was honoured after him; then *Jupiter* entered their List; and next to him *Minerva*: The People believing that *Apollo* could cure their Diseases; that *Mars* presided over War; that *Jupiter* was the supreme Deity; and that *Minerva* first taught Mankind Works and Manufactures.

Now the Power and Majesty of these, as well as of all the other *Gallick* Deities not named by *Cæsar*, for he has only enumerated the chief of them, was better known to the *Britons* than to the *Gauls*; and therefore upon the Certainty that the antient *Druids* of the *Britannick* Island were well skilled in the Mythology of the more Eastern Nations, I will, in the Description of those venerable Monuments round about the hot Springs of *Bath*, and such others in its Neighbourhood as have resisted the Effects of Time, and barbarous Hands, so as to preserve some Traces of what they once were, endeavour to point out their Founders and Uses in the obscure Period of our History; and not, as some have done, supinely give to *Cæsar*, and the *Romans*, what they don't appear to have arrogated to themselves.

FOR even *Tacitus* don't pretend that his Father-in-Law, *Agricola*, did any thing more than exhort and assist the *Britons* to build Temples, Houses and Forums, or Places to assemble in; or any thing more than employ his Care to have the Sons of their Chiefs taught the Liberal Sciences: The *Roman* Governor, and High Priest, in all this having in View to sooth a hostile People, and restore them to the Exercise of their Religion and Learning, after both had been abolished by the Order of *Claudius Cæsar*.

AGRICOLA likewise reduced the tributary Corn which the *Britons* supplied the *Romans* with, to the Quantity that was originally agreed upon; and took Care to cut off all other Causes of War between his own People and those he was appointed to subdue and govern.

THE *Britons* thus encouraged to Peace proceeded in their Buildings to sumptuous Structures for their Health and Pleasure; erecting stately Baths for the former, and magnificent Porticoes for the latter: In which Porticoes a brave People, till then unacquainted with Luxury, were led into all the Stimulations and Elegance of Banqueting; and thereby they were softened in Activity and Repose, with which their Bondage

dage to the *Roman* Empire will appear to have firſt commenced; as well as that *Bath* was the chief Scene of an Event ſo remarkable: An Event entirely owing to the Craft of *Agricola*, conſidered as the *Roman* High Prieſt, and not to his Power conſidered as the Soldier, and Stateſman of Conſular Dignity, to whom the Conduct of reducing and governing *Britain* had been committed on the Account of his conſummate Knowledge in the Field, as well as in the Cabinet.

CHAP. II.

Of the GODS, PLACES of WORSHIP, RELIGION and LEARNING of the antient *Britons*.

BATH claiming for its Founder one of the moſt eminent, and one of the moſt celebrated Philoſophers of all Antiquity; a ſhort Enquiry into the Gods, Places of Worſhip, Religion and Learning of the Inhabitants of the *Britannick* Iſland in thoſe early Ages of the World that preceded the Age wherein the *Druids* had their Riſe, ſeems neceſſary, in this Place, for the better underſtanding the Monuments with which King *Bladud* adorned his City; thoſe which for above five hundred Years drew the Prieſts from the Continent into *Britain* to be inſtructed at them in the Myſteries of the *Druidical* Profeſſion; and thoſe which continued a Nurſery for Learning for near ſix hundred Years after.

TOUCHING the GODS of the antient *Britons*, I ſhall firſt obſerve from ſacred Hiſtory, that as the Sun and Moon were placed in the Heavens, for Signs, for Seaſons, for Days, and for Years, ſo it is evident that God intended that Men ſhould obſerve the Motions and Influences of thoſe Bodies, to enable them to compute Time; to know when to Sow and Plant; and when to Reap and Gather: Mankind therefore meditating upon the Motions and Influences of the Sun and Moon, were not long before they miſtook them for the Supreme Gods; and there is not a Nation upon the Earth that hath not bowed the Knee to them as ſuch.

" THE *Egyptians*, ſays *Diodorus Siculus* in the firſt Chapter
" of his firſt Book, looked upon the Sun and Moon as the
" two chief Gods that were Eternal and Immortal; and held
" that their Attributes were a Spirit or quickening Efficacy,
" to which they gave the Title of *Jupiter*; Heat or Fire,
" which they called *Vulcan*; Dryneſs or Earth, to which
" they

" they gave the Appellation of *Metera*; Moisture or Water
" which they called *Oceanus*; and Air to which they gave
" the Name of *Minerva*."

Thus every material and distinct Thing that regarded the Globe on which we live, when God moulded it into its present Form, was esteemed to be part of the Deity; each became a God of itself; and Habitations were found for those Gods in the Orbs of the lesser Planets: So that the seven Planets, as *Albricus* the Philosopher attests, became the seven first Gods of the Pagan World; and Mr. *Sammes* telling us that the antient *Britons* looked upon the Sun and Moon as the King and Queen of Heaven; judging at the same time, *Jupiter*, *Mercury*, *Minerva*, *Venus*, and *Mars* to have been universal Deities; we may from thence conclude that they imagined the Spirit which animates all Creatures, as well as the Elements of Fire, Air, Earth, and Water to have been divinely influenced: And as such that they assigned the Essence of each of them a particular Habitation in Heaven along with the Sun and Moon, and placed them in the Orbs of the Planets *Mercury*, *Venus*, *Mars*, *Jupiter* and *Saturn*.

The Places of Worship, for the Adoration and Invocation of all those Intelligencies, which the *Britons* imagined to have presided in the Orbs of the heavenly Bodies, were such as the Patriarchs themselves set up, or adopted; namely single Trees and single Pillars: For after *Abraham* had made a Covenant of Friendship with *Abimelech*, King of *Gerar*, at a Well sunk by him for the watering of his Herds; had ratified it by an Oath; and had given the Well, expressed in *Hebrew* by the Word *Beer*, the Sirname of *Sheba*, i. e. an Oath, he planted an Oak Tree, or Grove, just by it; under the Shade of which he called on the Name of the Lord, and adored the everlasting God: *Isaac* did the same after he had built an Altar near his Father's Well and Tree: And *Jacob* had no sooner had his Vision in his Journey to *Mesopotamia* than he reared up a Stone; this he named the House of God; He then made a solemn Vow to invoke *Jehovah* at it with an Offering of the Tyth of whatever he should become Master of; and at his return to *Canaan* he built an Altar by his consecrated Pillar to enable him to fulfil his Vow.

Near Trees thus planted, or near others selected for their venerable Appearance, as well as for the Shade they gave, the *Jews* entertained Strangers; eat part of the Meat of the

Animals

Animals offered for Sacrifice; burnt their Incense; buried the Dead whom they most esteemed; and secreted such Objects of Pride as were incompatible with an humble Mind: Near one of them they erected a Pillar as a Testimony of their free and unanimous Choice to serve the God of *Israel*, and abandon all others: And by the same Tree and Pillar they formed their Republick into a Monarchy, and elected themselves a King.

From these Examples the Piety of the antient *Britons* undoubtedly led them to Plant, or set apart Trees, and to erect single Stones for Religious Purposes: These were the primitive *British* Temples; and Time itself hath not destroyed them, as the Trees and Pillars in our Church Yards, or other open Places of publick Resort in our Cities, Towns and Villages; and the Trees at the meeting of high Ways, do most abundantly testify.

These Trees, for the chief part, were consecrated to the Moon as a threefold Divinity that presided in Heaven, in the Earth, and in the infernal Regions; and they were esteemed as Statues of that Goddess under her Name of *Trivia*, tho' she was often represented by three Stones, as at *Trelech* in *Monmouthshire*: But the single Pillars were generally consecrated to the Sun; and when they were made tapering, and crowned with a Globe, they were looked upon as Statues of that God under his Name of *Belsamen*.

The Religion of the antient *Britons* consisted in their retiring to such Places as were venerable and solitary, and there worshipping their Gods, sometimes by themselves, and sometimes in Companies: For this was the Custom with the *Hyperboreans*, as *Pliny* informs us when he speaks of them as a blessed and happy People whose Country was open to the Sun, of a pleasant Temperature, and void of all noisome Winds, as well as hurtful Air; as a People that applied themselves to Labour only in the Summer Time, sowing in the Morning of that long Day, Reaping at Noon, and with the setting Sun, gathering the Fruits from the Trees; as a People that were utter Strangers to Discord, that felt no Sickness, and that enjoyed themselves in their Habitations during the whole Winter Season; and as a People that never died till they themselves thought proper to put a Period to their Lives: " Then, says our Author, the old Men, after
" a solemn Preparation, leaped from off a certain Rock into
" the Sea, and the Waters became an honourable and com-
" mon Place of Sepulchre to them."

The *Hyperboreans*, as Monfieur *Banier* obferves, were the moft religious People in the World; they never grew weary of Life till they had feen a thoufand Years compleat; and therefore a People thus reprefented could not be without the Belief of the Immortality of the Soul from the very firft time of their coming into the Ifland; which Point of Doctrine the *Britons*, from the remoteft Ages, have been celebrated for Profeffing: With this Belief they zealoufly adored their Gods, feeking their Aid on all Occafions, and attributing all the Good they received to them: Thefe they implored with Sacrifices under fuch Names as they, from time to time, thought beft expreffed the Nature of them; with the like Sacrifices they returned them their thanks; and with the firft Fruits of the Earth they made them grateful Offerings, as the fole Authors of every beneficial thing they gathered from it.

The Learning of the antient *Britons*, or rather of the firft Inhabitants of *Britain*, appeared to have been very extraordinary to fuch Writers as have endeavoured to fhew that we have had a Race of Kings before the Author of the *British* Hiftory commenced his Monarchy with a *Trojan* Prince, defcended from the great *Æneas*; for thofe Writers tell us, that *Samothes*, the firft King of the Ifland, afcended the Throne 945 Years before *Brute*, and that he was a great Scholar in Philofophy, Mathematicks and Religion; that his Son *Magus* was the fame; that his Grandfon *Sarron* founded Schools and publick Places for Learning; that his great Grandfon *Druis* gave the *Druids* their Origin, and was the Mafter of *Pythagoras* for his Doctrine of the Tranfmigration of Souls from one Body to another; and that *Bardus* the Son of *Druis* added Poetry, Mufick and Heraldry to the Learning of his Anceftors.

This pompous Account is entirely rejected by Mr. *Milton*, who will not give it the Room in his Hiftory, fo much as of a *British* Fable: It may neverthelefs pafs as a *Chaldean* Tale, wherein the Hiftory of King *Bladud*, and the *Athenian* Necromancers that affifted him in his Works of *Bath*, was wrapped up by *Berofus* in order to do honour to the Priefthood, and advance its Antiquity as high as the firft Monarchy that was eftablifhed in the Ifland.

The *Athenian* Necromancers I juft now mentioned, appear, from what Mr. *Sammes* writes, to have been four in Number; and *Bladud*'s taking them under his Protection when they were driven to the Neceffity of deferting their City,

muft

must have laid the Foundation for that particular Friendship which subsisted formerly between the *Hyperboreans*, and the *Grecians*; and more especially the *Athenians*, among whom our *British* Prince resided, and the Inhabitants of *Delos*: Now for the latter, Mythologists give a very good Reason, for they tell us that *Latona* made the Island of *Delos* her Place of Refuge when she was pursued by a Monster, named *Python*, which *Juno* made the Earth produce to be the Instrument of her Vengeance against her, and there she was delivered of *Apollo* and *Diana*: And for the former we find as good a Reason in the late Archbishop of *Canterbury*'s Antiquities of *Greece*; our Author telling us, in the Ninth Chapter of his second Book, that the *Athenians*, at a time when the Plague raged over all *Greece*, received an Oracle from the *Hyperboreans*, commanding them to make Vows and Prayers in behalf of the rest; and that after that they continued to send Gifts and Offerings thither, as they had formerly done to *Delphi*.

THE Birth of a God in any Country, denotes no more than the Introduction of his Worship into it, as *Herodotus* most expresly writes; from whence Monsieur *Banier* supposes the Worship of *Apollo* to have been propagated from the *Hyperboreans* to the *Grecians*; we may add of *Diana* also; and this so early as the Ages preceding the *Trojan* War, since *Pausanias* tells us that the *Delphian* Oracle was founded by two *Hyperboreans* named *Pegasus* and *Agyeus*; and since *Diodorus Siculus* assures us that the *Corinthians* applied to that Oracle for Directions how to dispose of the Bodies of the Sons of *Jason*, that were murdered by their Mother *Medea*: That very *Medea* who was Sister to *Circes* the Enchantress, and no less eminent in the Art of Witchcraft; and that very *Medea* who, by providing herself with a hollow Image of *Diana*, got access to *Pelias*, King of *Thessaly*, and made him believe that the Goddess in a Chariot, drawn through the Air by Dragons, had passed from the *Hyperboreans* over many Parts of the World, and had at length made choice of him, as the most pious Prince, to settle her Image with, and establish her Worship for ever: A Stratagem by which she was enabled, in the Evening of the Day of his entering the City *Iolcos*, to get the King murdered, and his Palace put into the Possession of the *Argonauts*.

WHEN the Worship of *Apollo* and *Diana* was once introduced into *Greece*, the *Hyperboreans*, to do Honour to their Gods,

Gods, sent Offerings to them; and these, as the *Delians* affirmed to *Herodotus*, were wrapped up in a Bundle of Wheat Straw, and so transmitted to *Delos*; two Virgins, accompanied with five Citizens, carrying the first Offering that was made; soon after which two other Virgins were dispatched to the same Place to make an Acknowledgment to *Lucina* for a speedy Delivery; and to these four Maidens *Callimachus* adds another, whose Name was *Loto*.

Argis and *Opis*, *Hyperoche* and *Laodice*, are the Names of the Virgins mentioned by *Herodotus*; and that Historian tells us, that the five Citizens that accompanied two of them to *Delos*, went under the general Title of *Peripherees*.

When the *Grecians*, about the Age wherein *Thales*, the *Milesian*, lived, found that the Solar Year, consisting of one entire Revolution of the Earth about the Sun, would not agree with the Lunar Year, consisting of twelve entire Revolutions of the Moon about the Earth, the Study and Endeavours of the Astronomers, of those Times, was to find out *Cycles*, or a certain Number of Lunar Years, wherein, by the Intercalation or Addition of one or more Lunar Months, the Revolutions of the Earth and Moon might be brought within the same Period. Now the first Attempt that was made for this Purpose, consisting of the Intercalation of a Month, at the End of a Cycle of two Years, as well as at the End of another Cycle of four Years, we may from thence fairly conclude that those Attempts were made by the Directions of the *Hyperboreans*.

By the five Peripherees that were sent to *Delos*, we are therefore to understand the Addition of five Days to the *Grecian* Solar Year, which, at first, contained no more than 360 Days, divided into twelve Lunar Months; by the two Virgins those Peripherees accompanied, the Cycle of two Lunar Years; by the two other Virgins, of *Herodotus*, the Increase of that Cycle to one of four Years; by *Loto*, the intercalated Lunar Month at the End of each Cycle; and by the sacred Things those Messengers carried with them, Offerings to *Apollo* of the first Fruits of their Corn, and an Acknowledgment to *Diana* of some other Kind.

This last Cycle was not long in use before it was doubled, and three Lunar Months intercalated, which brought eight Revolutions of the Earth about the Sun, and ninety nine Revolutions of the Moon about the Earth so near together, that it seems to have given Rise to the Fable, "That the *Hyper-*
" *borean*

Chap. II.   A Defcription of BATH.

"borean *Apollo* had killed the Monfter *Python*, or *Typhon*," and on this Victory the *Pythian* Games were inftituted; *Apollo* was from thence furnamed *Pythius*; the Mouth of the Hole or Cavern of the Earth which he had feized at *Delphi*, and made himfelf Mafter of, to deliver Oracles, had a *Tripod*, or three Legg'd Stool, covered with the Skin of the vanquifhed Monfter, placed over it for his intoxicated Prieftefs to fit upon, and catch the Divine Exhalation, or what the God dictated from the Cavern without Danger of falling into it and breaking her Neck, as many of her Order, during their Intoxication, had done; and the Prieftefs, whofe chief Qualities were Age, Poverty and Ignorance, had the Name of *Pythia* given to her.

THE *Pythian* Games were at firft celebrated near *Delphi* every Ninth Year, or rather when the Period of Eight Solar Years was compleat; and therefore, to the Honour of *Apollo Pythius*, an Octoftyle, Monopterick Temple was erected over the Oracular Cave at *Delphi*; and a Feftival, to be celebrated every Ninth Year, was inftituted in Memory of his Victory over the Monfter.

THE Profpect, or outward Appearance of this Temple, having been the very fame with that of the Temple mentioned by *Diodorus Siculus*, as belonging to *Apollo* in the *Hyperborean* Ifland; and the Cave from whence *Trophonius* delivered Oracles having been furrounded with white Stones, forming a Monopterick Temple, makes it much more than probable that the *Grecians* received the Idea of thefe kind of Structures from the *Hyperboreans*, if Hiftory had not informed us that *Abaris* erected Temples in feveral Parts of *Greece*, and if the *Grecians* had not reprefented the *Delphian* Temple as a Work performed by *Pteras* with Wax and the Wings of the Bees *Apollo* had brought from the *Hyperborean* Regions.

THE Monopterick Temple over the Oracular Cave of *Trophonius* became further remarkable from the Pillars with which it was compofed fuftaining Obelifks made of Brafs: And as the Name of thefe kind of Structures is compounded of two *Greek* Words, *Monos*, one, and *Pteras*, a Wing, is it not probable that *Abaris* had the Name of *Pteras* given him on Account of thefe fort of Temples, as well as the Wings with which he pretended to foar to the upper Regions of the Air, and waft himfelf aloft through that Element over Sea and Land from Mountain to Mountain; and from Country to Country?

By *Abaris* or *Bladud*'s presenting *Pythagoras* with the sacred Arrow of *Apollo*, we may suppose the *British* Sage to have communicated to the *Samian* Philosopher the Worship paid by the *Hyperboreans* to *Apollo* and *Diana*; together with the eight Years Cycle, as well as the Intercalation of three Months to bring the Revolutions of the Earth about the Sun, and the Moon about the Earth, within the same Period; and thereby to have enabled him not only to compleat that System of the Planetary World, to which succeeding Philosophers gave the Title of the *Pythagorean*; but appear to the *Crotoniates* for *Apollo* himself: For at this time I will not suppose any thing more to divest *Pythagoras* of the Honour of that System; and for the future shall only endeavour to shew by the antient *British* Works of *Bath*, and in its Neighbourhood, that King *Bladud* taught the same System in *Britain*, in the same Age that *Pythagoras* taught it in *Greece* and *Italy*.

THE chief Part of the Learning of the antient *Britons* consisted therefore in the Knowledge of the Motions of the Heavenly Bodies; and this, with the Arts of Divination, as well as the particular Worship they paid to *Apollo*, was most undoubtedly the Arrow that lay concealed in the *Hyperborean* Island; this was the Arrow with which the Cyclops, or the Days, Months and Years, made use of by the first *Grecian* Astronomers, to regulate the Course of the Earth about the Sun, with that of the Moon about the Earth, were destroyed; this was the Arrow that wounded to Death the Monster *Python*, and mounted the *Pythia* at *Delphi* upon a Tripod, in the midst of an Octostyle Monopterick Temple, to become the Mouth of the victorious God; this Arrow, or System of Knowledge, was the God *Belenus* of the *Britons*; and *Belenus* was adored in *Britain* with as much Pomp and Ceremony as at *Delphi* itself: *Apollo* attending the Grand Festival at the End of every Cycle of Years with his Harp; and spending his whole Nights, from the Vernal Equinox, in March, to the Rising of the Pleiades, about the latter End of *July*, in playing upon that Instrument; and in singing and dancing to it.

THE other Parts of the Learning of the antient *Britons*, in the Persons of *Samothes*, his four next Successors, and the nineteen Kings that followed the Giant *Albion*, will be shewn, from time to time, in the Description of their Works; and in Conclusion of this Chapter, I shall only for the present take notice, that as the Authors of the Fable of *Samothes*, make
him,

Chap. II.   A Description of BATH.   117

him, together with *Magus, Sarron, Druis* and *Bardus*, to have reigned 247 Years; so if we call those Years Lunar Months, for the time between every New Moon was, as *Pliny* attests in the 48th Chapter of his 7th Book, the full Period of the *Egyptian* Year, they will just amount to the twenty Solar Years that *Bladud* sat upon the *British* Throne.

THIS Prince seems to have been disguised under the Name of *Samothes*, either from the Island and City of *Samos* wherein *Pythagoras* had his Birth, and began to teach those things which have immortalized his Name; or from the other Island of *Samos*, so famous for the *Samothracian* Mysteries; and those Mysteries into which the *British* Sage was initiated.

CHAP. III.

Of King BLADUD's Works at BATH, and their constituting the Metropolitan Seat of the BRITISH DRUIDS.

PROPER Cisterns about the Heads of the hot Springs to receive the Water upon its breaking out of the Earth, were the first of King *Bladud*'s Works at *Bath*, as History and Tradition testify; over, or in which Cisterns we may suppose high Towers to have been erected, not only to render the Situation of the hot Waters conspicuous to People at a Distance from them, but to serve as Objects for Adoration; and to those Cisterns we may also suppose Drains to have been made to convey cold Water at Pleasure to the hot, since the Remains of a couple of Drains have been lately discovered running in direct Lines between the hot Springs, and a couple of cold Springs, about seven hundred Feet to the Northward of them; and since we have a Tradition in *Bath* that such subterranean Canals were made at the same Time as the Baths themselves.

COMMON Report, as the Author of the *Tour through Great Britain* observes, makes those Drains no other than necessary Contrivances to secure the hot Springs from the cold; however as the vulgar Opinion of most People formerly was, that the Bath Water received its Heat from Fires, contrived and concealed in some secret Place or other, by the magical Art of King *Bladud*, that Opinion must have taken its Rise from a secret Method made use of, in antient Times, to increase or abate the Warmth of the Water in the Baths, instead of

the

the visible and known Method now made use of to render the Water of the *King's* Bath temperate to the Bathers in general in it; or exceeding hot, when the Cases of some particular People require a hotter Bath than ordinary.

THE Form of the Baths of *Bath*, as they were made by their first Founder is uncertain; but as to their Use, the Author of the *British* History assures us, they were intended for the Benefit of the Publick. And as that Historian, and all other Writers of King *Bladud*, together with the aboriginal Inhabitants of the City, by their Tradition, unanimously join in making him a Magician, so we may look upon this Work as the Basis of his Magick, by enabling him to apply the hot Waters to cure the Diseases of Mankind; and from thence conclude, that *Bladud* assumed their medicinal Virtues to his own Power with the Gods; made the World believe it by abating or increasing their Heat at his Pleasure; and that all his other Works in or near *Bath* regarded Religion, Astrology and the Mathematical Arts.

FROM this Conclusion it is natural to suppose that the King, as he pretended to be endowed with the gift of Prophecy, took upon himself not only the Office of High Priest in *Britain*, to unite the Priesthood to the Royalty, agreeable to what is said of the *Hyperborean* Leader, and as *Darius Hystaspes* had done in *Persia*, in the last Year of his Reign; but constituted the four learned *Athenians*, that fled into *Britain*, the Heads of four Orders of Priests to act under him; It being well known that the *British* Priests were divided into four Orders, to wit, Philosophers, Divines, Prophets and Poets, and that all these were subject to an High Priest.

THE *British* King and High Priest had an Example for the Power he seems to have assumed over the Heat of the Bath Waters, in the Waters of the Sun in *Ammonia*, which were cold in the middle of the Day, and boiling hot in the middle of the Night, as *Herodotus*, l. 4. *Diodorus Siculus*, l. 17. c. 5. and *Quintus Curtius*, l. 4. c. 7. attest; those Waters having had Buildings near them, from whence boiling Water could be conveyed by Drains to the Cistern at the Head of the cold Spring, to give the Water of it the Heat it acquired, at the appointed Time.

THE Cisterns that originally received the Water of the hot Springs of *Bath* seem to have been only two in Number, one at the Head of the chief Spring, and one between the

Chap. III.   A Defcription of BATH.   119

two fmaller Springs: For when the Houfe now ftanding over-againft the South Side of Saint *John*'s Chapel was built, which I think was in the Year 1718, the Workmen, in digging for the Foundation, met with the Veftigia of a Bath; and the very Ciftern, moft probably, that held the Waters of the adjoining hot Springs.

As one of the *Britifh* Names of *Bath* demonftrates that the hot Waters, or fome of them, were confecrated to the Moon, under the Name of *Pallas*; and as one of the *Roman* Names of the City demonftrates likewife, that the fame Waters, or fome of them, were confecrated to the Sun; fo we may conclude that the Tower in or over the Ciftern thus difcovered, not only furmounted the Waters facred to the Moon, but was confecrated with them to that Luminary; and that the Tower in or over the Ciftern at the Head of the chief hot Spring, not only furmounted the Waters facred to the Sun, but was confecrated with them to that Luminary, as King of the Heavenly Bodies.

Now, in an Augural Line with the hot Waters and Towers thus confecrated to the Sun and Moon, and at the Diftance of about 3250 Feet from them, as we afcend the Hill now bearing the Name of *Lanfdown*, there are three large Stones lying upon the Ground, in a little Field by the Side of the Road, known by the Name of *Sols Rocks*, with a Foundation juft behind them, fhaped into a Circular Form: One of thefe Stones lies upon its Edge, and is fourteen Feet long, four Feet thick; the other two lie flat, and feem as though they had formerly been in one, of about thirty Feet long, feven Feet fix Inches Broad, and three Feet nine Inches thick: But now the Pieces are fomewhat thinner; and while one appears full eighteen Feet in Length between the extreme Points, the other meafures no more than thirteen Feet from End to End.

These three Stones, when erect and perfect, feem to have made a ftupendous Altar; and the circular Foundation behind them feems to have borne other erect Stones, which, in all Probability, were fet up by King *Bladud* for a Temple in honour of the Sun.

The Goddefs *Minerva* appears, by all Accounts, to have had a Temple erected to her Honour near the warm Fountains of *Bath*; and to the fame Goddefs, under her *Phœnician* Name of *Onca*, we have already fhewn that one of the Hills of the City was confecrated.

The

THE Hill of *Bath Onca* plainly intimates that the Goddess was highly honoured at the warm Fountains of the City; and tho' Tradition, as well as the modern Writers, place her Temple to the Eastward of those Springs, I am nevertheless inclined to believe that it stood to the Westward of them; since in digging for a Foundation for one of the late Duke of *Chandos*'s Houses, in the Year 1728, I met with the Remains of some Stone Walls which seemed to have been part of the Stereobata of no inconsiderable Temple.

THESE Remains were probably part of the Basis of the very Temple at *Bath*, wherein *Bladud* kept perpetual Fires burning; and the Circumstance annexed to that Historical Fact, of the Fuel never consuming to Ashes, but, on its decay, turning into Balls of Stone, seems to me to mean no more than this, That the Water of the adjoining hot Springs, or some other Water near them, was found to be of a petryfying Nature after passing thro' a certain Part of the Earth; the Moisture of the Western Division of the Body of *Bath* still growing into a perfect Rock of Stone against the City Wall just beyond the Place where the Water of the Hot and Cross Baths is brought through that Wall in its Passage to the River.

A Draught of this growing Rock may be seen in Doctor *Guidott*'s *De Thermis Britannicis*, P. 165; and its Situation being pointed out by the Letter o, in Doctor *Jones*'s *View of Bath*, the Vestigia of the imaginary Temple of *Minerva* were discovered just above it, and under the House by the Figures Number 11. These Ruins lay buried very low in the Ground, and several Feet under the Bottom of the Walls of the old House that was taken down; nor had I met with them at all if a Vintner of *Bath* had not, at that time, prevailed upon the Duke to expend so much Money as was necessary to make a Set of Wine Vaults under the Cellar Story of the new Building.

ABOUT eleven Years after the Discovery of these Works, we began to penetrate the Ground for Foundations for our new Buildings on the North Part of the *Ham*; and in digging into it we met with the Remains of divers old Walls, together with single Stones wrought in a curious Manner: Some of the Stones were twelve Feet under the Surface of the Land; and the whole seemed to me to claim a Parent of much greater Antiquity than the *Romans:* I will suppose these Walls and Stones to have been part of *Bladud*'s Palace, since the *Britons* always

Chap. III.   A Defcription of BATH.   121

always choofe to build near a Wood, or a River for Coolnefs; and the *Ham* is fo fituated that the *Avon* forms a Circular Line from the North Eaft to the South Weft Parts of that Meadow.

THE Word *Ham* is pure *Saxon*, and fignifies an eminent dwelling Place, fuch as a King's Palace; and as *Bladud* is faid to have built *Caerbren*, a Name which imports a King's Throne; his Temples compofed of Pillars, or Places of Addrefs to the Gods; and his Oracle, as well as Royal City, as above; fo I am inclined to believe that King *Bladud*'s Throne, or Palace, was placed in the *Ham*: That the Altar, or Rocks of *Solis*, with the Temple behind it, was his Place of Addrefs to the Sun by Sacrifice: And that the Temple lying to the Weftward of the hot Springs was his Place of Addrefs to the Moon; for *Caer* in the Highlands of *Scotland*, where *Irifh* is fpoke, is a Word now made ufe of to exprefs fuch erect Stones as this Altar, and thefe Temples feem to have been compofed of; as Doctor *Garden*, in his Letter to Mr. *Aubrey*, inferted in the laft *Englifh* Edition of *Camden*'s *Britannia*, p. 1256, particularly writes.

I am likewife inclined to believe that King *Bladud*'s Oracle ftood near the North Weft End of the *Ham*, and in a Piece of privileged Ground, a Place of Sanctuary no doubt, now bearing the Name of Grove; fince that Name points out not only a Parcel of Trees growing near one another, but a fingle hollow Tree, a Cheft, or a Pit to conceal fomething in; the Word Grove fignifying a Cave in the Earth, or any hollow Body, as well as a dark gloomy Wood, fuch as is impenetrable to the Beams of the Sun, as is evident from the Pits on *Mendip* Hills being ftill called Groves, the Miners Groviers.

THE Oracular Tree of the Foreft of *Dodona*, in *Greece*, was, as Monfieur *Banier* takes notice, no more than a hollow Tree, fuch as *Homer* tells us the *Hamadryades* were ufed to quit when their Inclinations led them to tafte the Pleafures of Love with the *Sileni* in Caves of the Earth; and in that Tree the Minifters of the Oracle, as our Author further obferves, hid themfelves when they gave their Refponfes to the Queftions afked by an old Woman that acted as the Prieftefs of *Jupiter* before it.

AT the Foot of this famous Tree there was a Fountain which run with a foft murmuring Noife, and that articulate Sound was fometimes taken for the Voice of the Oracle, and interpreted by the Prieftefs as fuch: And by the fame Tree

R   a

a Brazen Statue with a Lash in its Hand, and several Kettles near it, whence the Name *Dodona*, were suspended in the Air in such manner that the Figure, when agitated by the Wind, like the Clacks in Gardens or Orchards, struck against the Kettle that was next it; this communicating the Motion to the rest raised a clattering Din; and the Noise was sometimes taken also for the Voice of the Oracle, and interpreted by the Priestess as such.

The Predictions thus formed by the Priestess of *Jupiter* from the Voice of her Collegue in the hollow Tree, from the Purling of the Water, or from the Clattering of the Kettles, were delivered to those who came to consult the God either in Verse, when she was clear in the Answer he gave her; or by Lots when she feigned herself doubtful: And this having been a sort of Divination, to which *Pythagoras*, according to *Varro*, very much addicted himself; it was performed by casting something like Dice into Water, occasionally to sink or swim in that Element; and the Chance of the Cast, says *Pliny*, l. 2. c. 7. was taken for a God.

This Kind of Divination appears from hence to have been a necessary Attendant to Oracular Trees, Chests and Pits; and as such it seems to have been practised near *Bladud*'s Oracle at *Bath*, since a publick Way on the East Side of the Grove is, to this Hour, called by the Name of *Lot* Lane; and there is no doubt but that all the other Kinds of Divination were practised near the hot Springs, as *Coston* lying West and by North of them, and *Telsford* lying to the South South-Eastward of the same Fountains, were Places for Divining into the Will of the Gods.

I would now ask whether our Grove at *Bath* may not, with the highest Probability, be supposed to be that which belonged to *Apollo* in the *Hyperborean* Island, notwithstanding the Forests of *Kingswood* and *Selwood* demonstrate natural Groves, of vast Magnitude, to have lain near the Waters of the Sun? And I would also ask, whether there is not some Reason for one to suppose the Circular Foundation behind the Rocks of *Solis* the Basis of the renowned Temple, of a round Form, dedicated to that God in the same Island?

The first natural Grove I just now mentioned bearing a Royal Title; this lying to the Westward of *Caerbren*, or the King's City; a Town dignified with the Marks of Royalty lying still farther Westward; the Sea itself terminating the Line under the Name of *King Road*; and the whole lying

within

Chap. III. A Description of BATH. 123

within the Limits of fifteen Miles in Length; I would further ask whether the King's City, his Wood, his Town, and his Road, all lying Westward of one another, may not be supposed to have had their Rise at one and the same time, under one and the same Prince; and *King's Weston* to have been the chief Maritime Town of *Bladud*'s Kingdom when the *British* Court was seated about the hot Springs of *Bath?*

THE Mouth of the River *Avon*, just before it opens itself into *King Road*, hath been esteemed a sea Port from all Antiquity; it still makes the Port of *Bristol*; and what the contiguous Buildings of that City now are to the Port, the Buildings of *King's Weston*, in all Probability, formerly were, till the open and exposed Situation of that Town rendered it necessary for the Mercantile Inhabitants to remove to another that should be well skreened from the boisterous Sea Winds; Tradition telling us that after a laborious Trial between two Giants, named *Gorum* and *Vincent*, to cut a Channel from *King Road* to a convenient Place for making a Harbour, and erecting a Maritime Town, the latter prevailing brought the flowing Water of the *Severn* Sea to the Place where *Bristol* now stands.

KINGSWOOD seems to have been a Forest destined to hold the King's Game, rather than a Grove consecrated to *Apollo*; but *Selwood* having been formerly remarkable for a Chapel wherein the Bones of St. *Algar* were buried, and therefore, says *Leland*, in the seventh Volume of his *Itinerary*, frequented by the superstitious Multitude, that Forest was undoubtedly a Grove applied to Religious Purposes in Pagan Times, tho' its *British* Name of *Coitmaur* points out to us nothing more than its Magnitude; nor is there the least Reason to suppose it to have been used in such an eminent Manner as to become the Grove of *Apollo*.

THE Grove of that God was really artificial; and it was undoubtedly situated near the hot Fountains of *Bath*, in the Piece of privileged Ground now bearing the Name of *Grove*, and marked with the Letter n in Doctor *Jones*'s View of the City, as above: And as the Way on the East Side of our Grove, marked with the Figure 1, and still called *Lot* Lane, must have had that Name from the Practice of Divination by Lots in it, so the Name of *Ambrey* given to the Meadow marked with the Letter q, must have taken its Rise from an Ambre or rocking Stone formerly in that Field; and probably by the Letter r, where the *Ambrey* House now stands.

THE

THE Bishop of *London* takes notice of one of these Kind of Stones near *Buxton* Baths in *Derbyshire*; and though it is twelve Feet high, and thirty six Feet about, " yet a Man, says " he in the *Britannia*, p. 593, may move it with his Finger:" Many other rocking Stones are still remaining in *Cornwall*, and other Parts of the *British* Dominions; and they are known by the general Name of *Ambre*.

AMBRE is an old Country Word with us in the West of *England*, for a Cupboard; as such the abovementioned *Tom Coryat*, in the Beginning of his Book of *Crudities*, gives his Belly the Title of a capacious Aumbrie for the hungry Haddocks; so that the Word was not improper to express a sacred Inclosure wherein some spiritual Being was supposed to take up its Habitation; for as Monsieur *Banier* observes, the Pagans carried Superstition so far as to believe the Deities themselves resided in the Statues that represented them.

STILPO, the Philosopher, having publickly denied the Residence of *Minerva* in the famous Statue of that Goddess, made by *Phideas*, and set up in a Temple at *Athens*, erected to her under the Name of *Parthenis*, or the Virgin, was arraigned for his Infidelity and Presumption before the great *Athenian* Court of *Areopagus*; where he was obliged, in his Defence, to have recourse to a pitiful Evasion, and to say he had asserted the Statue was not a God, because it was a Goddess; which, however, did not hinder him from being banished.

THE Statues of the pagan Deities were as often simple Blocks of Stone, as Stones shaped by Art into the Human or any other Form. The Statues of *Hercules* and *Cupid* were nothing, as *Pausanias* affirms, but two Masses of Stone; " and " in one Place, says our Author, there are thirty square Stones " which had the Names of so many Divinities." *Lucian* goes further, for he tells us, that in the Temple of *Astarte*, *i. e.* the Moon, in the City of *Hierapolis*, in *Syria*, there were Statues which moved of themselves, and delivered Oracles.

THE Rocking Quality of the *British* Ambres, and such kind of moving Statues of the Gods, was owing to the exact Equilibrium given to them; and this was so well understood by the Antients, that as *Pliny* writes in the 96th Chapter of his second Book, there was a Rock of Stone near a Town called *Harpasa*, in *Asia*, which was so exactly counterpoised as to be put in Motion by the Force of a Man's Finger: And the same Author adds in the 7th Chapter of his 34th Book, that

the

Chap. III. A Defcription of BATH. 125

the Statue of *Hercules* made by *Lyfippus*, and fet up in the City of *Tarentum*, in *Italy*, might be eafily ftirred by the Strength of a Man's Hand, notwithftanding the Figure was forty Cubits high.

By the Name of *Ambrey*, in the Meadow and Houfe above defcribed, we have fomething more at *Bath* than the Shadow of this Mathematical Contrivance; a Contrivance whofe Effect, to this Hour, aftonifhes the generality of Mankind, and often draws the Admiration of the reft! What muft it then have done in pagan Times, when the high Prieft, arrayed in his facred Robes, put one of thefe rocking Stones in Motion by the flighteft Touch, as the Means of obtaining a tacit Anfwer to what he wanted to know of the imaginary God that refided in it?

This, as Mr. *Toland* remarks, could do no lefs than bring Criminals to confefs what could no other Way be extorted from them; and therefore the placing an *Ambre* at *Bath* was a Mafterpiece of King *Bladud*'s Magick; but whether the Equilibrium given to fuch rocking Stones was his own Contrivance, or the Invention of the Learned Men of the Eaft, let the Antiquity of the *Britifh Ambres*, compared with that of the rocking Stones, Statues, and even Temples of the Eaftern Nations determine.

The *Delphick* Temple was a rocking Edifice; for after the neceffary Preparations were made for confulting the Oracle of that Place, " the whole Temple of *Apollo*, by I know not " what Artifice, fays Monfieur *Banier*, trembled and fhook " to its very Foundation, as the Signal given by the God " himfelf of his firft Arrival in it; and a Laurel Tree at the " Entry of that Structure was no lefs agitated." Now as this Oracle was founded by the *Hyperboreans*, and as the Temple was built by *Pteras* with Materials brought by *Apollo* from the *Hyperborean* Regions, it muft neceffarily follow that the Motion given to the whole Structure was the Work of *Bladud*, let the Invention come from whence it will.

In a Line almoft direct North of the *Ambrey* Houfe at *Bath*, and at the Diftance of about three hundred Feet from it, a remarkable Tree was, till of late, upheld, under the Title of *Bel*, or *Belenus*'s Tree; and it grew by the Letter m in Doctor *Jones*'s View of the City: The Field next the *Ambrey* goes partly by the Title of St. *John*'s Meadow, and partly by that of the King's Meadow: And the River *Avon*

feparates

separates it from two other low Pasture Grounds, the one bearing the Name of *Bel* Meadow, the other that of the *Hays*; a Word implying Circles, or rather the Peripheries, Rings, or Out-Lines of such Figures.

BELENUS's Tree seems to have been planted, originally, in Honour of the Arrow, or that System of Knowledge of the Motions of the heavenly Bodies which was secreted with the *Hyperboreans*, and, perhaps for the most part acquired by the great Skill and Labour of *Abaris*, or *Bladud*, in his Astronomical and other Studies: And *Belenus*'s Meadow seems to have been set apart for the Seat of the God *Apollo*, while he was supposed to preside at the Festivals celebrated in Honour of him at the End of every Cycle of Years; the *Hays*, at the same time, serving the Multitudes that danced the *Hay-degines* at those Festivals; and more especially on the first of *May*, which is still called by the aboriginal *Irish*, as well as the Highlanders of *Scotland*, the Day of *Belen*'s Fire, because the Day was proclaimed by great Fires, lighted the Night before, in Honour of the Sun, upon Altars erected upon the Summits of our highest Hills.

AT the Tree sacred to *Bel*, *Apollo* principally, and all the other Gods collaterally, seem to have been invoked; while the *Ambre* below tacitly declared the Will of the Deities: And the Celebration of the *Neomenia*, when once proclaimed, was probably begun at this Tree by a solemn Offering of Cakes; the People compleating the Festival with Games and publick Entertainments in the adjoining Meadow, still carrying the Marks of Royalty in its Name.

THE perpetual Fires maintained in the Temple of *Minerva* at *Bath*, may be looked upon as the Emblem of the Goddess; since Fire was the Symbol of a Virgin; and since the Moon was worshipped in the City as a young Maid: But whether young Virgins had the Care of this Fire committed to them by King *Bladud*, according to the Example of his *Trojan* Ancestors in *Italy*, is a Point which I shall now reserve for further Examination; and for the present only take Notice, that the Priests who proclaimed the *British* Festivals seem to have been furnished with Fire at the Temple of *Minerva* to kindle the Fuel on their Altars, which bore the Name of Carns from their circular Forms; Carn, Karn or Cern, as the Bishop of *London* writes in the last *English* Edition of *Camden*'s *Britannia*, being a primitive *British* Word, signifying a Circle.

SOME

Chap. III.   A Description of BATH.

Some of these Carns made part of *Bladud*'s Works of *Bath*; and the first seems to have been erected on the Summit of a high Mount rising up on a declining Branch of *Mons Badonca* just above the Rocks of *Solis*, and a small Matter to the North East of them: For the Mount is still called *Beacon Hill*; while its original Name is retained in a Fountain, called *Carn Well*, to the Eastward, and in a Tract of Land, called *Carn Hills*, to the Westward of it, and within Musket Shot of the Center of the Mount.

The *British* Carns were nothing but Heaps of small Stones raised in a gentle tapering Manner, upon a Circular Basis, to a considerable Height; and then covered with large flat Stones to serve as Hearths for making the Fires upon. The Name of these Altars express their Form; and from them *Apollo* must have received his Sirname of *Carneus*, rather than from a Person who bore the Name of *Carnus*.

As we have now shewn the most apparent Marks at *Bath* of a King and a Palace; of a hollow Tree or Grove for an Oracle; of a Place for Divination by Lots; of a Tower and Tree consecrated to the Sun; of a Tower consecrated to the Moon; of an Ambre or animated Stone, as another Place of Residence for some superior Being to Man; and of Temples sacred to the Sun and Moon, with one Altar near that of the former to offer Sacrifices at, and another to make Fires upon to proclaim Festivals: And as all these may be comprehended under the most antient Name, given to the City, of *Caerbren*; so I shall offer it as a more than probable Conjecture that King *Bladud* built his Palace in the *Ham*; having the hollow Tree or sacred Grove of *Apollo*, with a Place for Divination by Lots, in Front to the Northward, as well as the Altar or Rocks of *Solis*, the round Work or Temple of the Sun, and the Altar or Carn: And having also *Belenus*'s Tree, with the animated Stone, the principal Bath surmounted by a Tower consecrated to the Sun, the inferior Baths surmounted by a Tower consecrated to the Moon, and a Temple of the same Luminary, all lying to the Westward.

When the King was thus seated, who can doubt of his placing the Priests appointed for the Service of some of the sacred Works that lay near the hot Springs in the Villages of *Haulway*, *Waldcot* and *Charlcomb*, or rather *Carncomb*; as the Name of the first implies the Street of the Sun, that of the second the small Cottages belonging to the Grove, and that of the third the Vale belonging to the Carn? Or who

can

can doubt of his placing such other Priests as were destined to watch for the first Appearance of *Onca*, or the new Moon, on the Top of the Mountain that was consecrated to her?

About the Middle of the Summit of this Mountain we see an antient Chapel turned to profane Uses! This Structure remains, to this hour, a part of *Waldcot*; four or five Houses about it make a little Hamlet; and there is still a yearly Assembly at it on the 10th of *August*, or the Feast Day of Saint *Laurence*: All this seems therefore to be the Continuation of something instituted in pagan Times, and leads me to a Belief that *Bladud* extended his Works to the furthest Extremity of *Mons Badonca*, or *Lansdown*, before he began any thing upon the other Hills of *Bath*.

Lan being a *British* Word signifying a Church or sacred Place, we accordingly find the Remains of a circular Work, of about thirty Feet Diameter, near the profaned Chapel on *Lansdown*: And we also find several Barrows or small semi-globular Mounts of Earth, and several Pits or small semi-spherical Concavities in the Ground near the same Structure.

This Circular Work was undoubtedly a Temple of the Moon; and the Pits seem to have been Altars sunk into the Ground for the Purpose of sacrificing to that Luminary when she disappeared towards the Change; as well as when she was invoked as Queen of the infernal Regions upon Acts of Necromancy, or calling up the Dead: For *Bladud* and his Collegues were great Necromancers; and the Professors of that Art offered their Libations and Sacrifices in Holes and Ditches directing downward, and contrary to the Altars that pointed up towards Heaven.

Upon the Southern Part of the Extremity of *Mons Badonca*, a Piece of Ground appears separated from the rest of the Down by an Intrenchment; this is divided in the middle by a strait Bank of Earth directing to *Cainsham*; and each Part is adorned with a Quadrangular Barrow. To the Westward of this Work, the Village of *Northstoke* is situated: And the hollow Stem or Trunk of the Tree that gave Name to the Place, must have been the Object of Adoration where Insence was burnt, or some other religious Ceremony performed in Honour of the Moon, as Queen of the heavenly Bodies.

To the Northward of this Intrenchment above this sacred Tree, we find a Work that makes a mere Labyrinth of
Holes,

Chap. III.   A Description of BATH.   129

Holes, Ditches, Banks, and Barrows; but, at the same time, Art discovers itself so much in the Figure of the Whole, as well as in the several Parts, that I shall make no Scruple in pronouncing it the Work whereby King *Bladud* and his Colleagues feigned themselves able to raise up all the Deities and Inhabitants of the infernal Mansions in the Practice of the Art of Necromancy: And in several other Parts of the Summit of *Mons Badonca* there are Barrows and Pits, as well as the Footsteps of divers Intrenchments, whose Uses shall be reserved for further Consideration, as the Works themselves seem to have been subsequent to the former.

THE Pagans watching for the first Appearance of the Moon, after a Change, upon their highest Hills; no Place on Earth could be more proper for that Purpose than the South-Westward Extremity of *Mons Badonca:* In the Intrenchment therefore that now appears on the Summit of that Part of the Mountain, we may suppose *Bladud* to have placed the Priests destined to watch for *Onca*'s first Appearance: And nothing seems more probable, than that the King seated the other Priests that officiated at the rest of the Works on the Top of this Hill in the Villages of *Langridge* and *Wolley,* both lying against the backside of it; as the Name of the first implies a Place belonging to some Temple or sacred Work; and that of the second, the Plant that was esteemed by our antient Priests as the greatest Gift of Heaven.

THE Works of *Mons Badonca* seem to have been succeeded by others raised in the Vale at the North East End of that Mountain; the King erecting a Fortress for the first, and placing it on the opposite Side of the *Avon* from *Waldcot:* This Fortress the *British* Writers called *Kaerbadus,* the *Saxons Bathwic,* Names to the same Import; for *Kaer* in the *British* Tongue, and *Wic* in the *Saxon* are synonymous, and signify a fortified Place; and *Badus* and *Bath* mean one and the same thing.

A computed Mile beyond this Fortress *Bladud* seems to have seated the civil Part of his Subjects; as the Name of *Hamton,* given to the Village, demonstrates a Connection between that Place and the *Ham* that made the Residence of the King: And such as were appointed for the Service of Religion, like the *Levites* among the *Jews,* together with such as were destined for War, he most undoubtedly placed on the Summits of two Hills, one to the Southward, and one to the Northward of *Hamton*; strongly intrenching both Bodies of People.

S

THE Southward Intrenchment, as it seems to have contained the People appointed for the Service of War, terminated the Summit of *Camalodunum* to the North; it is now called *Hamton Down*; and it shews the Footsteps of an infinite Number of Stone Walls: And the Northward Intrenchment, as it seems to have contained the People separated for the Service of Religion, terminated the Summit of a declining Branch of *Haul Down* to the South Eastward, and is now called *Solsbury* Hill.

THE chief Part of the Summit of the Mountain to which this Hill belongs, retains the Name of *Charme Down*, and thereon we see several Barrows, with the Footsteps of an infinite Number of Stone Walls, like those on *Hamton Down*; from whence we may for the present, at least, conclude, that upon the spacious Downs dedicated to the Sun King *Bladud* raised sacred Works, and practised that part of his Magick which went under the Name of Inchantments to draw the Gods down from Heaven to reside in them: The Works themselves lying in such a Form that they can claim for their Author nothing but an Inchanter, such as *Bladud* is recorded to have been, and such as he manifested himself to be by composing a Tract of Conjurations; for such a Book *Abaris* is said to have wrote.

WE may likewise conclude, that upon some Temple or sacred Work belonging to *Solsbury* Hill, the King lost his Life, by practising what was beyond the Ability of Man to perform, to give Rise to the Tradition concerning him which mentions his Death to have been occasioned by a Fall upon *Solsbury* Church: And it seems highly probable that *Swineswick* and *Tatwick* made the Places of Abode for such as attended the Works on *Haul Down*, as those Villages are situated at the Foot of the Western Side of the Mountain; as a House in the former still goes by the Name of King *Bladud*'s Palace; and as the Name of the latter points out not only the Mansion of *Mercury*, but Habitations for the several Ministers of that Messenger of the Gods, and Coadjutor to the Deity to whom the Hill above the Village was sacred.

THE Summit of *Camalodunum* being terminated to the North by an Intrenchment that contained the People appointed for the Service of War, the God, *Mars* himself, seems to have been honoured upon a small declining Branch of his Hill, issuing Northward from another of a much greater Size that runs Westward from the West End of the Body of the
Mountain:

Chap. III.   A Description of BATH.   131

Mountain: For there we find a deep Intrenchment surrounding a small Elliptical Area of about one hundred and eighty Feet in Length, by about one hundred and eight Feet in Breadth; and this bearing the Name of *Inglescomb* Castle, the transverse Diameter of the Work makes almost an East and West Line.

THE Center of this Castle is pointed out by an old Maple Tree in the midst of an elevated circular Work of about thirty Feet Diameter; to the Westward of which there is a Pit, or Dish-like Concavity, sunk into the Earth, and to the Eastward we find a circular Area raised upon it, whose Center is in a right Line with that of the Tree and Pit.

THIS Monument of Antiquity, according to the Tradition of the Inhabitants about it, was, in the Times of Yore, famous for a Well in it, wherein the People imagined great Treasures to have been hid, and reported that Lights in the Night time were often seen hovering about the Work; from whence we may fairly draw this Conclusion, that the whole Monument was a Work more than ordinary sacred in the Ages of Paganism; and that it was consecrated to *Camalos* the *British* God of War, the Tree in the Center having been the Image of the Deity; the circular Work it grows in, the Basis of his Temple; the circular Area to the Eastward, the Remains of his Altar; and the Pit to the Westward, the Well of the God where the Soldiery took their military Oaths.

BY these Works it seems highly probable that King *Bladud* established the Worship of *Camalos* at the North Westward End of the Mountain consecrated to him; and as the Name of *Welmarstan* implies the Town of *Mars*'s Well, who can doubt of its having been the Place of Habitation for such Priests as were appointed for the Service of the antient *British* God of War; and for administering the proper Oaths to all that entered themselves into the Army?

THE South Eastward Corner of the Summit of the Hill of that Deity presents us with the Ruins of a most stupendous Work; and with nothing less than the undoubted Remains of the great Court of Justice of the antient *Britons*, to which they annually resorted to have their Controversies decided;
" a Discipline, says *Cæsar*, transferred from *Britain* to *Gaul*;
" where every Body flew for Justice to the yearly Meeting
" of the *Gallick* Priests at a consecrated Place upon the Con-
" fines of the *Carnutes*, a People possessing the middle Re-
" gion of that Country."

THE

THE chief Judges of the *British* Court of *Camalodunum* seem to have been seated upon the decline of that part of the Hill lying between it and the Intrenchment that contained the People separated for the Service of War; and their Place of Habitation is come down to us under the Name of *Claverton*, or the Town of the *Claves*; a Name still preserved in the *Isle of Man*, where the Remains of the antient *British* System of Justice is allowed to exist; and is given to such Members of the chief Court of that Island, whose Province it is to hear and determine all Cases of Difficulty and Consequence arising in it.

THE annual Meeting of the Judges of *Mona* is on the Feast Day of Saint *John* the Baptist; their Tinwald, or supreme Court of Justice, is situated on a Hill near the middle of the Island; and this Court resembles the primitive *Athenian* Court of *Areopagus*; it being open and uncovered; and the *Claves*, with the other Judges of it, sitting under no other Canopy but that of Heaven.

NOW that the Court of Justice on the Hill of *Mars* at *Athens* should prove a Precedent for a Court of Justice on the Hill of *Mars* at *Bath*, seems next to Demonstration, as *Bladud* received part of his Education at *Athens*, and was assisted in his Works at *Bath* by four of the most learned *Athenians* of his Time; and as the *Claves* who principally sat in his Court of Justice resembled the Archons who principally sat in the Assembly of the *Areopagites* of *Athens*.

THE *Gallick* supreme Court of Justice having been situated upon the Confines of the *Carnutes* of that Nation, and taking its Original from the supreme Court of Justice of the *Britons*, it leads me now to shew, that this Court was situated upon the Confines of the *Carnutes* of our own Country; for as Mr. *Toland* writes, there were *Carnean* Priests among the *British* Druids; and such *Carnean* Priests as were appointed for the Service of the *Carn* at the East End of *Mons Badonca*, were seated in a Comb within half a Mile of the sacred Altar, while those that daily attended it assembled still nearer the *Carn* in a Dent of *Beacon* Hill, now called *Fryars* Hall, from a Tradition that it was antiently a Place for Fryars to meet in.

THE Mount that bore this *Carn* is but small and low in Comparison of the Mount now going by the Name of *Duncarn*, and rising up on the Extremity of a declining Part of *Camalodunum* branching South Westward from the Body of the Hill: This Mount undoubtedly bore the principal and most

Chap. III.   A Defcription of BATH.   133

moft celebrated *Carn* of the antient *Britons*; and three different Places juft beneath it retaining the Names of *Duncarton*, *Carnecot*, and *Priefton*, is the higheft Demonftration that can be produced of the Magnificence with which the *Carn* was attended, by the *Carnean* Priefts; a Body of Men, who by walking bare Foot over the Embers of the Exhaufting Fires on it, may be very juftly fuppofed to have fecured to themfelves fome of thofe great Privileges which *Cæsar* declares the *Druids* to have enjoyed; and fuch as *Pliny* tells us the *Roman* Senate ordained for the *Hirpins*; a fet of People, who by walking unhurt upon the burning Coals of the *Acervus*, or *Carn* on Mount *Soracte*, at the yearly Sacrifice celebrated by them on that Hill in Honour of *Apollo*, became venerable to the fupreme Council of the greateft Empire of the World.

THUS it appears, that the annual Affembly of the antient *Britons*, for the Decifion of Controverfies, was held upon the Confines of the *Carnutes* of our own Country; the fame as the annual Affembly of the antient *Gauls* was held for the fame Purpofe upon the Confines of the *Carnutes* of that Nation; and *Great Britain* may glory in having Monuments thus to prove her Right to the Inftitution and Practice of that Difcipline which *Cæsar* the High Prieft of *Rome*, from the Accounts of the *Gallick* Priefts, believed to belong to the Inhabitants of this Ifland.

BETWEEN the *Carn* and Tribunal on *Camalos*'s Hill, *Bladud* feems to have fixed a Stoke, or the hollow Trunk or Stem of a Tree; and to the North of that Stoke to have made a fmall Labyrinth of Pits, Ditches, Banks and Barrows; the King fixing the proper Priefts to attend the firft in Habitations round about the facred Tree, and feating fuch as prefided over the laft in a Vale below the Work; fome Houfes in it retaining, to this Day, the *Saxon* Name of *Barwick*, *i. e.* the Fortrefs, Manfion, or Village belonging to the Mounts or Barrows.

THE Conformity between thefe Works and thofe at the furtheft end of *Mons Badonca* feems to point out their Ufes; and even to demonftrate that they were applied for the Practice of the Art of Necromancy, as the Devil himfelf is introduced as a Labourer at the Completion of *Bladud*'s Works on *Camalos*'s Hill: For the laft material Work that feems to have been performed on that Hill, being a vaft Mount of Earth, there are People who tell us, that it was a fepulchral

Monument,

Monument, raised in Honour of some great Person; while others, who imagine it above the Power of human Art or Industry to raise so large a Hill, and yet believe it raised, ascribe it to the Devil, and say, that as he was going by that Place with a Wheel-Barrowful of Rubbish, taken up by him upon *Od Down*, he grew weary with his Load, and discharging it there made the round Mount that now appears; which, as it consisted but of one Barrowful of Rubbish, was therefore, say they, called *Barrow* Hill.

THIS remarkable Mount seems to me to have been King *Bladud*'s Sepulchre, for it stands within half a Mile of a Place called *Hakum* or *Hakim*, a Name expressive not only of a wise and learned Philosopher; but the very Title which is now given all over the East to *Zoroaster*: And it is so situated as to make the Angle of a Triangle with *Hakim*, and the Castle of *Inglescomb*.

BUT before *Bladud* met with his Tragical End, or had his Body deposited in this stupendous Mausoleum, he seems to have performed many other Works round about the hot Springs of *Bath*; and, after consecrating the Hills that continue the Curve Line on the Back of *Camalodunum* from the South West, round by the South, and by the East, to *Haul Down* at the North North East, and dedicating the first to the Twin Brothers, *Castor* and *Pollux*; the second to *Strenua*; the third to *Jou*; the fourth to the rising Sun, at the time of the Winter Solstice, by the Name of the King of the Heavenly Bodies; and the fifth to the same Luminary, at the time of the Summer Solstice; the King raised divers Altars and Mounts; sunk many Wells; and planted several Trees and a Stoke for the publick Worship of the Gods, if the Remains of such Monuments are of any Weight to support the Assertion.

THUS *Diana*, by her Sirname of *Limnatis*, will appear to have had her Grove, Stoke, or hollow Tree, in the Vale on the East Side of the Hill of *Strenua*, the Situation whereof is by Nature venerable, gloomy and every way applicable to the Luminary that presides over the Night: But the Summit of the opposite Hill, sacred to the King of the Heavenly Bodies, presenting us with a Situation quite the reverse to the former, and every Way applicable to the Luminary that presides over the Day, there the Rising Sun, at the time of the Winter Solstice, must have been hailed and saluted; and the Name of *Hays*, preserved in a few Houses

that

that make a little Hamlet, importing the Ring, Out Line, or Periphery of a Circle, makes it more than probable, that those Houses now supply the Place of an Altar and Monopterick Temple of the Sun; for the Service of which proper Priests were undoubtedly placed in the Village at this time bearing the Name of *Farleywick*.

BANNAGH-DOWN presents us with still more evident Marks of an Altar and Temple for hailing and saluting the Summer Rising Sun, than those at the *Hays* on the Hill next it, for hailing and saluting the same Luminary on his first appearing at the time of the Winter Solstice: For there we have Stones that go by the Names of the *Weather Bed* and *Grey Weathers*; and while *Titam* Hill, or the North End of the *King's Down* exhibits several Barrows, Banks, and other Works of the remotest Antiquity, the Eastward Part of the same Hill yields the Marks of a Well dedicated to *Mars*, and a couple of *Ash* Trees consecrated to the same God, the *Ash* Tree having been particularly sacred to him; and therefore against the North End of *Titam* Hill, the God of War had another *Ash* Tree set apart for his Honour.

OVERAGAINST this Tree, at *Akeham*, a Place lying at the Foot of the East Side of *Bannagh-Down*, and at *Oakford*, another Place lying at the Foot of the opposite side of the same Hill, the Goddess *Rhea* appears to have had *Oak* Trees set apart for her Honour also; for to her the *Oak* Tree was consecrated: If we proceed along the Valley Westward we shall find *Jupiter* to have had his Tree beneath the End of *Mons Badonca*, at a small Village called *Beach*, since to this God the *Beach* Tree was sacred: And if we pursue the Curve Line formed by all these Trees till we come almost to the West and by North of the Tree sacred to *Bel*, we shall meet with what appears to me to have been the last of King *Bladud*'s Works in that Part of his City which lay immediately round about the hot Springs.

THIS Work is a Semi-Globular Heap of Stones, raised on the Brow of *Pardies* Hill, *i. e.* the Hill of Swearing; it is an undoubted Monument of the most solemn Oaths of the antient Pagans; and the Custom of raising these Kind of Monuments, and swearing at them, seems to have taken its Rise in *Jacob*'s Days; the People in almost all succeeding Ages, during the Time of Paganism, practising it.

MOSES informs us, in the thirty first Chapter of the Book of *Genesis*, that when *Jacob* fled from his Father-in-law, *Laban*

pursued

pursued him to Mount *Galeed*, where they made a Covenant; previous to which *Jacob* set up a Pillar, and his Brethren raised a Heap of Stones; then the Terms of the Covenant were rehearsed: " Thou shalt not, said *Laban* to *Jacob*, afflict " my Daughters, or take other Women to Wives; then, " continues he, this Heap and this Pillar shall be a Witness, " that I will not pass over them to thee; neither shalt thou " pass over them to me for Harm; and the God of *Abraham*, " and the God of *Nahor*, and the God of their Fathers judge " betwixt us." *Jacob* assenting to the Terms thus proposed by *Laban*, swore to them by the Fear of his Father *Isaac*; and the Parties calling the Monument the Heap of Witness, they invoked God there to watch their Veracity in keeping the Covenant they had made, and in adhering to the Oath they had so solemnly taken.

Such Heaps of Stones as these are, in *Northumberland*, called *Lawes*; and, as Mr. *Camden* writes, they abound on the Mountains of *Redes* Dale, about the very Place where National Conferences were used to be held: Those Heaps of Stones were therefore raised as Monuments of the Agreements made formerly between the Lords Wardens of *England* and *Scotland*, on the Behalf of their respective Sovereigns; and are the most modern Instances, within my Knowledge, of King *Bladud*'s Institution, as above.

The former Works united made the Place which the *Saxons* called *Ackmanchester*, i.e. the *Oak* Men's City; and as those Works, independent of many others, bespeak a Royal Founder, and one that was also an High Priest; so if they are duly considered they will not only give the Priests of the *Oak* a more illustrious, and a more probable Origin than they have yet had, but constitute

Bath
The Metropolitan Seat of the
British Druids.

The same Works will furnish King *Bladud* with every thing that was necessary to that Form of Religion in which the second Part of his Magick consisted; as well as to the greatest Part of that Skill in Astrology, and the Mathematical Arts, which was requisite to compleat his Magical System; " and, in the Words of *Pliny*, bind the Senses of the antient " *Britons* with three of the surest Chains that were ever con- " trived or invented," since those People, by being Men of Sincerity and Integrity, untainted with Craft and Knavery,

and

Chap. III. A Description of BATH.

and Strangers to Excess and Luxury, as *Diodorus Siculus* have recorded their Character, in the 2^d Chapter of his 5th Book, were liable on every Occasion to be imposed upon by such as made Subtilty and Cunningness the chief Part of their Profession: For to see a Man drawing down the Gods from above; raising up the Dead from below; and obtaining Speech from a Dumb Tree, as well as Motion from a solid Mass of Stone, is seeing Trick and Illusion carried to its highest Pitch.

THE Pillars and other large Stones made use of in the Works above described, were indisputably fetched from *Far-Leigh*, or the *King's Down*; for to this Day there are Stones lying upon the West Side of that Hill, behind a large artificial Bank, ready wrought and prepared for Transportation of the same Size and Texture with the Stones now bearing the Name of *Sols Rocks*. And lest it should be hereafter imagined that the Stones now retaining the Name of the Sun were taken out of a Quarry just by them, I think it necessary to declare, that that Quarry was made by the Stone taken out of it to make the adjoining new Road, in the Year 1707; for before that Year the Road to *Lansdown* was considerably more to the Eastward of the Rocks of *Solis* than it is at present.

THAT the *Druidical* Profession had its Original in *Britain*, is sufficiently evident from what *Cæsar* writes, but much more so by the united Works of *Caerbren*, already described: With those Works the *British Druids* undoubtedly took their Rise; King *Bladud* appears manifestly to have been their Founder, and to have made *Bath* their Metropolitan Seat; and part of what he taught them was first communicated to him by the great *Pythagoras*; *Ammianus Marcellinus* telling us in the ninth Chapter of his fifteenth Book, that the *Samian* Philosopher instructed the *Druids* in their Laws and Customs: Then the *British* Priests who had been celebrated chiefly for their Piety, soon became eminent for their Learning; so eminent as to give *Pliny* Reason to say, " that a Man would " think the *Persians* first learned all their Magick from the " *Britons*:" And notwithstanding their Pupils, the Diviners, the Wisemen, and the whole State of the *Gallick* Clergy, went under a general Name importing Priests of the *Oak*, because, as the same Historian writes, they performed no Office of Divine Service, but under the Shade of Trees, or with Branches or Leaves thereof; yet, as Monsieur *Banier*

T   remarks,

remarks, the Antients sometimes distinguished them by other Titles, but such as always expressed their Functions.

THE FUNCTIONS of the Priests of the *Oak* will best appear from what *Diodorus Siculus* writes in the second Chapter of his fifth Book concerning them: For there we find the Philosophers represented as Men conversant with the Gods, and familiar in their Discourse with them; the Divines as Men acquainted with the Nature of the Deity; and that no Sacrifice could be lawfully offered unless it was presented by a Priest of one of these Orders.

THE Function of the Philosophers consisted therefore in presenting the Offerings of the People upon extraordinary Occasions; as well as in asking the Gods to grant them such good Things as they desired; and the Function of the Divines consisted in their presenting the Offerings of the People upon ordinary Occasions: The Priests of each Order performed their Offices by the help of a Grove or hollow Tree; and from thence they were denominated *Saronidæ*, *i. e.* Priests of the hollow *Oak*.

OUR *Sicilian* Author represents the Prophets as Men capable of foretelling future Events, by viewing the Entrails of the Victims offered up in Sacrifice; and the Poets as Men perfectly acquainted with the Virtues and Vices of the Laity, and very skilful in vocal and instrumental Musick: The Function of the Prophets consisted therefore in viewing the Entrails of the Victims slain in Honour of the Gods, and thereby disclosing the hidden Secrets of Futurity to the People; and the Function of the Poets consisted in collecting the Virtues and Vices of the Laity; in forming them into Songs to sing; in playing upon an Instrument like unto a Harp; and, with their Voice and Musick, in publishing the Praises of such as behaved themselves well, and the Dispraises of those that behaved themselves ill.

THESE Men were denominated Bards, a Name importing Poets and Songsters; and the Prophets having been known to the *Grecians* by the Name of *Ovaties*, to the *Romans* by that of *Vates*, Mr. *Toland* derives both from the *Celtick* Word *Faidh*, signifying a Person inspired by the Gods to reveal their Will.

SUCH were the Functions of the Disciples of the *British Druids*, and consequently such must have been the Functions of our Priests of the *Oak*, under the Superintendency of King *Bladud* their Founder; and nothing seems more probable than

Chap. III.   A Defcription of BATH.   139

than that his four *Athenian* Friends were the Heads of the four Orders the Priefthood was divided into; to each of which we may fuppofe the King to have given a Wand, together with a Ring, or an Egg, or perhaps both, as the proper Enfigns of their Superintendency.

That the chief Ensign of *Druidifm* was a Ring, pretended to have been generated by Snakes, in the Summer Time, is fufficiently demonftrated by a Tradition ftill fubfifting in our Ifland; and thus related by the Bifhop of *London* in the laft *Englifh* Edition of *Camden*'s *Britannia*.

"In moft Part of *Wales*, and throughout all *Scotland*,
" and in *Cornwall*, fays our Author in the 815th Page of the
" *Britannia*, we find it a common Opinion of the Vulgar,
" that about *Midfummer* Eve (though in the time they do
" not all agree) it is ufual for Snakes to meet in Companies,
" and that by joining Heads together and hiffing, a Kind of
" Bubble is formed, like a Ring, about the Head of one of
" them, which the reft by continual Hiffing blow on till it
" comes off at the Tail, and then immediately hardens, and
" refembles a Glafs Ring; which whoever finds (as fome old
" Women and Children are perfuaded) fhall profper in all his
" Undertakings. The Rings which they fuppofe to be thus
" generated, are called *Gleineu Nadroedh, i. e. Gemmæ An-*
" *guinæ*, whereof I have feen, at feveral Places, about twenty
" or thirty. They are fmall Glafs Annulets, commonly
" about half as wide as our Finger Rings, but much thicker;
" of a Green Colour ufually, though fome of them are
" Blue, and others curioufly Waved with Blue, Red and
" White."

Now Rings for the Finger having been firft made ufe of in *Samothrace*, from thence, fays *Pliny*, l. 33. c. 1. fuch Ornaments of the Hand were called *Samothracia*; and thefe may be very juftly fuppofed to have had Virtues peculiar to them, the Knowledge whereof, or the procuring fuch Rings, we may reckon among the *Samothracian* Myfteries into which *Bladud* was initiated; and from thence to have proved the Origin of the Snakes Rings with us, as well as of the Name of *Samothei* given to the *Britifh Druids:* For by this Name the antient Priefts of the *Oak* are fpoken of, as Monfieur *Banier* particularly remarks; and *Bladud* having been difguifed under the Name of *Samothes*, he was moft undoubtedly fo denominated from thefe Myfterious *Samothracian* Ornaments,

ments, which gave Rise to others pretended to have been generated by the same Reptiles that produced the Rings.

These were Eggs, and *Pliny* gives us the following Account of them in the third Chapter of his nine and twentieth Book: "In the Summer time yearly, an infinite Number of
"Snakes gather together in a round Form, entangling and
"enwrapping themselves one within another in the most
"artificial Manner: The Froth which they yield from their
"Mouths, and the Humour that comes from their Bodies
"incorporating together produces an Egg, and this they cast
"up on high into the Air, by the Force of their Hissing, at a
"certain Time of the Moon's Age, known only to the *Druids*
"themselves; and therefore one of them is always ready,
"with a good Horse near him, to watch the mounting up
"of the Egg, and to receive it in its Fall before it reaches
"the Ground, within the Lappet of a certain Garment: As
"soon as the Egg is thus catched, the Person that receives it
"must mount his Horse, ride away full Speed, make to
"some great River, and cross the same to preserve his
"Treasure; for the Snakes immediately disintangle them-
"selves, and, with the utmost Fury, pursue the Person
"who carries their Egg away till their Chase is stopped by
"the Water."

"One of these Eggs, says our Author, is of the Size of
"an ordinary round Apple; the Shell is of a Cartalagineous
"Substance; it is clasped all about with Concavities repre-
"senting those about the Legs of the Fish called a *Pourcuttle*;
"the Reality of it is always proved by its buoying itself up aloft
"in Water, and swimming against the Stream; and an Egg
"so proved, concludes our Author, became a sovereign Thing
"to procure a Person ready Access to Princes, to win their
"Grace and Favour, and to obtain the better of an Adver-
"sary in any Contest at Law."

The *Gallick Druids*, according to our Historian, wore these Kind of Eggs, set within Rings of Gold, as the Ensigns or Badges of their Profession; and therefore a Ring or an Egg, or both, of a wonderful Nature was the undoubted Badge of our antient Priests of the *Oak*; and was worn by the Superintendant of every Order, or the Head of every College, as his peculiar Mark of Distinction from the inferior Priests: And as the Snakes appear to have generated their Rings on the Eve of *Midsummer* Day; so it is highly probable that on the same Day they generated their Eggs likewise; and that
the

Chap. III.   A Defcription of BATH.   141

the three and twentieth of *June*, the Day preceding the Annual Meeting of the *Druids* to decide Controverfies, was the critical Time for watching for thefe Productions, the Poffeffion whereof enabled a Perfon to gain the Better of his Adverfary in any Conteft at Law : " I myfelf, fays *Pliny*, am able " upon my own Knowledge to aver, that *Claudius Cæfar*. " commanded a Gentleman of *Rome* to be put to Death for " carrying one of thefe Eggs in his Bofom at the time that " he pleaded his Caufe before him in Court."

THE PLANTS adopted by the *Druids* had Virtues no lefs extraordinary afcribed to them, than thofe afcribed to the Rings and Eggs that made the Badges of their Profeffion ; and thofe Plants having been chiefly *Miffeltoe*, *Selago*, *Samolus*, and *Vervain*; the firft they gathered with great Solemnity, and called it by a Name which in their Language imported *All Heal*, from an Opinion that it would cure all Maladies whatfoever.

NOTHING with the *Druids* was efteemed more facred than the *Miffeltoe* that grew on an *Oak* Tree ; this, or in fhort any thing elfe, fays *Pliny*, which they found growing upon that Tree, befides its own Fruit, they looked upon as a Gift from Heaven, and having gathered it when the Moon was juft fix Days old, it became, moreover, a fure Medicine to make the Barren inftantly Fruitful; and was a fovereign Counterpoifon againft all Vermin.

SELAGO appears by the Teftimony of *Pliny*, in the eleventh Chapter of his four and twentieth Book, to have been gathered with as much Solemnity as the *Miffeltoe* ; and the *Druids* difpofed of it as the only Prefervative againft all hurtful Accidents and Misfortunes whatfoever; thofe Priefts pretending that the Fume thereof was good for all the Infirmities and Difeafes of the Eyes.

SAMOLUS, according to our *Roman* Naturalift, was gathered with lefs Solemnity than *Selago* ; and the *Druids* difpofed of it as a never failing Thing to cure fuch Swine and Cattle as were afflicted with any Difeafe, and to fecure others from the like Maladies.

As for *Vervaine* the Solemnity obferved in gathering it about the rifing of the great Dog-Star, feems, by what *Pliny* writes in the ninth Chapter of his twenty fifth Book, to have far exceeded the Solemnity obferved in gathering any of the other Plants; for after a Libation of Honey with the Combs, offered to the Earth in the Dead of the Night, when

neither

neither Sun nor Moon appeared, every Plant had the Periphery of a Circle drawn round about it with an Inftrument of Iron, and the Perfon that plucked it up, immediately threw it aloft over his Head into the Air, making ufe of his left Hand only; after which the Leaves, Stalk, and Root of the Herb were feparated; and then every Part was dryed by itfelf in a fhady Place out of the Reach of the Beams of the Sun.

The *Druids* made ufe of this Plant in cafting Lots, in telling Fortunes, and in predicting future Events; and they difpofed of it as a Gift of Nature capable of rendering fuch People, whofe Bodies fhould be rubbed all over with it, able to obtain whatever their Hearts defired; to cure all Manner of Agues; to reconcile People in Enmity with each other; to make Friendfhip between whom they lift; and to give Remedy to any Difeafe whatfoever: Our famous Priefts pretending, at the fame time, that if any Dining Room fhould be fprinkled with the Water in which this Herb lay fteeped, all that fhould fit at the Table would become Pleafant, Merry and Jocund.

The Festivals of the *Druids* eftablifhed by the Founder of the Priefthood, and his *Athenian* Collegues, began with their Year; and this commencing with the Vernal Equinox, that day was determined by the fixth Day of the Moon's Age that happened on or neareft to the tenth of *March*; and was proclaimed the preceding Evening by kindling Fires on the feveral Carns; a Method obferved in publifhing moft of the Feftivals. Thefe Illuminations drawing the People together, *New Years Day* appears, from what Mr. *Toland* writes in his Hiftory of the *Druids*, p. 74, to have been then celebrated to obtain a plentiful Birth of every thing which the Earth was beginning to produce; the Priefts, during the Solemnity, prefenting the Laity with Portions of the *Miffeltoe* they had collected the Year before; and from thence, as Monfieur *Banier* remarks, the *New Years* Gifts we ftill make to thofe we value, had their Rife.

The fecond Day of the Year, or the feventh Day of the Vernal Moon, was celebrated in Honour of *Apollo*, the Son of *Latona*; and every fucceeding feventh Day of the fame Moon, as well as every feventh Day of every other Moon of the whole Year, became a Feftival in Honour of the fame Deity: All the Gods were complemented with a Feftival every

Chap. III.   A Defcription of BATH.   143

every Lunar Month, and thefe were celebrated at the Change of every Moon: And the End of every Cycle of Years proved a Feftival that crowned all the others, and was celebrated from the Day that ended that Period of Time, till *Apollo* was prefented with an Offering of the firft Fruits of the Corn that was gathered the next Harveft, and made up into Loaves of Bread.

THIS Offering was made between the Celebration of the Feftival obferved in Honour of all the Gods at the Change of the fixth Moon of the Year, and the Celebration of the next Feftival obferved in Honour of *Apollo*; it now bears the Name of *Lammas Day*; and the primitive Chriftians confecrating it to Saint *Peter in vinculis*, the *Britifh* Offerings of the Day were by them turned from Loaves of Bread to Money; and every Perfon fent his Penny to *Rome*, till King *Henry* the Eighth put an End to the Cuftom.

THE Sifter of *Apollo* having been the Goddefs invoked by Women in Childbed, under her heavenly Name of *Lucina*, we may fairly conclude, that the Acknowledgment made to her at *Delos*, by the two *Hyperborean* Virgins for a fpeedy Delivery, confifted of an Offering of the firft Fruits of *Miffeltoe*; the Plant that had Efficacy afcribed to it fufficient to make the Barren Fruitful; and the Plant that was gathered with the greateft Solemnity upon the fixth Day of the Moon's Age, and in all Probability it was of the fixth Moon of that Year that made the firft of the Cycle invented for harmonizing the Spheres.

WHEN the Vernal Equinox and Vernal Month began on the fame Day, as was nearly the Cafe in the Years 1733 and 1744, the fecond monthly Feftival in Honour of all the Gods began upon the firft of *May*; and according to *Toland* it was celebrated to obtain a profperous Growth to what the Earth had produced: *Midfummer* Day, according to the fame Author, was celebrated to draw down a Bleffing on the Fruits then becoming ready for gathering: And on the firft of *November* the People returned Thanks for having finifhed the Harveft, and thereby feen a happy Conclufion of the Summer. " It was at this time, fays our Author, that every Mafter of " a Family was religioufly obliged to purchafe a Portion of " the Fires remaining on the Carns to kindle the Fire anew " in his Houfe, which was purpofely extinguifhed the Night " before, and this, for the enfuing Year, was to be lucky and " profperous to him."

THIS

THIS Custom was observed in the Eastern Nations; for Monsieur *Banier*, in treating of *Vesta*, and the *Vestals*, informs us, that the sacred Fire preserved by private People at their Places of Abode was maintained at the Gate of every House; "and hence, says our Author, if we may believe *Ovid*, "came the Name of *Vestible*."

UPON the sixth Day of the Moon's Age the *Druids*, as *Pliny* writes in the four and fortieth Chapter of his sixteenth Book, began their Months, their *New Years*, and their several Ages; which, as he says, had their Revolution every thirty Years. Now when the Vernal Equinox and Vernal Month commenced together, the middle Day of Summer fell on the 24th of *June*, and on the sixth Day before the Change of the fourth Moon; and the first of *November* made the Day succeeding that which compleated the first eight Lunar Months of the Year, or the seventh Day of the ninth Moon, a Festival Day sacred to *Apollo*; and therefore from his antient *British* Name of *Haul*, as well as from the solemn Dismission of the People with confecrated Fire, upon the happy Conclusion of the Summer, that Day was called *Hallamas*, 'till it was dedicated to all the Christian Saints; after which it was indifferently called *All-Saints-Day*, or *All-Hallows* Day.

As often as the sixth Day of the Vernal Moon falls on the Day of the Vernal Equinox, so often *Easter* Day will fall on the Feast Day of the Annunciation of the Blessed Virgin; and from that Union of Days it seems evident, that the same Method that was observed by the antient *Druids* in fixing their Festivals, still continues for fixing *Easter*, but with a Proverb attending it, that whenever the Lord falls in the Lady's Lap, something extraordinary will happen to *England*.

IN such Years the sixth Day of the Rising of the great Dog Star answers the five and twentieth of *July*; and therefore as this Day happens three Days before the Change of the Sixth Moon of the Year, the preceding Night was a fit and proper time for the Nocturnal Ceremony of gathering the *Vervain* so useful to the *Druids* in casting Lots, in telling Fortunes, and in predicting future Events.

THE Victims offered at the *Misseltoe* Solemnity on the sixth Day of the sixth Moon of the Year, answering the third of *August*, were Milk-white young Bullocks, such, says *Pliny*, as never drew in Yoke, or had their Heads bound by the Horn; now that we had a Place near the hot Springs of *Bath*

appropriated

Chap. III.   A Description of BATH.   145

appropriated for such Sort of Cattle, let a Hamlet of *Wellow* bearing South South West, three Quarters Westerly, from the warm Fountains, at the Distance of four Miles and a half from them, and still retaining the Name of *White Ox Mead*, determine.

THE *Druidical* Priesthood having by the Ensigns of their Profession, as well as their extraordinary Plants been furnished with an universal Remedy against all Maladies in Man and Beast; with what would render the Barren Fruitful, prove a Counterpoison against all Vermin, and secure the human and several other Species from all Manner of Diseases; with what would make People prosperous, reconcile Enemies, and establish mutual Friendship; and with what would gain Mankind ready Access to Princes, win their Grace and Favour, and enable them to gain the better of their Adversaries in any Contest at Law: And the Priesthood having been so well connected, that Law or Policy required a Priest of every Order to be present at every Sacrifice, it became so venerable to the Laity, that they soon thought it expedient to exempt the *Druids* from attending the Army, as well as from paying Taxes; and yet they permitted them to enjoy all manner of Immunities: All Points of Difference they submitted to their Arbitration, whether it related to Life or Death, to Titles to Lands, or to the Extent of Confines; and whosoever refused to abide by their Sentences, let his Degree be high or low, was shunn'd and despised by his Countrymen, rendered incapable of suing for his Right, and not permitted to discharge any Office in the Common-wealth: Nay such high Regard was paid to them by Enemies, as well as Friends, that if two Armies were ready to engage, with their Swords drawn, and Spears presented one against another, if a Philosopher, or a Bard stept in between them, he instantly pacified the contending Parties; as if some wild Beasts, says *Diodorus Siculus*, had been tamed by Inchantments.

THE Author of this Priesthood could not have chosen a better Thing for the Basis of the Magick, which he practised and taught, than the hot Waters of *Bath*; nor have had a better Situation to fix all the Apparatus for an Oracle upon a Plan conformable to that of the Oracle of *Jupiter Ammon* in *Egypt*: For if *Diodorus Siculus*, and *Quintus Curtius*, may be depended upon, it will appear from their Writings, that there was a Temple just by the Waters of the Sun in *Ammonia*; that the Temple which contained the Oracle was at

U   some

some Diſtance from it; that the King's Palace was near the Oracle; that the Palace had a Caſtle contiguous to it; that Trees were planted by the ſacred Waters; that the Grove of the God extended fifty Furlongs in Length, by fifty Furlongs in Breadth; and that this Region was the Metropolitan Seat of the *Ammonian* Kings.

HERE we have an illuſtrious Example for all King *Bladud*'s Works round the hot Springs of *Bath*; *Pythagoras* had been in *Egypt* before *Cambyſes* committed his Outrages in that Country; and from that Philoſopher *Bladud*, when he was in *Greece*, or when he viſited his Colleague at *Crotona* in *Italy*, might have got the ſame Account, that the above Writers did afterwards procure concerning the ſacred Grove of *Jupiter Ammon*; which, at the ſame time that it became the Seat of the *Ammonian* Kings, it became likewiſe the Metropolitan Seat of the Prieſts of *Jupiter*; yielding Habitations for ſuch as were appointed for War, together with thoſe that were ſet apart for the Prieſthood; and all theſe were diſperſed in Villages round about the Oracle, Palace, and ſacred Waters of the Sun.

THE forming of the *Druidical* Prieſthood and the Works neceſſary for it, undoubtedly furniſhed *Beroſus* with Matter for the Hiſtory applied by him to the firſt five Kings of the Iſland; and on this Suppoſition *Bladud*, or *Samothes* reigned ſix and forty Lunar Months before the Arrival of his Colleagues from *Greece*; then taking *Magus* to his Aſſiſtance, they in one and fifty Months more compleated all the magical Works about the hot Springs of *Bath*, and *Magus* ſeems thereupon to have been appointed the Head of that Order of Prieſts who ſhould have an immediate Intercourſe with the Gods.

SARRON ſeems to have received Inſtitution at the ſame time with *Magus*, and to have been appointed the Head of that Order of Prieſts which was to preſent the Offerings of the People, ſince the Prieſts of both theſe Orders went under the Title of *Saronidæ*; and with them the King's Oracle ſeems to have been perfected.

THE Prieſts of the hollow *Oak* were ſet upon founding Schools and publick Places of Learning, and this ſeems to have taken up the next ſixty one Months; at the End of which Period of Time *Druis* received Inſtitution as the Head of an Order of Prieſts that were to attend the Sacrifices, and judge of future Events by obſerving the Entrails of the Victims;

Chap. III. A Description of BATH. 147

tims; and fourteen Months after him *Bardus* was put at the Head of the original *British* Priests, who, till then, sang the Praises of the Gods, and the Beauty of the Works of Nature; but afterwards the Praises of such as behaved themselves well, and the Dispraises of those that behaved themselves ill, were introduced into their Songs, and became the chief Parts of them.

THE Priesthood thus compleated, seems to have continued seventy five Months before *Bladud*, in practising his Magick, broke his Neck; and this Accident happened to him after he had reigned twenty Solar Years, or two hundred and forty seven Lunar Months, corresponding exactly with the Number of Years the first five Kings of the Island are recorded in History to have sat upon the Throne; *Berosus* telling us that *Samothes* held the Scepter forty six Years, *Magus* fifty one Years, *Sarron* sixty one Years, *Druis* fourteen Years, and *Bardus* seventy five Years.

CHAP. IV.

Of King BLADUD's Works near BATH, and their constituting the University of the BRITISH DRUIDS.

BALE, and several other Writers, having for their Author *Merlyn* of *Caledon*, tell us, that King *Bladud*, after his Return to *Britain*, from *Greece*, planted a University at *Stanford*, and appointed learned Men, who professed the Liberal Sciences, to teach them to his Subjects: The Author of the *British* History adding, that *Bladud* himself taught Necromancy in his Kingdom.

Now about eight Miles westward from the hot Springs of *Bath*, there is a remarkable Place called *Stantondrue*; a Name importing the *Oak* Men's Town built with Stone, as that of *Ackmanchester*, imports the *Oak* Men's City; and to come at it, we must first cross the River *Avon*; and after that another River that runs into the *Avon* at *Cainsham*, between *Bath* and *Bristol*; by the Side of which River *Stantondrue* is situated.

THE Passage over this last River might formerly have been called *Stanford*, from its having been a Ford for People to cross over that River who went from *Bath* to *Stantondrue*; for such as came from this Place towards *Bath*, called the Fords, by which they crossed the River, after the Names of

U 2 the

the Places to which the Roads through thofe Fords led. For Example, as the Intrenchment on *Camalodunum* had, to the Eaftward of it, high and ftupendous Cliffs, fo the Ford over the River that runs by *Stantondrue*, had the Name of *Pens*, *i. e.* Cliffs of Hills, given to it, and was called *Pensford*, becaufe the Road from *Stantondrue* to thofe Cliffs croffed the River there.

AGAIN, the Place where fuch as came from *Stantondrue*, to the Rocks of *Solis*, croffed the *Avon*, was called *Solsford*; becaufe the Road from one Place to the other croffed the River there.

THUS it appears that there was antiently a Communication between the Works round about the warm Fountains of *Bath*, and thofe of *Stantondrue*; and therefore at this Place it feems next to Demonftration, that King *Bladud* feated his *Athenian* Colleagues, to inftruct his Subjects in the Liberal Sciences; and there made them a Model of the Planetary World for that Purpofe; fince the Remains of fuch a Model is now to be feen in the Village; and the *Druids*, as *Pomponius Mela* writes, profeffed to know not only the Form and Magnitude of the whole Univerfe in general, and of the Earth in particular, but alfo the Courfes of the Stars and their Revolutions.

THE Remains of this Model bear the Name of the Wedding, from a Tradition that as a Woman was going to be married, fhe and the reft of the Company were changed into the Stones of which they confift: " No one, fay the Country " People about *Stantondrue*, was ever able to reckon the " Number of thefe metamorphofed Stones, or to take a " Draught of them, tho' feveral have attempted to do both, " and proceeded till they were either ftruck dead upon the " Spot, or with fuch an Illnefs as foon carried them off:" This was ferioufly told me when I began to take a Plan of them, on the 12th of *Auguft* 1740, to deter me from proceeding: And as a Storm accidentally arofe juft after, and blew down Part of a great Tree near the Body of the Work, the People were then thoroughly fatisfied that I had difturbed the Guardian Spirits of the metamorphofed Stones, and from thence great Pains were taken to convince me of the Impiety of what I was about.

I proceeded with my Work as often as the Weather would permit, and having been more than ordinary exact in the Survey, I can, with the greateft Certainty declare, that upon the Vertex of a fmall round Hill at *Stantondrue*, there are

now

Chap. IV. A Defcription of BATH. 149

now to be feen the Remains of eleven large Stone Pillars, and the Place for a twelfth; each of which feems to have been fix Feet fquare, and the whole to have made the Periphery of a Circle of 140 Feet Diameter; which is the exact Diameter of the Infide of the *Pantheon* at *Rome*, between the Bafis of the Columns, *Mons Dezgodetz* having meafured the Diameter of that Temple, in one Place, at 132 Feet one Inch, by the *French* Standard.

The Circle thus limited I have marked in the following Plan with the Letter A; and one of the Stones lying by the Letter G, is of a different Kind to any of the reft.

To the North Eaft of the Circle A, and upon the Decline of the Hill, there is another Circle of about 378 Feet Diameter; this in the Plan, Plate N° 1. 2. I have diftinguifhed with the Letter B; and the Stones now remaining in the Periphery of it, being twenty in Number, anfwer to the Divifion of 81 equal Parts, in the Circumference, and to no other Divifion of above one hundred that I have tried: The moft remarkable Stone in the Out-Line of this Circle ftands at the Letter I; and overagainft it, at the Letter K, there is another of a different Kind, and of the fame Sort with the Stone by the Letter G, in the Circle A. From the Center of one of thefe Circles, to that of the other, is 714 Feet; and if we extend a Line from one Center to the other, and produce it North Eaftward beyond the Letter C, it will terminate on a large flat Stone, called *Hakills*, or rather *Hakims* Coit, now lying on the Brow of a Hill, upon the North Eaft Side of the River by which *Stantondrue* is fituated: And this Stone, tho' greatly delapidated, is ftill ten Feet long, fix Feet broad, near two Feet thick, and lies about 1860 Feet from the Center of the Circle B.

At the Diftance of 375 Feet Eaftward from the Center of the Circle B, we come to the Center of a third Circle, marked in the Plan, Plate N° 1. 2. with the Letter D. This Circle is bounded by eight Stones, of fix Feet Square, and is 96 Feet, or juft 60 *Jewifh* Cubits in Diameter from the middle of one Pillar, to that of the other: The whole Diameter of 102 Feet feems to have been ftill increafed to 107 Feet by a Border marked with a dotted Line in the Plan; and this Circle appears to have been furrounded with the four Concentrick Peripheries L, M, N, O; the firft of which confifting of 27 Pillars, was 214 Feet Diameter in the Clear; the fecond confifting of 28 Pillars, was 248 Feet Diameter in

the

the Clear; the third confifting of 29 Pillars, was 282 Feet Diameter in the Clear; and the fourth confifting of 30 Pillars, was 316 Feet Diameter in the Clear; but with the Pillars the Diameter of this Out-Line of the Work was augmented to about 322 Feet: For one of the Pillars is now ftanding, and it is about three Feet thick.

THE eight Pillars of the Circle D are alfo now remaining, four in an erect Pofture, the other four lie flat upon the Ground; but of the 114 Pillars that formed the four Concentrick Rings about it, Time and barbarous Hands have left no more than the Fragments of 12, of which 7 are erect; and thefe Remains anfwer no other Divifions, as I could difcover by innumerable Trials, but thofe of 27, 28, 29, and 30, for the Pillars of the firft, fecond, third, and fourth Circular Line.

ONE of the great Pillars in the Circle D feems to me to have been 25 Feet high, and ftood by the Letter F; but the other feven don't look as though they had exceeded 12 Feet in Altitude above the Ground.

Now if we draw a Line from the Center of the Circle D, to the Center of the Circle B, and produce it Weftward 992 Feet, it will terminate on three Stones in a Garden by the Parifh Church of *Stantondrue*; two of which Stones are erect, and the other lies flat on the Ground: And if we draw a Line North Weftward, from the Center of the Circle A, to the Diftance of about 3250 Feet from that Circle, it will terminate on two Stones lying flat on the Ground, in a Field called the *Lower-Tining*. A Line extended from the Center of the Stone by the Letter F, in the Periphery of the Circle D, to the Center of that Circle, and produced to P, makes a Perpendicular to the Line A, B, C; and a Line extended from the Center of the Stone by the Letter G, in the Periphery of the Circle A, to the Center of that Circle, and produced to Q, makes a Perpendicular to the Line D, B, E: In the laft Place a Tangent Line drawn from the Periphery of the Circle A, to that of the Circle B, cuts in upon the Circle D, about fix Feet.

IN a Line between *Hakim*'s Coit, and the Circle D, we may fuppofe a Stone to have been placed at the Diftance of about 230 Feet from that Coit; and at a like a Diftance from the three Stones in the Garden at E, we may alfo fuppofe a Stone to have been placed, fo as to have lain in a Line between thofe three Stones, and the Circle A; which Suppofitions

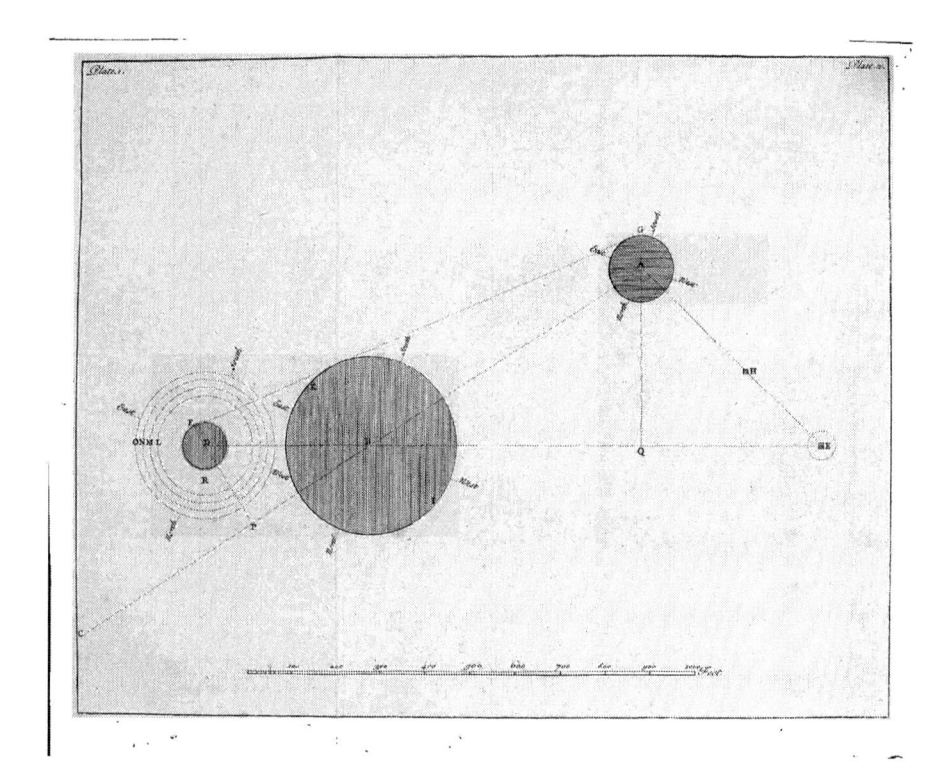

Chap. IV. A Description of BATH. 151

tions I could make very probable, but shall suspend my Reasons, 'till I have further examined into those Things on which I found them.

THESE Works together will not only appear little inferior to any of the great Works of Antiquity, for Magnitude; but form a perfect Model of the *Pythagorean* System of the Planetary World, as I just now asserted; and therefore I have brought them into one general Plan, as in Plate N° 3. 4.

A. The Circle on the Vertex of the Hill, of 140 Feet Diameter.

B. The second Circle of 378 Feet Diameter.

C. The Stone called *Hakim*'s Coit, lying in a Line with the Centers of the Circles A, B, and at the Distance of about 1860 Feet from the Center of the Circle B.

D. The third Circle of 102 Feet Diameter.

E. The three Stones in the Garden by the Church, and in a Line with the Centers of the Circles D, B.

F. The two Stones in the Field called the *Lower-Tining*, and lying at the Distance of about 3250 Feet from the Center of the Circle A.

G. The Stone supposed to have been placed about 230 Feet from *Hakim*'s Coit at C, and in a Line between that Stone and the Center of the Circle D.

H. The Stone supposed to have been placed about 230 Feet from the Stones at E, and in a Line between those Stones, and the Center of the Circle A.

THIS Circle being supposed to represent the Sun, the Circle B, according to the *Pythagorean* System, will image the Earth, and the Circle D the Moon; the supposed Stone at H will represent the Planet *Mercury*, the Stones at E the Planet *Venus*, the supposed Stone at G the Planet *Mars*, the Stone at C the Planet *Jupiter*, the Stones at F the Planet *Saturn*, and the dotted Peripheries of Circles will denote the Orbits of the several Bodies in that System; the dotted Periphery H. I. being the Orbit of *Mercury*, E. I. of *Venus*, B I. of the Earth, D I. of the Moon about the Earth, G I. of *Mars*, C I. of *Jupiter*, and F I of *Saturn*.

THE Distances between the several Bodies in the *Pythagorean* System, we may learn from *Pliny*, who tells us, l. 2. c. 21 and 22, that the Sun is treble the Distance to what the Moon is from the Earth; that from the Earth to *Venus* is eight Parts; from the Earth to *Jupiter* seventeen of the like Parts; from the Earth to the *Zodiack* twenty two of the
same

same Parts; that *Venus* is distant from *Mercury*, just the same as *Mars* is from *Jupiter*; and that each of those Distances is two of the like Parts.

Now if we turn to the general Plan of the Works of *Stantondrue*, we shall find that the Distance between the Center of the Circle B, and the Circumference of the Circle A, is just 644 Feet; and that the Distance between the Center of the Circle B, and the outward Line of Pillars round the Circle D, is just 214 Feet; so that from the Center of the Circle B to the Circle A, is a Trifle more than treble the Distance to what it is from the Center of the Circle B, to the outward Line of Pillars round the Circle D, conformable to the Distances between the Earth, Sun, and Moon in the *Pythagorean* System.

Moreover, if we suppose the Stones at C and E to have stood on Eminences of about 60 Feet Diameter, as it is very probable they did, then the Distance between the Circumference of the Circle B, and that of E, will be 773 Feet; and the Distance between the Circumference of the Circle B and that of C, will be 1641 Feet; which being divided into seventeen Parts, eight of such Parts is within a few Inches of 773 Feet: So that, in our antient Works, the Distance between the Circles B and E being divided into eight Parts, the Distance between the Circles B and C are seventeen of the same Parts; which is conformable to the Distances between the Earth and *Venus*, and the Earth and *Jupiter*, in the *Pythagorean* System.

Again, as *Pythagoras* held the Distance between *Venus* and *Mercury*, and between *Jupiter* and *Mars*, to be two of such Parts as are contained in the Distance between the Earth and *Jupiter*, when that Space is divided into seventeen, so the clear Distance between the Circles C and E, and the supposed Stones at G and H, in the Works at *Stantondrue*, must have been about 194 Feet; and if to this we add thirty Feet for the Semi-Diameter of each Circle, and six Feet to the Center of each Stone; then from the Center of the Circle C, to that of the supposed Stone at G, as well as from the Center of the Circle E, to that of the supposed Stone at H, will be 230 Feet, and extend to the very Places where those imaginary Stones appear to me to have stood.

The Circle A is bigger than the Circle D, as the apparent Body of the Sun is bigger than that of the Moon; the Diameter of the Circle D, is near of the same Proportion to

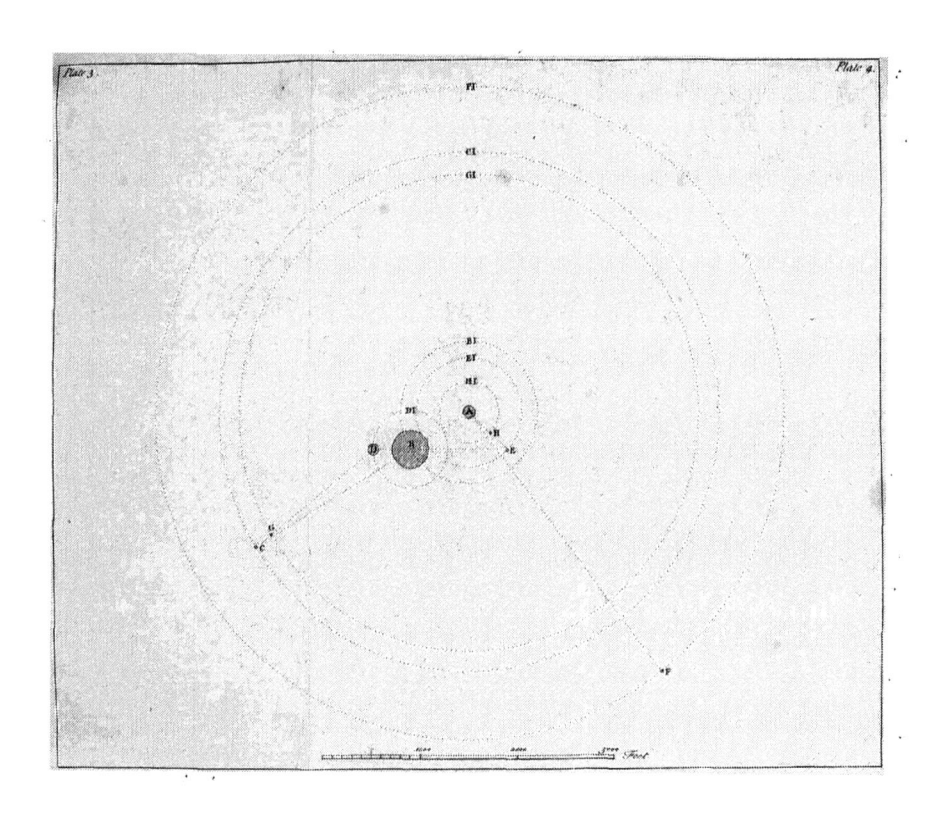

Chap. IV.   A Defcription of BATH.   153

that of the Circle B, as Aftronomers make the Diameter of the Moon to be to that of the Earth; and the Diftance between the Center of the Circle A, and the Stones at F, exceeds the Diftance between the fame Center and the Stone at C, in or near the fame Proportion that the Diftance of *Saturn* from the Sun, exceeded the Diftance of *Jupiter* from the Sun, in the *Pythagorean* Syftem.

THAT the Works of *Stantondrue* form a perfect Model of the *Pythagorean* Syftem of the Planetary World, I fuppofe will now be granted: To the South Eaft of which Works there is a high Hill called *Stantonbury*; and to the North Eaft there is another Hill bearing the Name of *Meafe-Knoll*, and making the Eaftward Point of *Dundry* Hill, but fevered from it by a Ditch, and a large artificial Bank of Earth, known by the Name of *Meafe-Knoll-Tump*; from whence we fee the Rocks of *Solis*, and moft of the other Works by *Bath*.

STANTONBURY and *Meafe-Knoll* are both intrenched, or the latter is rather terraffed at the Top, and both feem to have been fubordinate Works to thofe of *Stantondrue*; to the Southward of which there is another fubordinate Work called *Stantonwick*.

THE Way to *Meafe-Knoll* is called *Hare-Lane*: The Word *Hare* imports an Army, or a Lord; and the Word *Meafe* fignifies an eminent Dwelling-Place: So that as the Summit of *Meafe-Knoll* fhews an Intrenchment, we may affign it to fuch as were feparated for the Service of that Syftem of Learning that was taught at *Stantondrue*: And on the other Hand, we may affign *Stantonbury* for a Camp, for that Part of the Army which was at the difpofal of the learned Men at *Stantondrue*; whofe Place of Habitation was undoubtedly at *Stantonwick*.

IN plowing the Ground of *Meafe-Knoll*, as well as that of *Solfbury-Hill*, the People frequently turn up burnt Stones, and often find other Marks to prove each Place to have been long inhabited: The former, according to a Tradition among the People of the Country thereabouts, was the Refidence of one *Hakill* a Giant, who is reported to have tofs'd the Coit that makes Part of the Works of *Stantondrue* from the Top of that Hill to the Place where it now lies: He is alfo reported to have made *Meafe-Knoll-Tump* with one Spadeful of Earth; and to have had the Village underneath that Hill given him by the King, for fhewing him a Specimen of his great Strength; which Gift *Hakill* looked upon but as a fmall

X   Reward

Reward for what he had done, and therefore, say they, he called the King's present *Norton-small-Reward*. It is the same Place that the old Inhabitants of *Bath* called *Hog's-Norton*; and the Reality of *Hakill* is so firmly believed in that part of the Country, that, to this Hour, his Effigie is preserved and shewn as a great Piece of Curiosity, in the Parish Church of *Chew*, about a Mile from *Stantondrue*.

Now the great Resemblance and the manifest Connection between the Works of *Bath*, or the *Oak* Men's City, and those of *Stantondrue*, or the *Oak* Men's Town, built with Stone, makes it much more than probable, that all those Works were founded by one and the same Person, and for the same Purposes; to wit, to cure the Diseases of the People, to honour the Gods, and to instruct Mankind in the Liberal Sciences: For these *Oak* Men and their Founder, like *Zoroaster* and his Disciples in *Persia*, like *Pythagoras* and his Disciples in *Greece*, and like *Zamolxis* and his Pupils in *Thrace*, had their Cave to retire to, which is to this Day called *Oaky Hole*, and is situated by the City of *Wells*; out of which Cavern the Stone for the greatest Part of the Works at *Stantondrue* seems to have been taken, as any body must acknowledge that will but compare the Stone at each Place together.

The predominant Colour of that part of the Stone in the Works of *Stantondrue*, supposed to have been taken from *Oaky Hole*, is Red; and it is so exceeding hard, that it will polish almost as well as some of the purple *Italian* Marble, and is as beautiful: The other Stone is of two Colours, White and Grey; the white Stone seems to have been the Produce of *Dundry* Hill; but the grey Stone resembles the Sand Rocks about *Stantondrue*, and seems to have been taken from them.

PLINY, informs us in the second Chapter of his thirtieth Book that the Magical Art, as published by *Osthanes*, was practised in seven different Ways; first by the Means of Water, called Hydromancy, and lastly by that of Axes, called Axenomancy: Now as the prodigious Cave of *Oaky Hole* is the Source of the River *Ax*, which empties itself into the Sea, not far from the Village of *Bleydon*, is it not the highest Demonstration that that Den was the Place where the *Druids* practised Part of their Magick, and initiated their Disciples into the Mysteries of that Art? The chief Part of the rest they undoubtedly taught them at *Stantondrue*; where we may

suppose

Chap. IV. A Description of BATH. 155

suppose the High Priest had his College in the Circle B, Plate N° 1. 2, composed of 81 Cells, placed against the 81 Stones of which that Circle was composed; one Cell against the Stone at the Letter I, for himself, the Remainder for the Superintendants of the four Orders of Priests, and their Assistants.

The first Lesson the *Druids* set their Pupils, was to learn a considerable Number of Verses by Rote; "which some, "says *Cæsar*, have spent twenty Years about; for, as our "Author adds, they never committed them to writing, "though they were well skilled in the *Greek* Characters, and "made use of them on all Occasions, that did not regard the "Mysteries of their Religion and Learning:" But notwithstanding those Priests would not commit the Knowledge they taught their Pupils to writing, yet they took Care to record it in a more effectual Manner, by making their Works Expressive of it; and therefore those of *Stantondrue* may be looked upon not only as the very *Epitome* of the Learning, which the most antient *Druids* were eminent for, but point out, and represent the Gods, whom the *Britons* imagined to have resided in, and to have animated the Orbs of the Sun and Moon, as well as of the Planets *Mercury*, *Venus*, *Mars*, *Jupiter* and *Saturn*. We may therefore look upon the Circle A, in the general Plan, Plate N° 3, 4, to have been a *Duodecastyle* Monopterick Temple of the Sun, and the Circle D to have been an *Octostyle* Monopterick Temple of the Moon standing in the midst of a Court surrounded with a treble Porticoe: That the Stones at E was an Altar belonging to the former, and consecrated to *Venus*; the Stone at C, part of an Altar belonging to the latter, and consecrated to *Jupiter*; the imaginary Stones at G and H, Tables for the Use of those Altars, and consecrated to *Mercury* and *Mars*; and that the Stones at F are the Remains of an Altar made use of upon extraordinary Occasions, such as when the *Britons* offered up their human Sacrifices, and consecrated to *Saturn*.

The *Druids*, as we have already observed from *Pliny*, gathered their *Misseltoe*, when the Moon was just six Days old; and upon the same Day of her Age, they began their Months, their new Years, and their several Ages; which, as our Author says, had their Revolutions every thirty Years. Now if we examine the Works at *Stantondrue* we shall find by the Plan Plate N° 1, 2, that the Diameter of the Circle D, with the four Concentrick Peripheries of Circles round it, it, was divided into six equal Parts, two of which were given to the Body of the Temple D, two to the Court above it, marked with the Letter R, and two to the treble Porticoe that surrounded the whole.

AGAIN, the Periphery or Circular Line O, as it seems to have been composed of thirty Pillars, so it answers the Number of Years deem'd an Age; and the eight Pillars which bounded the Body of the Temple, answer the Cycle in Use before *Meton* published his of nineteen Years: The twelve Pillars that made the Periphery of the Circle A, answer the twelve Months of the Year; and the three Stones that made the Altar E, agree with the Number of Months intercalated every eight Years to bring the Revolution of the Earth about the Sun, and the Moon about the Earth within the same Period: The Days of the several Months made use of by the Antients, seem to have been expressed by the Pillars of the treble Porticoe round the Court of the Temple D; and there is no doubt but the Circle B, which represented the Earth, was made so as to express the Days of the Solar Year, since that Circle, at the Center of the Stones in its Periphery, is just 365 *Jewish* Yards in Circumference.

THUS the Works of *Stantondrue*, at the same time they represent the *Pythagorean* System of the Planetary World, they also point out the Computations of Time to bring the Motions of the chief Bodies in that System within the same Period; they are those Computations which the *Grecians* followed before *Meton* published his Cycle of nineteen Years, in the Year 430 before the Birth of Christ; and therefore they undeniably prove those Works to be older than the Year in which *Meton* published his Cycle, since that Cycle appears in most of the other antient Works of the Kingdom.

BY these Computations the Celebration of Festivals was fixed, they were the grand mystical Numbers of the antient *Britons*, and that they preserved those Numbers in their sacred Works, is very evident from an Example in *Cardiganshire*, mentioned by the Bishop of *London* in his *Britannia*, Page 773. It is nineteen Stones answering *Meton*'s Cycle of nineteen Years, and they are called by the Name of *Meini Kyvrivol*, or the numerary Stones.

THE Temple of the Moon at *Stantondrue* being just sixty *Jewish* Cubits Diameter, and surrounded with four Rows of Pillars, it exactly answers the Temple which *Cyrus*, by his Decree in the Year 536 before the Birth of Christ, directed the

Chap. IV. A Description of BATH. 157

the *Jews* to build at *Jerusalem* as above; and therefore *Cyrus*'s Decree for the Temple of *Jerusalem* must have been a Guide to the Builders of the Temple of the Moon at *Stantondrue*; wherefore these Works were of a later Date than *Cyrus*; and if we put them between that Monarch, and *Meton*, it will not only fall in the Year 483 before the Nativity of our Lord and Saviour; but amount almost to the highest Proof that *Bladud* began his Reign about the time I have already mentioned, to wit, the Year 483 before the Birth of Christ.

At *East* and *West-Harptree*, in the Midway between *Stantondrue*, and *Oaky-Hole*, we find the Remains of divers old Works, made with the same, or almost the same Kind of Stone with the Rocks of that Cave; and the Top of *Mendip* Hill, between *Harptree* and *Oaky-Hole*, is covered with a vast Number of Barrows, which few People have yet taken Notice of. *Harptree* must have therefore been a superb College of the Bards, or original *British* Priests, founded by King *Bladud* at the same time with his other Works, the better to draw those Priests into his System of Religion; and the Name of that Place seems to have arose from the Musical Instruments the Bards made use of, and the Trees under which they, in all Probability, performed some of the religious Ceremonies of their Order.

I would now ask, whether the collected Works of *Ackmanchester*, *Stantondrue*, *Oaky-Hole*, and *Harptree*, may not be fairly denominated the City in the *Hyperborean* Island, consecrated to *Apollo*? And whether the Citizens, from the Name of the last Work, don't appear to have been most of them Harpers, agreeable to what *Diodorus Siculus* writes of them?

Now since the founding of *Stantondrue* falls in with the Reign of King *Bladud*; since that Work is a Model of the *Pythagorean* System of the Planetary World; points out the Solar Months of the Year; the Days and Nights in the same Period of Time; the Lunar Cycle; the Moon's Age when the *Druids* began their Times and Festivals; the Days of their different Months; and eighty one detach'd Houses for an High Priest's College, on the same Plan with that of the *Jews*, that of *Zoroaster*, and that attending the Oracle of *Jupiter Ammon* in *Egypt*; each of which was composed of eighty Priests of an inferior Order, as we may see in the second Book of *Chronicles*, c. 26. v. 17. in *Prid. Con.* p. 1. b. 4.

b. 4. and in *Diod. Sic.* l. 17. c. 5: And since there is an apparent Connection between the antient Works of *Ackmanchester*, and those of *Stantondrue*, it seems manifest that the latter constituted the University of the *British Druids*; that this was the University which King *Bladud*, according to *Merlyn* of *Caledon*, planted; that it was at *Stantondrue* the King seated his four *Athenian* Colleagues; and that they were not only the Heads of the *British Druids* in those early Ages, but, under *Bladud*, the very Founder of them.

In *Caerbren* or the King's City, consecrated to *Apollo*, and thus containing a Seminary for the chief Youth of the *Britannick* Island, I will therefore leave the Flower of an honest plain Race of People under the Care and Instruction of four Orders of Men, whose Business it was, not only at this Place, but wherever their Doctrine prevailed, to sing their Praises; to foretell the Event of their Offerings; to make a Tender of their Sacrifices; and to ask such things of the Gods for them as they desired, and stood in most need of: To the united Works of *Caerbren* we may bring the *Druids* of *Gaul*, to receive the Instruction which *Cæsar* says they came frequently into *Britain* for: And if what *Cicero* says, when he tells us that the *Druids* were the Inventors of Mythology, be true; and if it be also true that *Abaris* wrote a Book of Theogony; we may, to the same Works, bring the whole Pagan World to be trained up in the Knowledge of sacred Things.

After the Death of King *Bladud*, in the Year 463 before the Birth of Christ, we may suppose nineteen *Samothean* Kings, or Arch *Druids*, to have presided at *Stantondrue*; the last of which having been named *Phranicus*; and he having held the Scepter in Right of his Wife, resigned his Government, and betook himself to the Continent 698 Years after the Death of *Bardus*: Call these Years Lunar Months, and they will amount to little more than 58 Solar Years; they will bring us down from *Bardus* to the Year 405 before Christ's Nativity; and in that Year it is highly probable the *British Druids* communicated the Cycle of nineteen Years to the *Gallick* Priests, gave the seven Intercalatery Months *Atlas* for their Father, and placed them in the Heavens in those Stars which bear the Name of the *Pleiades*.

To *Meton* and *Euctemon* the *Grecians* ascribed the Invention of this Cycle; and Sir *Isaac Newton* tells us that they, in order to publish it, observed the Summer Solstice in the

Year

Year of *Nabonaffar* 316, anfwering the Year 430 before the Birth of Chrift; fo that the firft Cycle in *Greece* ended about the Year 411, and the *Grecians* gave that Period of Time the Name of the GREAT YEAR; we call it the GOLDEN NUMBER, and *Diodorus Siculus* affuring us that *Apollo* came into the Ifland to celebrate the Feftival at the Completion of it, feems a fufficient Demonftration that this GOLDEN NUMBER was of *Britifh*, inftead of *Grecian* Original.

CHAP. V.

Of the *Grecian* Ornaments with which the antient Works of *Bath*, and in its Neighbourhood, were adorned.

BY the Teftimony of *Diodorus Siculus* we find that fome of the *Grecians* paffed over to the *Hyperboreans* and enriched their Temples with divers Prefents offered to their Gods; the chief of which Deities having been *Apollo*, and he having had a ftately Grove, with a renowned Temple, of a round Form, beautified with many rich Gifts, we may therefore fuppofe his Statue to have made the principal Part of thofe Prefents; and more efpecially fince a curious Brafs Head gilt with Gold, was found buried in *Bath*, on *Thurfday* the 12th of *July* 1727, about 5 o'Clock in the Afternoon, at no lefs than 16 Feet in Depth from the Surface of one of the publick Streets of the City, by Workmen who were then employed, at the Expence of the Chamber, in making the common Sewer, which, in that Year, was driven under Ground from the Bridge to High Street.

THIS Head reprefents that of a Beardlefs young Man with long curled Hair; and fo the *Grecian* Sculptors always reprefented *Apollo*; it is carefully preferved in the Council Houfe in the *Guild-Hall* of the City; and the Society of Antiquaries thought it incumbent in them to caufe a Profile of it to be engraved, the better to confecrate it to Eternity.

THIS valuable and curious Piece of Sculpture was found in a Line between the *King*'s Bath and *Belenus*'s Tree: And as the peculiar Quality attributed to the *Hyperborean Apollo* was the Cure of Difeafes, fo he became the Father of *Æfculapius*, the *Grecian* God of Phyfick; of which God we had formerly a Bas Relief in *Bath*, and Mr. *Camden* defcribes his Image to have been infolded with a Serpent, juft as *Ophiuchus* is reprefented in the Heavens, among the Northern Conftellations.

lations. This Bas Relief adorned the inner Side of that Part of the Wall, furrounding the Body of the City, which extends from Weft Gate to South Gate; it feems to have been found between the Year 1542, when *Leland* was at *Bath* collecting the Antiquities of the Place, and the Time when *Camden* was in the City, making his Obfervations; fince the former don't mention it in his *Itinerary*; and the latter defcribes it in his *Britannia*: But it was loft before Doctor *Guidott* wrote of the Antiquities of *Bath*, and before any real Draught was made of it; fo that any Reprefentation of it already publifhed, or that may be made hereafter, can be only imaginary.

LELAND takes Notice of the Image of *Hercules*, holding a Serpent in each Hand; as well as of a naked Man grafping a couple of thofe Vermin; and tells us, the latter was placed in the City Wall, not far from the North Gate, the former in the fame Wall between the South and North Gates. This naked Image, as *Camden* writes, was of *Hercules*, and feems to have reprefented him in the Action of his crufhing to Death the two Serpents that *Juno* fent to devour him, while he was young and naked in Bed; and our Author affures us that he faw another Image of the fame Hero holding up his left Hand, with his Club in the Right. Both thefe Images were placed in that Part of the Wall which lies between the North and Weft Gates; and in fome Part of the City Wall Mr. *Camden* obferved a third Image of *Hercules* holding a Serpent in his Hand, which, to him, appeared almoft defaced by Time; and, in all Probability, reprefented the Hero when he flew the *Hydra* of *Lerna*.

LELAND likewife takes notice of the Image of *Laocoon* embraced with two Serpents; this, fays he, was placed near Weft Gate; and *Camden* tells us that he faw a Figure of *Medufa*'s Head with her fnaky Hairs.

ALL the Figures of *Hercules*, as well as thofe of *Laocoon*, and *Medufa*, have been long fince loft; fuch of them as are not mentioned in the *Itinerary*, were undoubtedly found between the Year 1542, and the time that *Camden* wrote; and we may conclude with *Leland*, that as they were gathered out of the old Ruins of the City, they were placed in the Wall that encompaffes it, in Teftimony of the Antiquity of the Place: No real Draught of any of thefe Figures have been preferved; and they, with the Brazen Head, and Bas Relief of *Ophiuchus*, are here offered to the Confideration of the

Learned

Learned and Curious in Antiquities, as part of the Anathemata which the *Grecians* prefented the *Hyperboreans* with; and they are offered, for the moſt part, as *Symbols* proper to the hot Waters of *Bath*: For the Image of *Hercules* cruſhing the two Snakes that *Juno* ſent to devour him while he was young and naked in his Bed; the Image of the ſame Hero as he ſlew the *Numean* Lyon, as he killed the *Hydra* of *Lerna*, and as he carried away the Dog *Cerberus*, means no more than a beneficent Power, ſome great Gift of Nature, that relieves and preſerves Mankind when they are afflicted with bodily Diſeaſes; as ſuch the Antients placed *Hercules* along with *Ophiuchus* in the Heavens, where he appears with *Aquila* the *Britiſh* Prophet, and *Sagitta* the ſacred Arrow of *Apollo*, as a Northern Conſtellation decked with the Enſigns of his Victory over the King of Beaſts, and over the Guardian of the Gates of Hell.

Those Enſigns are a Club in the right Hand, the Head of *Cerberus* in the Left, and the Skin of the *Numean* Lion over the Body; and ſo Mr. *Camden*'s defaced Images were, in all Probability, decorated.

Laocoon, as well as *Abaris* or *Bladud*, was a Prieſt of *Apollo*, and both of *Trojan* Race: The former was alſo the Prieſt of *Neptune*; and he having darted his Javelin at the wooden Horſe which the *Greeks* left in the *Trojan* Camp, we are told that that Action was puniſhed the Day before the Deſtruction of *Troy*, while *Laocoon* was officiating at the Altar of *Neptune*, by two hideous Serpents, who firſt fell upon his two Sons, and after having piteouſly devoured them, ſeized upon *Laocoon* himſelf, as he was coming to their Relief, and cruelly ſtung him to Death. This was undoubtedly a Symbol to deter Men from Acts of Impiety, ſince *Laocoon*'s Action was interpreted and believed to be ſuch by the *Trojans* themſelves, notwithſtanding the Figure of the Horſe was impoſed upon them as an Inſtrument of Treachery inſtead of a Monument of Peace, or an Offering to *Minerva*, as the *Grecians* pretended.

The Figure of *Medusa*'s Head was the ſtrongeſt Symbol of the Power of Inchantment, ſince it was believed that all thoſe who looked upon the real Head were inſtantly turned into Stones. A notable Metamorphoſis of this Kind was performed in the Banqueting Hall of *Perſeus*, while the Nuptials between him and *Andromeda* were celebrating: For *Phineas*, to whom *Andromeda* had been promiſed, entring that Hall with a Band of armed Men, and beginning a bloody Fight, *Perseus*, in Danger of being overcome by Numbers, had immediate recourse to *Medusa*'s Head, the Sight whereof petrified *Phineas* and his Associates, who instantly became so many Blocks of Stone.

JUST such another Metamorphosis still appearing at *Stantondrue*, demonstrates to what a high Pitch the Art of Magick was advanced in *Britain*, when the Priests of that Place feigned the Stones, of which the Work consists, to have been a company of People turned into solid Blocks of Marble, and other Kinds of Rock, while they were going in Procession to the proper Place for solemnizing a Marriage between one of them, and her intended Bridegroom: And nothing is more probable than that the Power of effecting such Metamorphoses was ascribed to the *Druids* whenever they should produce the Figure of the *Medusa*'s Head, preserved no doubt, in their Capital Temple at *Bath*, and existing in the City till after the Time of Mr. *Camden*, as above.

CHAP. VI.

Of the Devastations as well as Restorations of BATH in the Days of the antient BRITONS.

WHEN the Line of *Bladud* became extinct in the Person of King *Porrex*, and *Britain* was thereupon inflamed with a Civil War, under no less than five Cotemporary Princes, *Dunwallo Molmutius* had no sooner ascended the Throne of *Cornwall* than he marched an Army into the Territories of the other contending Princes; and by destroying their Towns and Cities, he reduced the People under his Obedience: The Hero then preparing himself a Crown of Gold, forthwith mounted the Throne of *Porrex* with the Ceremonies of Coronation; and restoring the Kingdom to its antient State, established a Body of Laws for the better Government of it; built a Temple in Honour of the Goddess *Concord* in the City of *Trinovantum*; and dying after a long and glorious Reign, his Body was deposited in that City near the Temple which he himself had built.

BATH, by the Name of the City of *Trinovantum*, or the City in the turning Vale, must have suffered Desolation by the Hands of *Dunwallo*; but this Prince restoring it again, the City became the Capital Seat of the *British* Kings; *Belinu* the Son of *Dunwallo*, in the midst of his Affluence of Riches, after the Destruction of *Rome*, adorning and augmenting it; and *Lud* the Son of *Heli* becoming famous in the Century preceding the Commencement of the Christian Æra for the Building of Cities, he particularly distinguished himself by increasing that of the turning Vale, which the Author of the *British* History assures us, in the 20th Chapter of his 3^d Book, grew so eminent for its Structures, as well publick as private, that no City in all the foreign Countries could shew more beautiful Palaces.

THIS Magnificence seems to have drawn the *Belgic Gauls* into *Britain* that *Cæsar*, in the 5th Book of his *Commentaries*, tells us came here either to plunder or invade the Island; and particularly *Divitiacus*, whom our Author, in the second Book of his *Commentaries*, declares to have been once the most potent Man in *Gaul*, and Sovereign of the *Sueffones*.

THIS Prince obtained considerable Possessions while he remained in *Britain*; and all the *Belgæ* that came into the Island in a hostile Manner, took care to compromise Matters with the *Britons* so as to settle among them; and then applying themselves to the Cultivation of the Earth, the generality of them retained their antient Names wherever they settled; the *Cangi*, a small Colony of the *Belgæ*, in particular; our learned Antiquary, Mr. *Camden*, telling us that those People were seated near *Oaky-Hole*; " for, says he, there " seems to be the Remains of the Name *Cangi*, in some " Places thereabouts, as in the Hundreds of *Cannington* and " *Canings*, in *Wincaunton*, which is sometimes called *Cangton*, " and *Kaingsham*, as much as to say, the Mansion of the *Cangi*."

THE High Priesthood of *Gaul* was annexed to the Sovereignty in the Person of *Divitiacus*; and *Cæsar*, the High Priest of *Rome*, assuring us, that the *Gallick Druids* went into *Britain* to qualify themselves in their Profession, who can doubt of *Divitiacus*'s being of the Number to enable him to lead the *Cangi* thither?

DIVITIACUS was the Person that led that Colony of People into *Britain*; and after he had fixed their chief Seat at *Cainsham* in *Somersetshire*, he seems to have penetrated the Country Westward as far as *Cannington* in the same County; and Eastward as far as *Bishops Cannings* in *Wiltshire*; the *Gallick* King and High Priest giving his own Name to the *Devises* near that Village.

THIS will appear probable enough when we trace the Remains of the Name *Cangi* all along that Tract of Country which lies between the Mouth of the River *Avon*, and the Hundred of *Canings*: For we find it firſt at *Briſtol*, in *Caning's* Marſh, at the Foot of *Brendon* Hill; next in *Cainſham*, and *Chewton-Cainſham*; then in the Town and Hundred of *Calne*; afterwards in *Biſhops Canings*, and the Hundred of *Canings*; and, in the laſt Place, in *Keine*, *Keinell*, *Alcannyng* and divers other Villages, all bordering upon the ſacred Works of the *Britons*, as tho' the *Cangi* had pitched their Stations with a Deſign to invade or plunder the *Britons* attending thoſe Works.

Now that this was the End and Deſign of the *Cangi*, ſeems evident from this, that every Place, bearing their Name, is near a Fortification contiguous to ſome *Britiſh* Temple or Altar; and it is highly pleaſing to obſerve how the *Cangi* were all along kept in the Valleys, while the *Britons* maintained the higher Ground, and, in all Probability, thereby preſerved the ſacred Works that lay within the moſt antient Limits of *Caerbren*; as well as thoſe that made the Colleges for the Arch Prieſt of every Order to exerciſe the Functions aſſigned them by their Inſtitution.

ONE of theſe Colleges was ſituated on *Exmore*, at the South Weſt Corner of *Somerſetſhire*; another on *Saliſbury* Plain, in *Wiltſhire*; and a third on *Marlborough Downs*, in the ſame County. The Works on *Exmore* ſeem to have made the College where the Prophets, ſtiled by the *Romans* Extiſpices, foretold future Events, by viewing the Entrails of the Victims offered in Sacrifice: The Works on *Saliſbury* Plain ſeem to have made the College where the Divines performed the Offices aſſigned to their Order, and pretended to raiſe up the infernal Deities from below: And the Works on *Marlborough Downs* ſeem to have made the College where the Philoſophers officiated, and made Mankind believe them capable of drawing down the Celeſtial Gods from above.

DIVITIACUS, as an High Prieſt, deſirous of perfecting himſelf in his Profeſſion at the *Britiſh* Schools, ſeems to have taken up his Abode at *Cainſham* while he attended the initiating Cave of our Prieſts of the *Oak*, their Univerſity, their Metropolitan Seat, and the College of the Poets at *Harptree*: *Cannington* ſeems to have been a Place of Reſidence for him while he attended the College of the Prophets on *Exmore*: And the *Deviſes* was his chief Place of Habitation while he

attended

Chap. VI.   A Description of BATH.

attended the College of the Philosphers on *Marlborough Downs*; and the College of the Divines on *Salisbury* Plain.

AT this College the *Gallick* High Priest acted the Part of a *Gallick* King that had introduced himself into *Britain* for the Sake of Plunder and Dominion; Mr. *Andrew Paschal*, in a Letter to Mr. *John Aubrey* bearing Date from *Bristol* the 2^d of *December*, A. D. 1689, mentioning an Anonymous Author, who, in a Manuscript Discourse upon *Stonehenge*, declares that a bloody Battle was there fought between an illustrious Hero that bore the Name of *Stunings*, and *Divitiacus*; in which the former got a compleat Victory over the latter.

UPON this Defeat it seems highly probable that *Divitiacus* returned to *Gaul*; and that the Faction which rose up in that Country, and stripped him of all his former Glory, began upon the News of his ill Success in *Britain*.

THE *Gallick* King and High Priest, when divested of his Sovereignty, took a Journey to *Rome* to implore the Assistance of the Senate, which he could not obtain; but on *Cæsar*'s Arrival in *Gaul* the Posture of Affairs was, by his Favour, changed again; and *Divitiacus* having been restored to his antient Dignity, became an inviolable Friend ever after to the *Roman* General and High Priest.

WHILE the *Gallick* Prince, thus restored by *Cæsar*, remained in *Britain*, he qualified himself so well in the Art of Divination, that *Cicero*, after he had conversed with him, ascribed the Invention of that Art to the Priests of the *Oak*; and his Defeat at *Stonehenge* was probably the Cause of the Difference between *Lud*, whom *Cæsar* calls *Imanuentius*, and his Brother *Cassibellaun*, or *Cassivellaunus*, as *Cæsar* writes his Name: For the *Belgæ* flying to the Temples in the capital City of *Lud*, for that Sanctuary which the *Molmutine* Laws had provided for People in Distress, *Trinovantum* itself was besieged, the Country Towns about it were ravaged, the King was slain, and his eldest Son *Androgeus*, or *Maudubratius*, to avoid his Father's Fate, in a short time fled to *Gaul*; and putting himself under the Protecton of *Cæsar*, obtained a Promise of Friendship from that great Soldier.

THE Devastations committed at this Time were probably made good upon *Cassibellaun*'s Election to the Crown of his Brother; since the *British* History represents him as a King that began his Reign with such Acts of Generosity and Magnificence as rendered him famous in distant Kingdoms: And the same History informs us that the King having, from an Impulse of Piety, bestowed the City of *Trinovantum* upon *Androgeus*, who can doubt of his having first repaired it?

THE Account of *Cæsar*'s Invasion of *Britain* making the Beginning of the fourth Book of the *British* History, by the 8th Chapter of that Book the *Trinovantum* to which *Cassibellaun* summoned the Nobility of *Britain*, with their Wives, to offer solemn Sacrifices to their tutelar Gods for their Deliverance from the *Romans*, upon *Cæsar*'s return to *Gaul*, appears to have been a different Place from the *Trinovantum* bestowed upon *Androgeus*, as the capital City of his Father, whom *Cæsar* stiles King of the *Trinobantes*; " a People, " says our Author, that possessed one of the most considerable " Provinces of the Island:" But no part of this Province could extend any thing near the Place where *London* is now situated, since the *Thames* divided *Cassivellaunus*'s Territories from those possessed by the *Belgick Gauls* next the Sea Coast; and since his Dominions were so large as to extend fourscore Miles into the Island.

THE City of *Trinovantum* bestowed upon *Androgeus* was undoubtedly *Caerbren*, or the City of *Bath*, in its antient State; and the Court of *Camalodunum* must have been that which the young Prince insisted upon having *Evelinus* tried in for killing *Hirelglas*, when *Cassibellaun* ordered the Matter to be brought before him and the Nobility, at the Time that they were all assembled at *Trinovantum*; *i. e.* at some winding Valley perhaps in the King's own proper Territories.

CHAP. VII.

Of the Devastations as well as Restorations of BATH in the Days of the ROMANS.

THE *Cangi* that were protected at the Temples of *Caerbren* returning to their Original Seats, on *Cæsar*'s laying his Injunctions upon *Cassibellaun* not to injure *Androgeus* or the People under his Dominion, they so increased in the compass of about ninety Years, that on *Claudius Cæsar*'s ascending the Throne of the *Roman* Empire, A. D. 40. they became not only a powerful People of themselves; but by extending their Settlements, they laid the Foundation of the *Belgick* Kingdom in *Britain*, which, as Mr. *Camden* writes, contained all *Somersetshire*, *Wiltshire*, and part of *Hampshire*;

that

that is all the Land immediately furrounding the Metropolitan Seat of the Arch *Druid* of the Ifland, and the Colleges of his feveral Orders of Priefts, their initiating Cave, and their great School of Learning.

TACITUS, in the Life of *Agricola*, affures us, that the great *Julius Cæfar* was fo far from conquering *Britain*, that he became Mafter of nothing but its Coaft; and that it was the deified *Claudius* who accomplifhed the Undertaking, after affociating *Vefpafian* into the Direction of the Defign. " With-
" out either Battle or Bloodfhed, part of the Ifland, fays
" *Suetonius*, fubmitted to the Emperor within a few Days of
" his landing upon it;" and *Claudius* having begun Hoftilities to obtain the reft, returned to *Rome* the fixth Month after his Departure from thence, leaving the Government of what he had acquired to *Aulus Plautius*; under whofe Command *Vefpafian* purfued the War, fought thirty pitch'd Battles with the Enemy, fubdued two powerful Nations, and took above twenty Towns, together with the *Ifle of Wight*.

OSTORIUS fucceeding *Plautius* in the Government of the conquered Provinces of *Britain*, and in the Command of the Army, his firft Exploit was in defeating the *Icenians*; and *Claudius* having determined to abolifh the Religion of the *Britifh Druids*, as *Tiberius Cæfar* had abolifhed the Religion of the *Gallick* Priefts of the *Oak*, and the Practice of every thing in *Gaul* belonging to their Profeffion; *Oftorius*, for this End, led his Army next againft the *Cangians*; and in the ninth Year of *Claudius*'s War in *Britain*, A. D. 50, he wafted their Territories, committed general Spoil, and then planted a Colony, powerful in the Number of *Veterans*, at *Camalodunum*, i. e. *Mars*'s Hill; erecting a Statue to the Goddefs *Victory*, as *Tacitus* informs us in the twelfth and fourteenth Books of his *Annals*.

VARIOUS have been the Conjectures touching the Situation of this Hill; but *Pliny* telling us that the Town of *Camalodunum* ftood about two hundred Miles Southward of the Ifland of *Mona*; and that Diftance and Bearing from the Middle of the Ifland bringing us to the City of *Bath*, and the curving Mountain juft before it, ftill retaining for its Initial the *Saxon* Name of *Mars*, is a fufficient Demonftration that the *Camalodunum* of *Tacitus* was this very Mountain.

BATH, in its moft antient State, was therefore the principal Place that was wafted and fuffered general Spoil, when *Oftorius* led the *Roman* Army againft the *Cangians*; and
nothing

nothing can bear stronger Testimony of the Arms of those mighty Conquerors, than the Remains of the Works already described round about the hot Springs: For the Rocks of *Solis* lye prostrate upon the declining Ground below that which made their antient Basis; and the portable Stones of the Works that were levelled to the Surface of the Earth on the Summit of *Haul Down* appeared, till lately, in great Abundance, in a Kind of Walling practised by the *Romans* about eighteen hundred Years ago, and described by *Vitruvius*, l. 2. c. 8. and after him by *Palladio*, l. 1. c. 9. under the Title of *Reticulatum*, or Net Work; of which I don't remember ever to have seen another Example.

Some of the Blocks of Stone that made the great Court of Justice on *Camalodunum* are still lying against the South Side of the Hill; but, for the most part, they are eaten into by the devouring Jaws of Time, and look like so many Honey Combs: And these Blocks of Stone, with an infinite Number lately taken away to make the adjoining publick Road, and to adorn the Gardens of the Curious in Nature's Imperfections, lay in such a confused Manner as though they had been the Rocks fabled to have been piled up by the Giants against Heaven, and then hurled down by the Thunder of *Jupiter*.

History gives us a just Idea of the Power of the Machines of War made use of by the *Romans*; these Blocks of Stones are an Instance of it; and the conquering Arms of those mighty People appear still stronger at *Bath* in the Streets of the present Town, as well as in the Bowels of the Earth, as often as they are searched; both clearly shewing that a Consular Army, of two Legions, encamped on the Ruins of that Part of the City immediately surrounding the hot Springs.

To make this as obvious as possible Plate N°. 5, 6, exhibits the Plan of a *Roman* Camp, as the same is described by *Polybius*; this was delineated by a Scale of five hundred Feet in an Inch; and therein

A. Is the Prætorium, or General's Tent.

B. The Street called the *Principia*, and containing one hundred Feet in Breadth.

C. The Street, of fifty Feet in Breadth, that divided the two Legions.

D. D. The Tents of the Tribunes.

E. E. The Tents of the Cavalry.

F. F. The

Plate 5. Plate 6.

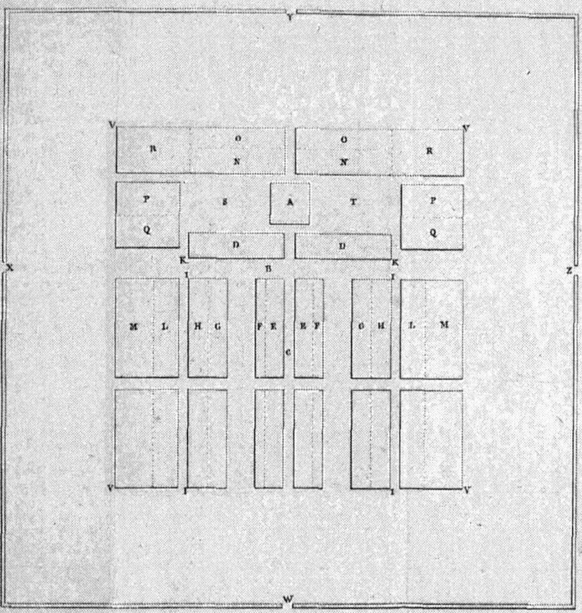

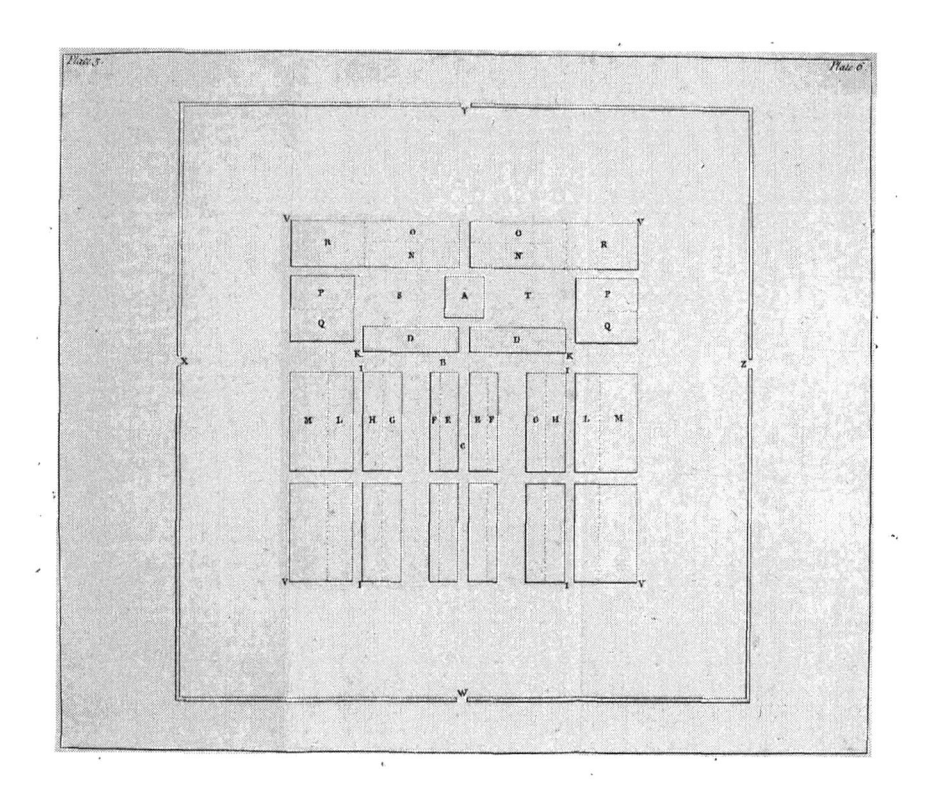

Chap. VII.   A Defcription of BATH.   169

F. F. The Tents of the Triarii.
G. G. The Tents of the Principes.
H. H. The Tents of the Haftati.
I. I. I. I. A Square of 1050 Feet containing the Troops of two Legions.
K. K. The Front Line of the Camp; from which, to the Back of the Prætorium, is 383 Feet 4 Inches; and this, with the Breadth of the Street B, and the Depth of the Square, I. I. I. I. makes the whole Depth of Ground, occupied by the two Legions, amount to 1533 Feet 4 Inches.
L. L. Tents of the Cavalry of the Allies.
M. M. Tents of the Infantry of the Allies.
N. N. Tents of the extraordinary Horfe of the Allies.
O. O. Tents of the extraordinary Foot of the Allies.
P. P. Tents of the Flower of the Foot.
Q. Q. Tents of the Volunteers.
R. R. Tents of the Foreigners, or Allies.
S. Ground for the Market, Altar, &c.
T. Ground for the Quæftor, &c.
U. U. U. U. The whole Camp of two *Roman* Legions, with their Allies, forming a Square of 1816 Feet 8 Inches; round which there was a void Space of 600 Feet broad; out of which the Thicknefs of Parapet, or Breaft-Work being taken, the clear Area of the Camp, with the Space round it, remained 3000 Feet in Length, and 3000 Feet in Breadth: The Camp was made approachable by four Gates, marked with the Letters, W, X, Y, and Z; and it was juft of the fame Size that *Mofes* directed the *Jews* to build their Cities, viz. 2000 Cubits Square.

The Liberties of the Camp extended ten thoufand Paces from the Army; and if we fuppofe each Pace to have contained three of fuch Feet, as *Villalpandus* deduced from the Congius of *Vefpafian*, then the Diameter of the Camp, with its Liberties, muft have been 21,000 Paces, or about 20,550 *Englifh* Yards, by the Standard in the *Exchequer*; which is equal to 11 Miles, 2 Furlongs, and 310 Yards.

Now if we compare the Plan I have been defcribing, with the Streets of *Bath*, as expreffed in Doctor *Jones*'s View of the City, we fhall find that the Street called the *Principia*, and the Street that divided the two Legions in the *Roman* Camp, are anfwered by the Street traverfing the City of *Bath* from Eaft to Weft; and by *Stall Street*, which, from the Middle of the former Street, runs directly South; or at least those two Streets are so situated, that they make Right Angles with one another.

The Name of *Stall*, by which the last Street is called, seems to have taken its Origin from the Stalls of the *Roman* Horse, encamped on each Side of it; and that Part of this Street, which extends beyond *South Gate*, is commonly called *Horse Street*; a Circumstance sufficient to confirm the Rise of the former Name, and prove it to have been from the Stalls of the *Roman* Horse.

The South East Corner of the General Hospital, or Infirmary, lately built in *Bath* just under the Figure 6, is in a right Line with *Stall Street*; and that Point, in Respect of the two Streets of the Town which I have been describing, answers the Center of the Prætorium of the *Roman* Camp: Accordingly, in digging the Foundation for that Hospital, in the Year 1738, I found the Vestigia of Part of the Prætorium, which I then measured by an *English* Foot, and delineated the same, as in the following Plan, Plate N° 7, by a Scale of twelve Feet in an Inch.

A. The Foundation of the Altar, which was placed near the General's Tent; and, in all Probability, served also for an Hypocaustum.

B. B. B. Holes where the Clay Pipes were fixed, to convey hot Air to the several Rooms of the Prætorium; many of which Pipes were dug up, and they were of a square Form; some six Inches Diameter, some nine Inches, &c.

C. A deep Hole of Ashes.

D. D. Two Ditches, each two Feet six Inches broad.

E. E. *Mosaick* Pavements; the first six Feet broad, the second eighteen Feet broad, and formed by Circles, like the *Mosaick* Pavement which was discovered, A. D. 1692, in the Grounds of *Henry Tomkins*, of *Kaer-Leon*, in *Monmouthshire*, Esq; and of which there is a Draught in the last *English* Edition of *Camden*'s *Britannia*, p. 833: But the Circles in that Pavement are formed upon a Diameter less than an *English* Foot; whereas those of our Pavement in *Bath*, are two Feet nine Inches Diameter: So that I am apt to think the Circles in the former Pavement were just a *Roman* Foot Diameter; in the latter three of the same Feet, or one Yard Diameter.

F. Two Steps, of six Inches Rise each Step.

G. A Floor, paved with common Stone, whose Level was twelve Inches higher than the Floor E, E.

H. A Wall three Feet two Inches thick.

North

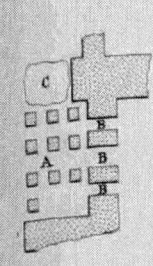

C
A B
B
B

H

G

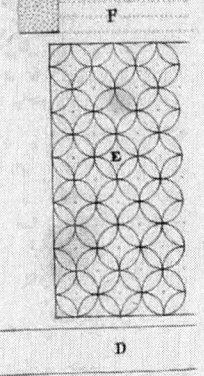

F
E

East

D
E
D

South

Chap. VII.   A Description of BATH.   171

THE Corner of the Hospital is a small Matter to the South East of the first Letter D; and under the South West Corner of the same Hospital, we found Wheat, the evident Marks of the Market which was always kept next the Prætorium, and the Altar, in the *Roman* Camp.

THE Wheat, the *Mosaick* Pavements, and the Foundation of the Altar, were about six Feet below the Surface of the Ground; under which it was at least three Feet to the Gravel, or natural Soil. Answering the Street behind the Prætorium, which led to the Gate Y, in the Plan, Plate N° 5, 6, a Road runs Northward, till it intersects the great Road, called the *Foss Way*, and this was formerly well known by the Name of *Foss Lane*.

IN the Year 1592 two antient Inscriptions was dug up in a Field at *Waldcot*, lying contiguous to the *Foss Way*; in the Year 1708, a third was dug up in the Way itself, a little beyond *Waldcot*; and these Inscriptions, says *Martiniere* in his great Geographical and Critical Dictionary, Vol. II. Page 146. prove that the second and twentieth Legion had heretofore their Quarters in the City of *Bath*.

THESE Circumstances, united, are next to Demonstration that a *Roman* Camp was pitched at *Bath*; and it seems highly reasonable to believe that *Ostorius*, after thus trampling on the Metropolitan Seat of the *British Druids*, could have been no less severe to the *Druids* themselves. *Suetonius* declares that *Claudius* utterly abolished *Druidism* as a Religion most detestably inhuman; " for, says *Tacitus*, they sacrificed " their Captives in Groves consecrated for that abominable " Purpose, and, in order to discover the Will of the Gods, " consulted the Entrails of Men:" As publick Murderers *Ostorius* seems therefore to have brought the Heads of the Authors of it to publick Execution, as the only Expedient to abolish a Religion that made Practices of the greatest Cruelty, Acts of Holiness; and in its Stead introduce the Religion of the *Romans*; *Tacitus* telling us that the chief End of the General in planting a Colony at *Camalodunum*, was to inure the *Britons* to the Laws and Jurisdiction of the *Romans*.

THE Arch *Druid* and the Heads of his four Orders of Priests seem to have suffered Death on *Haul Down*, between the Summit of the Mountain, and *Solsbury* Hill, in a Place now retaining the Name of *Slaughter Lane*; and to have been afterwards buried on *Pardies* Hill, by the Heap of Witness:

Five Monuments of Ignominy now lying on the Brow of that Hill, in a right Line; and thefe being Heaps of Stones, we may fuppofe them to have been piled up on the Bodies of the flaughtered *Druids*, by the cruel Hands of the *Romans*, by whom they fell.

ALL Antiquity attefts, that it was a Cuftom with Conquerors, and abfolute Princes, to throw Heaps of Stones upon the Bodies of the moft Eminent among the vanquifhed, as well as on the Carcaffes of thofe who were notorious Offenders againft the Law : *Joſhua* informs us in the 8th Chapter of his Book, that he ordered the Body of the King of *Ai* to be laid at the Entring of the Gate of the City, and a Heap of Stones to be raifed thereon, as a Token of his Victory over him : *Joſhua* alfo writes, that after he had ordered *Achan* to be ftoned to Death, for embezzeling the confecrated Spoil, he directed a Heap of Stones to be piled on his Body : And the Author of the fecond Book of *Samuel* tells us, that as foon as *Joab*'s Armour-Bearers had killed *Abſalom*, they put him into a Pit, and then raifed a great Heap of Stones on him.

THE learned Annotator on *Camden* fuppofes all thofe Heaps of Stones upon the Tops of Hills in *Wales*, and elfewhere, called *Carns*, to be Memorials of the Dead; and, in his *Britannia*, p. 699, tells us, that it was cuftomary to throw Heaps of Stones on the Graves of Malefactors, and Self-Murderers: " Traytors, adds he, are, by the *Welch*, called *Karn Vradwyr*; " Thieves *Karn Lhadron*; and the moft paffionate Wifhes a " Man can exprefs to his Enemy is, that a *Karn* be his " Monument."

HEAPS of Stones, having been thus Marks of the higheft Infamy, as well as Trophies of the greateft Victories, Heaps of Earth were efteemed quite the reverfe; and, in antient Times, the laft Funeral Rite which a Perfon could pay to his Friend, or a People to their Sovereign, was to raife a Monument of Earth to his Honour. This was the laft Compliment that was paid to *Hector*, as *Homer* teftifies in the laft of his *Iliads*, thus rendered by Mr. *Pope*,

" Laft o'er the Urn the facred Earth they fpread,
" And rais'd the Tomb, Memorial of the Dead.

This was the laft Compliment that was paid to King *Bladud*, as above : And we may fuppofe the fame Compliment to have been paid to the fucceeding *Britiſh* Kings *Cunedagius*, *Gorboduc*, *Dunwallo Molmutius*, *Guintelinus*, *Gorbonion*, and *Lud*, who were all interred at *Trinovantum*.

WHEN

Chap. VII.   A Defcription of BATH.

WHEN *Oſtorius* decamped from about the hot Waters of *Bath*, and led his Army againſt the *Brigantes*, he built, or ordered a Town to be erected upon the Lines of his Camp for the Colony that ſupplied the Place of his Legions; but this, as *Tacitus* declares in the fourteenth Book of his *Annals*, was not defended by a Ditch, or Paliſade; and, conſequently, it was but a weak and defenceleſs Place: It was, however, adorned with a ſtrong and magnificent Temple, built and dedicated to the Honour of *Claudius Cæſar*; and this Structure ſeems, for the chief Part, to have been raiſed with the Stones that made the round Temple of *Apollo* behind the Rocks of *Solis*. The Author of the *Britiſh* Hiſtory makes *Arviragus*, the Great Grand Son of *Lud*, the Builder of a Temple in Honour of *Claudius*; and by his telling us that it was erected in a City built by the Emperor, and called after his own Name, the City of *Claudius* muſt therefore have been that which was erected by *Oſtorius* at *Camalodunum*.

THE Veterans of this new planted Colony ſoon thruſt all the old Inhabitants of the Country out of their Houſes; exterminated them from their native Lands; and the Prieſts culled out for miniſtering in the Temple erected in Honour of *Claudius*, under the Cloak of Religion, devoured the whole Subſtance of ſuch as were ſubject to the *Roman* Power: So that notwithſtanding the *Britiſh* Nobility frequented the *Roman* Temple at firſt, and even adored *Claudius* as a God for his having remitted to them the Confiſcation of their Goods, " Yet, ſays *Tacitus*, that Temple was ſoon looked upon by " the *Britons*, in general, as a Bulwark of Domination " eſtabliſhed over them without End:" *Arviragus*, according to the *Britiſh* Hiſtory, was buried in it; and Mr. *Holinſhed* making that Prince the ſame with the *Praſutagus* of *Tacitus*, his Death muſt have happened while the Temple ſubſiſted, and within a few Years after it was finiſhed.

DURING thoſe Tranſactions that brought Deſolation upon the Metropolitan Seat of the *Britiſh Druids*, and ſeated a *Roman* Army, and a *Roman* Colony on its Ruins, the Prieſts of the *Oak* in general, the Fugitives that would not ſubmit to the *Roman* Power, and the Revolters from it, flew to *Pliny*'s Iſland of *Monapia*, now the *Iſle of Angleſey*, for Refuge, whereby that Iſland ſoon grew powerful in Inhabitants; and there the Refugees not only enjoyed their Religion and their Laws, but ſupplied the new Revolters with Succours till *Suetonius Paulinus*, a General of the higheſt Renown in the Science of War, aſ-
failed

failed the Island, defeated the Inhabitants with a cruel Slaughter of the *Druids* and all that resisted him, abolished their Places of religious Worship, and established a Garrison over the Vanquished.

But while *Suetonius* was thus employ'd, Tydings were brought him of the sudden Revolt of that Part of *Britain* which had been subdued and reduced to a *Roman* Province; and the *Britons* taking Arms under the Conduct of the renowned *Boadicea*, Queen of the *Icenians*, and Wife of *Prasutagus*, then lately deceased, they immediately fell upon the Colony of *Camalodunum*, took the Temple by Storm after a two Days Siege, and razed and burnt every thing the *Romans* were Masters of; the *Britons*, at the same time, killing, gibbeting, burning, and crucifying their Enemies with the Vengeance of Men determined to extirpate the whole Race of People against whom they had taken up Arms; nor did their Rage cease till they had killed seventy thousand Souls, all *Romans*, or Confederates of *Rome*.

This happened just after *Nero* had burnt the City of *Rome*; transferred the Guilt of that Action upon the Christians; and began his Persecution of them: Then the Ruins of the *Roman* Town of *Camalodunum* covered the Ruins of the Metropolitan Seat of the *British Druids*: But before this happened *Joseph* of *Arimathea*, with eleven others, all Disciples of Saint *Philip* the Apostle, came into *Britain*; and fixing himself and Brethren at *Glastonbury*, in the very Heart of all the *Druidical* Works above-mentioned, they there preached the Christian Faith to the *Britons*; *Arviragus* granting them that Town for a Place of Habitation, together with the Land about it for their Maintenance; and the Christian Teachers immediately erecting a small Church, and the first that was built in the Island.

But notwithstanding the King's Bounty was such, yet he would not Embrace the Faith himself; and it seems probable that he permitted it to be preached in Opposition to the *Roman* Paganism; for which, when *Arviragus* died, Vengeance was executed against his Family: His Wife underwent the ignominious Violence of Stripes; his Daughters were ravished; and his Relations were treated as Slaves till they flew to Arms in the Absence of *Suetonius Paulinus*, when he led the Army against the *Isle of Anglesey*.

It was under this General, while he commanded in *Britain*, that *Cnæus Julius Agricola* learned the first Rudiments

of

of War: By commanding afterwards the twentieth Legion, on *Vespasian*'s Acceffion to the Throne of the *Roman* Empire, and by taking a higher Command under *Petilius Cerealis*, *Agricola* was deem'd equal to the Office of Governour of *Britain* by common Fame, which, in this Inftance, says *Tacitus*, directed the publick Choice: And *Agricola*, at the fame time that he was promoted to the Government of the Ifland by the Emperor *Vespasian*, was alfo invefted with the Pontificate, whereby he came into *Britain* under the threefold Capacity of Governour, General, and High Prieft. His Arrival here happened about the Middle of Summer, in or about the Year of Chrift 78; and the General, after leading his Army againft the *Ordovicians*, conceived a Defign to reduce the *Ifle of Anglefey*, and make his Peace with the main Body of the *British Druids*, which he had no fooner done, than he determined, as he was acquainted with the Temper of the People in his Province, to cut off all the Caufes of War.

This was the Work of the Winter; the following Summer he employ'd, in firft alarming the Enemy, and then in fparing them, thus to tempt them with the Sweetnefs and Allurements of Peace; and accordingly feveral Communities fubmitted themfelves to him. The fecond Winter he purfued other Meafures to footh the *Britons*, by firft privately exhorting, and then publickly affifting them to build Temples, Houfes and Forums: He likewife employed his Care to have the chief Youth of the Ifland inftructed in the Liberal Sciences; and the *Britons* thus allured proceeded in their Works of Architecture to magnificent Galleries, and to fumptuous Baths.

By thefe Works the Metropolitan Seat of the *British Druids*, their Univerfity and their feveral Colleges were reftored, that the national Religion of *Druidifm* might be again practifed in Oppofition to Chriftianity to footh the Clergy; and to the *Roman* Paganifm to footh the Laity, and prevent their Subftance from falling into the Hands of Men that tricked them out of it under the Cloak of Religion.

Thus, says *Tacitus*, *Agricola* won the Affections of the *Britons*, and thereby captivated and enflaved them to the *Roman* Power.

In the Reftoration of *Bath*, under *Agricola*'s Government, the *Britons* built fuch Houfes as were neceffary for the immediate Dwellings of the *Druids*, fo as to anfwer the Lines of the City, while it remained the Town of *Camalodunum*; preferring

ferring the Streets and other open Parts of that Town to all other Confiderations for Places to offer their Incenfe at, to confult their Gods, to kill their Sacrifices, and to offer fuch Sacrifices: And there feems to be no doubt of their having made two Cifterns to receive the Waters of the hot Springs, adorned with a Tower in the Middle of each Refervoir; one Ciftern to receive the Water of the chief Spring, and the other to receive the Water of the two other Springs. The Towers fo built we may fuppofe to have been again dedicated to the Sun and Moon; and, at the fame time, to have reprefented thofe two Luminaries, as covering Waters that were looked upon to be Attributes of them.

THE chief hot Spring was inclofed according to the Plan, Plate N° 8, 9, of which there are three Sides almoft entire, and the Foundation of the fourth, or South Side, is very vifible. This Bath was, and is now juft fixty of fuch Feet in Length, and forty of fuch Feet in Breadth, as *Villalpandus* deduced from the *Congius* of *Vefpafian*; and this Circumftance alone, is next to Demonftration, that the *Britons*, affifted by the *Romans* in that Age, were the Builders of fo much of the prefent Walls, as anfwer and correfpond with the Plan, which was drawn by a Scale of twelve Feet in an Inch.

THE four Rooms, like Baftions, at the four Corners of this Bath, and marked with the Letters, A. A. A. A, were for People that went into the Bath to undrefs and drefs themfelves in: The Niches at each End were feven in Number; and on each Side there were twelve of the fame Receffes, all of a form, truly worth our Obfervation; for the Aperture of every Niche is three Feet broad, every Niche is three Feet deep, and the circular Part is juft three Feet fix Inches Diameter.

THE Form of the Ciftern that received the other Springs is no ways to be attained; tho', in general, it was Rectangular, and the Niches in the Walls were of the fame Ovenlike Shape with the Niches in the Walls of the principal Bath: Thefe Receffes were undeniably calculated for Shelter and Warmth; and therefore the Baths themfelves muft have been open and uncovered, contrary to the Method obferved by the *Romans* in their artificial warm Baths.

NOW, as there is not the leaft Shadow to fuppofe the feveral Places fet apart for Religious Purpofes, in *Agricola*'s Days, ever after altered, in Point of Situation, or the facred Works abridged, at leaft not till the Diffolution of Monafteries,

Plate 8. North Plate 9.

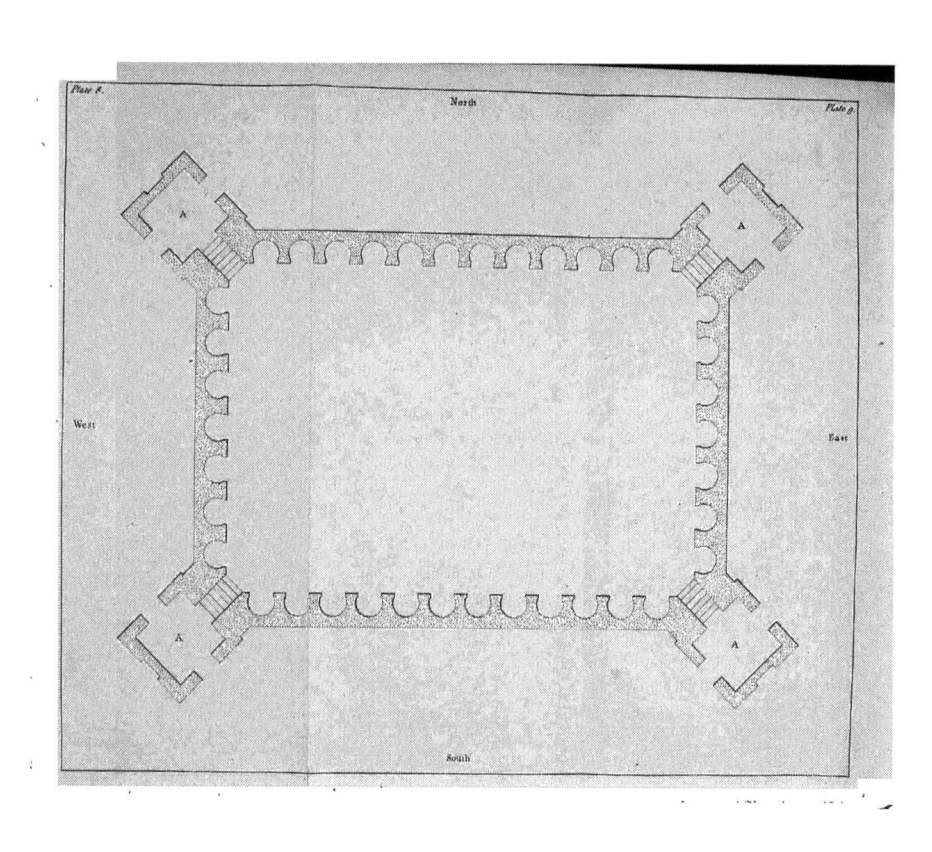

West East

South

Chap. VII.   A Description of BATH.

ries, &c. in the Reign of King *Henry* the Eighth; I have therefore taken the Centers, and Central Lines of the Churches, Towers, remarkable Trees, and Ambrey-House at *Bath*, and have placed them in the following Plan, Plate N° 10, 11, as they stood in respect to the Lines of the *Roman* Camp as it was turned into a *Roman* Town; and upon those Centers and Central Lines, I have delineated such Altars, Trees, &c. as were probably built and planted for religious Uses.

This Plan is drawn by a Scale of 250 Feet in an Inch; and

A. Is the principal Bath which was dedicated to the Sun, and represented that Luminary.

B. The inferior Bath, filled by the Water of the two hot Springs issuing out of the Earth at C and D; this was dedicated to the Moon, and it represented that Luminary.

E. An Altar for sacrificing to the Moon.

F. An Altar for sacrificing to the Sun.

L. A Tree dedicated to *Belenus*.

M. A Grove, or hollow Tree.

N. An Ambre, or Rocking Stone.

O. The Back of the Prætorium.

P. The Street of fifty Feet broad, that divided the two Legions.

Q. The Depth of the Camp, to the lower End of the sixth Maniple.

R. The Street of 100 Feet broad, called the *Principia*, which was so much frequented by the Officers, and common Men of the *Roman* Army, that a Number of Soldiers were appointed to sweep and cleanse it every Day in Winter, and Water it in Summer, to prevent Dust.

S. The Street called *Quintana*, because it opened beyond the fifth Maniple, and divided the several Bodies that composed the Legions into two equal Parts: At the East End of this Street, the Palace of the *British* Kings seems to have been situated, and on the Ruins of it we may suppose the Forum to have been built, which *Agricola* excited the *Britons* to erect for a Place of publick Assembly near the Waters of the Sun.

T. T. The Streets of 150 Feet broad, between the Triarii and Principes.

The Distance between the Back of the Prætorium, and the lower End of the Ground covered by the sixth Company in the *Roman* Camp, was just 1133 Feet four Inches; and the Breadth of the Land covered by the Legions amounted to 1050 Feet: This Spot of Ground, though scarce able to contain one of the publick Baths of *Rome*, was so extremely well disposed that it contained Lodgments for a *Roman* General, twelve Tribunes, 330 Horsemen, and 3480 Footmen; admitting, at the same time, of open Places for a Market, Tribunal, and other publick Works; and therefore the same Spot of Ground covered with Houses instead of Tents would admit of Habitations for a large Body of People, besides those that belonged to the Priesthood.

SUCH was the Form, and such was the Size of the Body of the Metropolitan Seat of the *British Druids*, when it was first restored under *Agricola*; and as the Inhabitants increased we may suppose the Villages round about it to have been peopled, till the City extended to the Limits of the Land that made the Liberties of the *Roman* Camp: Nor could the City have been long in thus extending itself, since the Incitements to draw the *Britons* together were exceeding great, and since their assembling for Inactivity and Repose was the End and Design of the *Romans* in exciting and assisting them to erect Buildings for publick, as well as private Uses.

NOTWITHSTANDING the Veterans of the Colony of *Camalodunum*, that exterminated the *Britons* from their Houses in the Villages round about the hot Springs, enjoyed those Habitations no longer than ten or eleven Years, yet they seem to have adorned them as Possessions perfectly secured to them and their Posterity; for in many of those Villages *Mosaick* Pavements and other Ornaments peculiar only to the *Romans* are continually discovering themselves.

COIL seems to have been the first *British* King that resided at *Bath* after its Restoration under *Agricola*; he began his Reign, A. D. 125, and the *Romans* permitting the *Britons* to be governed by their own Laws, King *Coil* is said to have formed a particular Charter for the Government of the Inhabitants of *Bath*.

THIS Monarch, according to the Tradition of the Inhabitants, was crowned in *Bath*, and in Memory of it, and of his giving the City its first Charter, his Statue is still preserved by the Citizens in the Front of the *Guild Hall*. He was succeeded by his only Son, named *Lucius*; who, abandoning *Druidism*, embraced the Christian Faith; and *Congell* the Author of *Monkery* in *Britain*, seems to have seated himself near the hot Springs of *Bath* to draw the *Druids* into a Discipline,

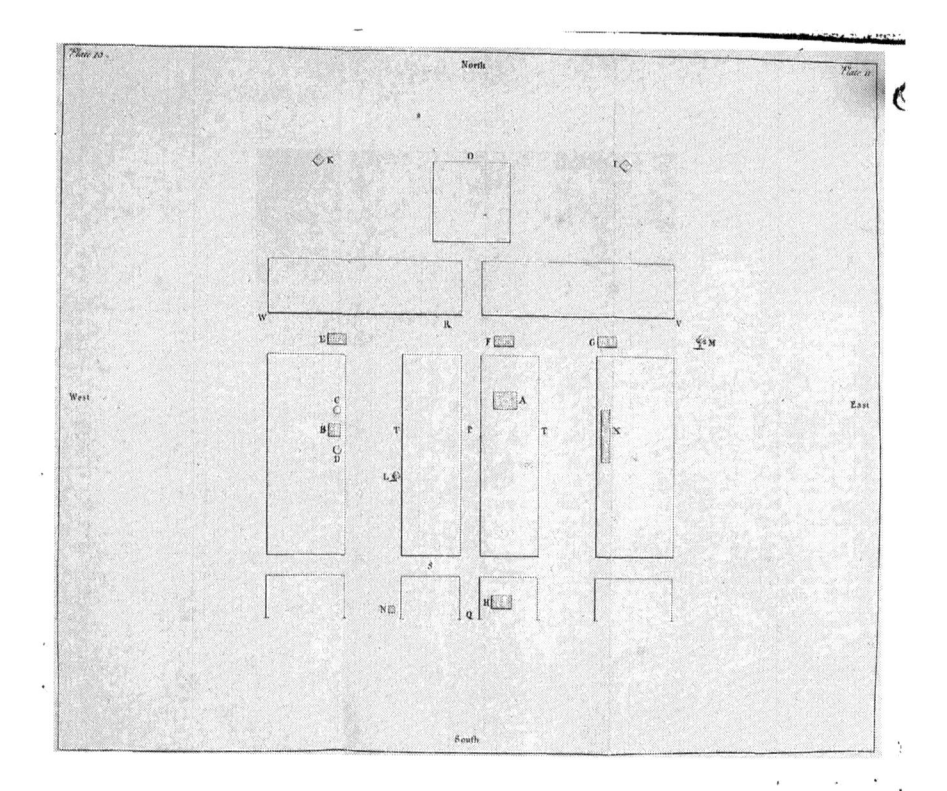

Chap. VII.   A Defcription of BATH.

Difcipline, exercifed in folitary Places under the Shade of Trees, like part of their own : For a Village in a large Wood bearing South Eaft and by Eaft from the Center of the City, and lying at no greater Diftance than three Miles from that Point, ftill retains the Name of *Congell*, as well as the Wood itfelf.

CONGELL feems to have had another Seat about twenty Miles weftward of this, at a Place now called *Congerfbury* ; and there, according to one of the *Glaftonbury* Chronicles, St. *Fagan* and St. *Deruvian* founded the See of the Bifhop of *Somerfetfhire*, A. D. 167 : But be that as it will, *Druidifm* ftill prevailing at *Bath*, the City continued the Metropolitan Seat of the Priefts of the *Oak*, till the Age preceding *Auguftin* the Monk; the *Saxons* calling it by the Name of *Achmanchefter*, *i. e.* the *Oak* Mens City, from the vaft Number of Priefts that dwelt in it; and *Solinus*, a *Roman* Writer, celebrating the publick Baths of the Place as the greateft Curiofity in *Britain*; our Author declaring, in his *Polyphiftoria*, that the hot Springs of our Ifland were richly accommodated with all Manner of Conveniences for the Service of Mankind ; and Mr. *Camden* declaring it to be out of all doubt that the Springs fo accommodated were thofe of *Bath*.

THE Fame of thefe *Baths* was fuch that the very Ways leading to them were, by the *Molmutine* Laws, made Places of Sanctuary. To *Dunwallo* the *Fofs* Road beginning in his Hereditary Dominions, and leading through *Devonfhire* and *Somerfetfhire* to *Bath*, is attributed ; by the *Britifh* Hiftory it appears that his Son, *Belinus*, improved that Road, extended it, and made three other principal Roads to traverfe different Parts of the Kingdom ; and fucceeding Princes made divers publick Ways that led to our hot Fountains, of which the Road, called *Achmanftreet*, that leads from *Buckinghamfhire* through *Oxfordfhire* to the *Foffe*, and fo on to *Bath*, is an inconteftible Proof; that Road, in the time of the *Saxons*, taking the Name of *Achmanftreet*, from its leading to *Achmanchefter*.

WE have another ftrong Proof of what I have afferted in the *Via Badonica*, or Road from *London* to *Bath*, defcribed by Doctor *Stukeley* in his *Itinerary*, p. 132 ; and by the *Itinerary* of *Antoninus* it appears that a Road led from the Waters of the Sun to *Venta Silurum*, or the Port of the *Silures*; this, according to Doctor *Gale*, paffed through *Abone* to *Trajectus*; but that learned Gentleman was miftaken in making *Hanham* the *Abone* of his Author: For this Place, with a *Saxon* Termination, lies on a *Foss* Road leading from *Bath* to the Passage over the Mouth of the *Severn*, it stands six Miles from *Bath*, nine Miles from the Water Side, and is wrote *Abotston*, but pronounced *Abson*.

CHAP. VIII.

Of the Devastations as well as Restorations of BATH in the Days of the SAXONS, DANES, and NORMANS.

BATH having been strongly besieged by the *Saxons* in the Year of Christ 520, it then suffered no inconsiderable Depredations before King *Arthur* raised the Siege, drove the Enemy to the Summit of *Mons Badonca*, and there defeated them: But four and fifty Years after that, the *Saxons* coming against the City under the Conduct of their Kings *Cuthwin*, and *Ceawlin*, they carried Fire and Sword to the Heads of the hot Fountains, and laid every Part of *Achmanchester* in Ruins.

THE great School of Learning of the *British Druids* survived their Metropolitan Seat about five and twenty Years, and subsisted till *Augustin* the Monk came into *Britain*, and, by the Order of *Gregory* the *Great*, silenced it for the same Reasons that *Galileus* was condemned by the Inquisition of *Rome* in the Year 1633; namely because the *British* Priests of the *Oak*, as well as the *Florentine* Mathematician, believed the *Pythagorean* System of the Planetary World, and instructed their Pupils in it.

AFTER this Transaction *Augustin* desired to have a Conference with the *British* Bishops at a particular *Oak Tree*, situated, according to *Bede*, in the Confines of the *Wiccians* and *West Saxons*: " Admitting this *Oak*, says the Bishop of " *London*, in the *Britannia*, p. 630, to be in *Hewiccia*, it " must needs have stood in that Part of *Gloucestershire* which " bounds the Counties of *Wilts* and *Somerset*:" And our Author further observes that some have conjectured, that *Augustin*'s *Oak* may have been in a Parish called corruptly *the Rock*.

Now in a North East and one Quarter easterly Line from the hot Springs of *Bath*, and at the Distance of four Miles and a Quarter from them, the Counties of *Wilts*, *Gloucester*, and *Somerset* meet together in the Middle of the great *Foss Road*

Road on the Summit of *Bannagh Down*: Three Quarters of a Mile Weftward of this Point we have a Place called *Oakford*; and another Place, called *the Rocks*, lies half a Mile from *Oakford*, and at the fame Diftance from the Meeting of the Counties: From all which it féems much more than probable that here *Auguftin* had his Congrefs; and where could he have held it ſo properly as at the antient Metropolitan Seat of the *Britifh Priefts* of the *Oak*, when it was in the Poffeffion of the Pagan *Saxons* that he was fent into the Ifland particularly to convert?

But whether *Auguftin*'s *Oak* grew at *Oakford* in the Vale on the Weft Side of *Bannagh Down*; at *Oakham* in the Vale on the Eaft Side of the fame Hill; at *the Rocks* near the Top of the Mountain; at a Place called *Cold Afton*, from its high Situation, and, perhaps, from *Auguftin* the Monk; or in *Monks Wood* in the Vale at the North End of *Haul Down*, is a Point referved for further Confideration: Tho' at, or near one of thofe Places, we may, with the higheft Probability, fix it; and a Tradition ftill fubfifting touching *Monks Wood*, feems to point out the very Affembly that was held at *Auguftin*'s *Oak*.

This Congrefs muft have drawn that Bifhop of *Menevia* into *Somerfetfhire* who had been Abbot of *Glaffenbury*; became the Succeffor of Saint *Dubricius* two Years after the Deftruction of *Achmanchefter*; and was raifed to the Rank of a Saint, by the Name of *David*, for his great Ability in working Miracles: And nothing is more probable than that this *Britifh* Bifhop at the firft Conference that was held at *Auguftin*'s *Oak* joined with the *Roman* Monk in preaching to the unconverted *Saxons*, as well as in turning the Sacred Works of the Pagans from Heathen to Chriftian Ufes: So *David* feems particularly to have been employed in turning the facred Works about the hot Springs of *Bath* from the Service of Idols to that of the true God; for the Monks, in fucceeding Ages, affirmed that he, by his Prayers, cured the Waters round about *Bath* of their Defection, and gave fome of them perpetual Heat and healing Virtues.

The Fact feems to be, that Saint *David*, by confecrating the hot Waters to Chrift, cured them of their Defection; and by clearing the Heads of the Springs of the Rubbifh that lay about them, reftoring the chief Bath, and making new Ones to receive the leffer Springs, the Bifhop gave the Water the Liberty of difplaying its Heat and Virtues, which it

could

could not do while the Springs lay buried in the Ruins of the City.

To Saint *David* we may therefore attribute the Separation of the hot Waters that, till then, rofe up in one Ciftern confecrated to the Moon, and the making a Ciftern at the Head of each Spring: One of thofe Cifterns feems to have been of a Triangular, and the other of a Quadrangular Form; each new Ciftern, as well as the Ciftern at the Head of the chief Spring, feems to have had a Tower erected in the Middle of it; and thefe were finifhed at the Top with Croffes as Marks of the Converfion of the hot Waters from Pagan to Chriftian Ufes: In effect, the Baths that made fo confiderable a Figure, among the curious Works defcribed by *Solinus*, were reftored by Saint *David* only as fimple Cifterns; and thofe Conveniences with which they had been richly accommodated for the Service of Mankind in the Ages of Paganifm, were left in their Ruins, lay neglected, and were foon forgot.

From reftoring the Baths, and converting the hot Waters to Chriftian Ufes, we may very juftly fuppofe Saint *David* to have proceeded to a Reftoration and Confecration of the other Pagan Works of the City; and more efpecially the Altars of the Sun and Moon: The Altar marked with the Letter E, Plate N° 10, 11, feems therefore to have been covered with a Church, dedicated to Saint *Michael*; and the Altar marked with the Letter F, had a Church raifed over it dedicated to Saint *Paul*.

Now if we allow five Years Time, from Saint *Auguftin*'s coming into *Britain*, to the Completion of thefe Works at *Bath* by Saint *David*, it will bring us down to the Year of Chrift 601; and it is very probable that upon the Divifion of *England* into Parifhes, which was begun about A. D. 636, thefe Churches were made Parochial, and fome others built.

Just eighty Years after St. *Auguftin* came into *Britain*, and in the Year 676, *Ofbrich*, a petty King of the *Wiccii*, founded and built a Nunnery at *Bath*, together with a Church dedicated to St. *Peter*; and in the Book of the Antiquities of the City *Leland* found it recorded, that at that time *Theodorus* was Arch-Bifhop of *Canterbury*; and that one *Bertane* was the firft Abbatiffe of the Monaftery, which was placed to the Eaftward of the chief hot Spring, and is marked in the Plan, Plate N° 10, 11, with the Letter X. He likewife found it recorded, that while *Theodorus* was Arch-Bifhop, one *Ethelmod*, a great Man, gave, by the Leave of King *Ædelrede*,

Chap. VIII. A Description of BATH.

rede, Lands to one *Berneguid*, Abbatiſſe of *Bath*, and to one *Fuleburs*.

About one hundred Years after *Oſbrich* began his Works at *Bath*, viz. about the Year of Chriſt 775, *Offa*, King of the *Mercians*, rebuilt the Church of Saint *Peter*, in a much more magnificent Manner than what it was before; and, as *Leland* conjectures, ſet Secular Cannons in it: But this Church was deſtroyed in the *Daniſh* Wars, in the Year 878, when King *Alfred* was driven to take Shelter at a neat Herd's Cottage in the *Iſle of Athelney*, near *Taunton* in *Somerſetſhire*.

After this the *Saxons* ſurrounded the Body of the City with a Ditch, a Wall, and a Rampier of Earth: This, with the higheſt Probability, is ſuppoſed to have been done by King *Alfred*, among thoſe Places began' to be fortified by him, in the Year of Chriſt 887: And the Wall thus built was carried from the Work at I, in the Plan, Plate N° 10, 11, to K; from thence it extended to W; thence in a Curve Line to Q; ſtill curving on by M to I; the King, at I and K, erecting two Towers for the Defence of that Part of the Wall; and giving to that at I, the Name of *Counter*'s Tower, and to that at K, the Name of *Gaſcoyn*'s Tower, the Baſis of which ſtill continues; but *Counter*'s Tower was deſtroyed about five and forty Years ago by Mr. *William Webb*, a Maſon now living.

The Earth that came out of the Ditch on the Outſide of the Wall, raiſed a Rampier within it; the Marks of which are ſtill viſible in ſeveral Places: And four Gates having been left in the Wall for Entrances into the City; one of thoſe Gates was left at Q; another juſt above the Letter M; a third to the Weſtward of I; and the fourth near the Letter W.

This Wall deſerves our particular Notice, for its having been built in an Age when the Maſon's Trade was ſo little practiſed in *England*, that (as *Rapin* writes, Vol. I. B. 4.) it was a Rarity to ſee a Houſe built with other Materials than Timber: " It was King *Alfred*, ſays he, that introduced
" into this Kingdom the Cuſtom of building with Stone and
" Brick; and that Monarch ſeeked all Occaſions of inviting
" into his Dominions Foreigners that were eminent in their
" Profeſſions, to inſtruct his Subjects, on whom he ſettled
" Penſions to the Amount of the ſixth Part of his whole
" Income. He likewiſe took particular Care to have always
" about him the moſt noted Architects and Workmen; kept
" them

"them employed with the sole View of improving their
"Skill, and appropriated the sixth Part of his Estate to pay
"them." The Works performed in the Reign of *Alfred*,
may be therefore looked upon as the Fountain from whence
most of our old Buildings were derived; and the Wall that
surrounds the Body of *Bath* is a Piece of Work so good in its
Kind, that, in my Opinion, it can claim no other Original
than the Hands of King *Alfred*'s Workmen, with Materials
collected chiefly from the Ruins of the antient Works of the
City: So that those who would have this Wall a *Roman*
Work, had better pretend it *Egyptian*; and tell us it was
built by their *Æsculapius*, or those under him, because History
makes that Person the Author of such Kind of Works.

WITH the Wall the Heart of the City was restored to a
higher Degree of Magnificence than it had been in for 300
Years before: But the King contracted the antient Limits
of the Place, and reduced them to a small Berton on the
Outside of the Wall that surrounded the Body of it; the rest
he formed into a separate Jurisdiction; denominated it the
Hundred of *Bathforum*, from the Forum that was built in it
at the Instigation of *Agricola*; and in the Church of Saint
Peter, *Edgar*, according to the *Saxon* Chronicle, was crowned
King of *England*, with great Solemnity, upon the 11th of
May, A. D. 973.

THIS Monarch, by all Accounts, had a great Veneration
for *Bath*; he expelled the secular Cannons from Saint *Peter*'s
Church; placed Monks of the Order of Saint *Benedict* in their
Room; appointed an Abbot to preside over them; and gave
the City its second Charter; in Memory whereof the Statue
of that *Saxon* Monarch is still preserved, in the Front of the
Guild Hall; in the Monkish Times the Inhabitants, in all
their religious Ceremonies, prayed for the Soul of King *Edgar*;
and when *Leland* wrote the 2^{d} Vol. of his *Itinerary* they
pursued the Custom of electing, yearly, on *Whitsunday*, a
King among themselves in joyful Remembrance of *Edgar*,
and the richest Men of the Town made it a Rule to feast
their Monarch, with all his Adherents.

THE *Bath* Monarchy devolving upon Mr. *Nash* on his
first coming to the City on the 4th of *August*, A. D. 1704,
that Gentleman enjoys it to this Hour; but without any of
the antient Perquisites; and it may be very justly said, that
this *Bathonian* Sovereign hath often fed those that should have
feasted him.

THE

Chap. VIII.   A Description of BATH.

THE first Abbot of *Bath*, according to Mr. *Willis*, in his Account of the Conventual Cathedral Churches, p. 219, was *Elphegus*, or *Elphage Prior* of *Glastonbury*, preferred from hence to the See of *Winchester*, A. D. 984, and afterwards translated to *Canterbury*: But before our Abbot was removed from his Abbacy Sir *William de Mohun* built the Priory of *Dunster* to the Honour of St. *George*, and then annexed it as a Cell to the Abbey of *Bath*, to which it belonged till the final Dissolution of the Monastery, in the Year 1539.

AFTER *Elphage* was made Arch-Bishop of *Canterbury*, he, about the Year 1010, rebuilt the Monastery of *Bath* in a very sumptuous Manner: But this Structure, with every other part of the City, was brought to its final Ruin, by *Robert de Mowbray*, Earl of *Northumberland*; who having raised a warm Rebellion against *William Rufus*, he, with his Uncle, *Geoffrey* Bishop of *Constance*, came from *Bristol* to *Bath*; and, as *Holinshed* writes, took the City, which they plundered and burnt in the Year of Christ 1088; *Alfius* having been then Abbot of *Bath*, and a Spectator of that dreadful Desolation; the Terrour of which instantly sent him to his Grave.

NINE Years before this happened, and upon the Return of *William* the *Conqueror* from the Siege of *Dolle*, A. D. 1079, Arch-Bishop *Lanfrank* called a Council of the Clergy at *London*, in which, says *Holinshed*, it was ordained that for the Honour and Dignity of the Church certain Bishops Sees should be removed from small Towns into Cities of more Fame; and in particular that the See of *Wells* should be removed to *Bath*: *Giso* was at that time Bishop of *Wells*; but he dying not long after the *Conqueror*, was succeeded in the Year 1088, by *John* of the little Farm, born at *Tours* in *France*, and therefore commonly called *John of Tours*.

THIS *John of Tours* practised Physick at *Bath*, and, as Mr. *Collier* writes in his *Ecclesiastical History*, acquired a considerable Fortune by it before he was preferred to *Wells*: So that the Doctor's Views of further Acquisitions from the Use of the hot Waters strongly prevailed with him to restore the City, and, conformable to the Order of the Council of the Clergy, to fix his Pontifical Seat in it. In this Design, the Bishop was encouraged by the Monks of *Bath*, who not only solicited him to unite the Abbey and Bishoprick together, but gave him 500 Marks, the Value of 20000 Sheep in those Days, to enable him to purchase the former: And King *William Rufus* having presented *John of Tours* with the Ruins of the City, the Charter made on that Occasion in the Year 1090, ran in Words to this Effect.

"WILLIAM King of *England*; To O, Bishop of *Sarum*, and L, Abbot of *Glastonbury*; to A, the Vicount, and to all the Barons *French* and *English* of *Somerset* and *Wiltshire*, Greeting. Know ye that I have given to God and Saint *Peter* in *Bath*, to *John* the Bishop and to his Successors, for the Augmentation of his Pontifical See, all my City of *Bath* in free Alms for the Health of the Souls of my Father, of my Mother, of myself, and of my Predecessors and Successors: 1 have given it, I say, to him in as free and honourable a Manner, as I hold any City in *England*, with all its Appurtenances, whatsoever I or my Father have enjoyed or possessed there, with all the accustomed Rights both within and without the same, with the Toll Money arising as well in the Fields as the Woods, as well in the Market as the Meadows, and other Lands, that with the greater Honour he may fix his Pontifical Seat there."

THE Bishop upon this Grant, and another in the same Year of the Abbey, for the Money furnished by the Monks, rebuilt and enlarged the Church of Saint *Peter* to above 300 Feet in Length; erected a stately Palace on the West Side of it; and in the Year 1094, he, according to *Holinshed*, began to inhabit in his new Dwelling-Place, taking upon himself the Title of the first Bishop of *Bath*. He also rebuilt the Monastery, and constituted one of the Monks a Prior to act under him; whereby the Monks of *Bath*, after having had Abbots over them for about 110 Years, were put under the Government of Priors, subject to the Bishop of the Diocess.

BESIDES these Works, *John of Tours* made two new Baths within the Limits of the Monastery, for the Use of the Publick; calling one the Abbot's Bath, the other the Prior's Bath; and these existing for at least 500 Years, were fed by the Water of the *King*'s Bath, to which they became temperate Baths, just as the *Cross* Bath is to the hot Bath, and enabled the Bishop to adapt the hot Waters to all manner of Cases and Constitutions.

BY these publick Works, and by the private Dwellings erected in Consequence of them, the City of *Bath* was soon restored to a greater Degree of Magnificence than before it was burnt by the Rebels; which new erected City and all Things belonging to it, King *Henry* the first not only confirmed to the Bishop, upon his coming to the Throne; but,

Chap. VIII. A Description of BATH. 187

on the 6th of the Ides of *August*, A. D. 1111, and in the 12th Year of his Reign, re-confirmed the same, with a Grant of the Hidage of 20 Hides of Land for the better Support of the Pontifical Dignity. The Charter on this Occasion ran thus.

"In the Name of the Father, the Son, and the Holy
" Ghost, Amen. Henry by the Grace of God King of
" *England*, To all Arch-Bishops, Bishops, Abbots, Earls,
" Barons, and his faithful Subjects *French* and *English* of his
" whole Realm of *England*, Greeting. Be it known unto
" you, That that Gift which I have given to God and Saint
" *Peter* in *Bath*, where my Brother *William* and I have con-
" stituted and fixed the Episcopal See of all *Somersetshire*,
" which was formerly at the City called *Wells*, to wit, that
" City and all things belonging to the Ferm of the same
" City, I give and confirm to our Lord Jesus Christ; to
" *Peter* his blessed Apostle; and to *John* the Bishop, and his
" Successors for their perpetual Right and Heritage. I Grant
" also the Hidage of twenty Hide Lands belonging to the said
" City; and all Pleas, Laws, Courts of Justice and Customs
" thereto belonging wholly and altogether; and whatsoever
" besides my Father, my Brother, or myself have enjoyed
" in the said City; all these I fully and wholly give to God;
" and grant to the Church of the same City, to *John* the
" Bishop and to his Successors, to the Intent it may be for
" established and perpetual Alms for the Souls of myself;
" my Wife and my Children; and also of my Father, my
" Mother, and my Brothers."

About five Years before the Date of this Grant, and in the 12th Year of the 2d Indiction after the Council of the Clergy at *London*, A. D. 1079, *John of Tours*, touched with a Remorse of Conscience for depriving the poor Monks of what he had bought with their own Money, divided the old Possessions of the Monastery with the Prior he had made, and granted him and his Successors some others, in Lieu of those he kept, in Words to the following Effect.

" In the Name of the Father, the Son, and the Holy
" Ghost. I *John* by the Grace of God, Bishop of *Bath*,
" To all Bishops my Successors, to all the Sons of the Holy
" Church, Greeting. Be it known unto you all, that for
" the Honour of God and of Saint *Peter*, I have laboured,
" and at Length effected, with all decent Authority, that
" the Head and Mother Church of the Bishoprick of *Somerset*
" shall

"shall be in the City of *Bath*, in the Church of Saint *Peter:* To which Holy Apostle and to the Monks, his Servants, I have restored their Lands, which I formerly held unjustly in my own Hands in as free and ample Manner as *Alfius* the late Abbot held them before me: And if I have improved them, and whatsoever of mine shall be found thereon, I give to them, to their own Use and Property. I also give them for farther Supply of their Food and Cloathing, and to increase the Convent of the Holy Brethren serving God there, and to re-imburse the Treasury what I took from the Church, those Lands which I have acquired by my own Travail, or bought with my Money; To wit, those five Hides in *Weston*, which I purchased of *Patricius de Caurcia*, and the Land of *Hugh* with the Beard, to wit *Claferton*, *Docne*, *Mersfield* and *Eston*, together with *Herley* and *Arnemude* on the Sea-Coast, and whatsoever belongs to them, and one House in *Bath*, and one other House in *Winchester:* But as to the City of *Bath*, which first of all King *William*, and after him his Brother King *Henry*, gave to Saint *Peter* for their Alms, I have, pursuant to my Vows, determined that all Issues and Profits arising from it, be laid out in perfecting the Work I have begun in Church Ornaments of Copes, of Cloaks, of Screens, of Traplings of Tapestry, of Crucifixes, of Robes, of Chalices, and of Phylacteries: And whatsover of my own I have added to the Episcopal Chapel, my whole Armory, my Cloaths, my Bowls, my Plate, and all my Houshold Furniture, I give to Saint *Peter* and his Monks for ever to their own Use and Property, for the Remission of my Sins. Whosoever therefore shall infringe on this my Gift, may the Curse of God and of his holy Apostles and Saints light on him, and by the Authority of me, tho' a Sinner, let him be accursed and for ever cut off from the Community of the Church. Done A.D. 1106; in the Reign of *Henry*, Son of *William* Duke of *Normandy*, and King of *England*, *Anselm* being Arch-Bishop; of my Ordination the 19th; and of the Indiction the 12th. And that this my Deeds may remain more firm and unshaken, I have, with my own Hand, signed it with the Sign of the Holy Cross."

The Bishop survived this Grant about 17 Years; and when he died in the Year 1123, he was buried in the Middle of the Presbytery of the Church of Saint *Peter*, by him rebuilt:

built: A noble Tomb was some time after erected over his Grave, with his Image lying upon it; and both remained entire till after the Dissolution of Monasteries: *Leland* says, he saw the Image, and tells us that Weeds then grew about the Tomb!

By the Means of this Bishop, *Bath* became a City for Men separated for the Service of Religion under the *Norman* temporal Government, the same as it was when the *Saxons* called it *Achmanchester*, or the *Oak* Men's City; but its Glory was soon eclipsed; for *John of Tours* was no sooner dead, than great Contentions arose between the Monks of *Bath*, and the Cannons of *Wells* for the Priority in the Election of a new Bishop; and in the midst of these Disorders the City, with St. *Peter*'s Church, were again burnt down about the third Year of King *Stephen*, and *Bath* remained an Heap of Rubbish till *Robert* the third Bishop put an End to the Disputes, by obtaining of the Pope that the See should be in both Places; but that the Name of *Bath* should be preferred in the Title: This done the Bishop rebuilt the Monastery, Palace and Church, about the Year 1140, and lived till the 13th Year of King *Henry* the 2d, A. D. 1167.

CHAP. IX.

Of the Additional Works to BATH, between the End of the NORMAN Government and the Removal of the Episcopal See to WELLS.

KING *Henry* the second kept the Bishoprick of *Bath* and *Wells* void for some Years, at Length it was given to *Reginald Fitz Joceline*, a *Lombard*, who, notwithstanding his Partiality to *Wells*, rebuilt the small Churches of Saint *Mary* and Saint *Michael* within the Walls of *Bath*; and near the latter he, in the Year 1180, founded an Hospital with a Chapel thereunto belonging, which he dedicated to Saint *John* the *Baptist*: He afterwards obtained of King *Richard* the first the Manors of *Curry*, *Wrentick* and *Hatol*, to augment his Bishoprick, which in the Year 1167, produced L 434. 11. 8. and then he was translated to *Canterbury*; but dying at *Dogmersfield* in *Hampshire*, was buried at *Bath* on *Christmas-Day*, A. D. 1191.

This Prelate was succeeded in the See of *Bath* and *Wells* by *Savaric*, Abbot of *Glastonbury*; who favouring *Wells*, as his

his Predeceffor had done, had Art and Intereft enough with King *Richard* to exhange the City of *Bath* for *Glaftonbury* as an Addition to *Wells*, and fo *Savaric* took upon himfelf the Title of Bifhop of thofe Places.

THE City thus coming into the Hands of the Crown, King *John*, while he was Earl of *Moreton*, founded a Benedictine Priory at *Waterford*, and another at *Cork* in *Ireland*, which he annexed as Cells to the Abbey of *Bath*; and foon after he came to the Throne he granted the Citizens a new Charter.

IN the feventh Year of the Reign of this King, A. D. 1205. *Savaric*, the Bankrupt Bifhop of *Bath*, for fo Sir *John Harrington* ftiles him, died; and he was fucceeded by *Joceline de Wells*, who immediately removed his See to *Bath*, and fo became the fixth Bifhop of the Place, juft one hundred Years after *John of Tours* had, by his Grant, fixed the Pontifical Seat of all *Somerfetfhire* in it, with a folemn Curfe againft the Perfon who fhould, in the leaft, infringe on what he had done, as well as a ftrict Command to excommunicate and cut off any fuch Perfon from the Communion of the Church.

THE new Bifhop in the next Place agreed with the Monks of *Glaftonbury* to put Matters on their former footing, and to fuffer their Reftitution, in Confideration of their giving him fome good Manors to augment his Bifhoprick of *Bath* and *Wells*, which they very readily confented to do; and gave him the Manors of *Congrefbury*, *Cheddar*, and *Axbridge*: So that the Rents of the Bifhoprick, in the 14th Year of King *John*, A. D. 1212 amounted to L 640. 6. 9: But it was fix Years after that before Pope *Honorius* the third granted his Bull to diffolve the Union of the Churches which had been made by the Intrigues of *Savaric* the Bifhop.

ABOUT the Time of this Diffolution, *Necham*, Abbot of *Exeter*, celerated the Virtues of the hot Waters of *Bath*, and exploded the common Opinion of their being made hot by Art, in Words thus tranflated by the Bifhop of *London*, and inferted in the *Britannia*:

" Scarce Ours to *Virgil*'s Baths the Preference give,
" Here old decrepit Wretches find Relief.
" To Bruifes, Sores, and ev'ry cold Difeafe,
" Apply'd, they never fail of quick Succefs.
" Thus human Ills kind Nature does remove;
" Thus Nature's Kindnefs human Arts improve.
" They're

Chap. IX. A Description of BATH.

" They're apt to fancy brazen Stoves below,
" To which their constant Heat the Waters owe.
" Thus idle Tales deluded Minds possess,
" But what? We know that 'tis a Sulph'ry Place."

THE City now flourishing, *William Button*, the tenth Bishop, augmented his Bishoprick with the Manors of *Bicknaller*: So that by the Acquisition of these new Manors to the other Estates of *Bath*, the City grew into such Repute towards the latter End of the thirteenth Century, that in the 26th Year of the Reign of King *Edward* the first, A. D. 1298, it sent Citizens to serve in Parliament; a Priviledge granted to it at the Instance of *Robert Burnel*, the eleventh Bishop of *Bath*; who was first Treasurer, then Lord Chancellor of *England*, and, on the King's claiming the Crown of *Scotland*, became his Spokesman on that Occasion upon the second of *June*, in the Year 1291.

WILLIAM DE MARCHIA succeeding *Robert Burnel* in the Bishoprick of *Bath*, as well as the high Office of Lord Treasurer, he obtained a Grant from the King, in favour of his Abbey, of two Fairs, the one to be held in *Berton*, i. e. in the Meadow now called the *Ham*, the other at *Lyncomb*; and this appears to have been all the Augmentation that was made to the Possessions of the Abbey since the Time of *John of Tours*.

UPON the Death of *John de Drokensford*, the 14th Bishop of *Bath*, on the 9th of *May* in the 3d Year of King *Edward* the third, A. D. 1330, the Issues of the Bishoprick, for that Year, amounted to L 534. 6. 10¼ exclusive of the Value of the Grain, of sundry Kinds, growing on 4898½ Acres of Land when the Bishop died; the Weeding, Reaping and Gathering in of which cost L 173. 0. 5; which demonstrates a vast Increase in the Revenues of the Bishoprick: And now the holy Brethren of the Abbey, seized with a Spirit of Industry, began to Increase the Revenues of their House; for the Art of weaving Woolen Cloth was no sooner brought into *England* than they encouraged and practised it at *Bath*, and from hence it was carried to *Bristol* immediately after the Parliament had passed an Act, in the Year 1337, to encourage that Trade: The Shuttle, the chief Implement of which, was introduced by Prior   , with the Arms of the Abbey, as an Ornament in the Front of the Abbey-House, and there it still remains, a Trophy of the Industry of the Monks of *Bath*.

IT

IT is very certain that King *Edward* the third granted the Corporation of *Bath* a Charter, but the Date I have not been able to come at, tho' by the best Account I can get it was in the Year 1361; and if my Information be right several Tenements were, by that Charter, made over to the Corporation, under the reserved Rent of between 19 and 20 Shillings a Year to the Crown, for the Reparation of the Church of St. *Michael* without the North Gate; and for the Maintenance of the Poor of that Parish in particular, and of the City in general. The Rents accruing to the Parish by these Tenements in the Year 1374, amounted to no more than *L* 2. 14. 8. *per Annum*; but as the Leases were renewed, the Rents were increased; so that by the Year 1527, they amounted to *L* 11. 1. 8. and the Tenements were then thirty two in Number, of which fifteen were situated in *Waldcot*, and *Waldcot Street*, and were let for *L* 4. 18. 4; Eleven fronted *Broad Street*, the Rent of which amounted to *L* 4. 16. 8; Four stood in *Frog Lane*, and were let for *L* 1. 1. 2. and the other two were situated in *Stall Street*, the Rent of which having been *L* 0. 5. 6. made up the above Sum of *L* 11. 1. 8.

THAT part of the Income of these two and thirty Tenements, which was to be applied towards the Maintenance of the Poor, was laid out, for the most Part, upon the Bread, which in former Times was distributed to the People at the Church-Doors, during the Time of *Lent*, in large Loaves; but of late Years in small Rolls: And in Honour of the Royal Donor *South Gate* was rebuilt, A. D. 1363; the King's Statue, in a sitting Posture, having been then placed in a Niche over the Middle of the Aperture, with a Statue of the Bishop, as Lord Abbot of *Bath*, on one Side; and the Statue of the Prior, his Deputy, on the other Side.

AT the same time a Stone Bridge, with a Chapel and Gate upon it, was built over the River *Avon* to make a more convenient Communication between the City and *Lyncomb*, during Fair time, than by crossing the River at the Ford just above it; this Work was immediately dedicated to Saint *Laurence*; and about the same time *John Boccace*, an *Italian* Writer, described the Origin of the hot Springs and City of *Bath*, with the Virtues of the Waters, in Words supposed to be spoken by King *Bladud*; and thus recited by Doctor *Guidott*, from some printed Copy of *Boccace*'s Works as translated by *Daniel Lidgate*, Monk of St. *Edmundsbury*, in the Year 1432.

"SOME

Chap. IX. A Description of BATH.

" Some say, I made the holesom Baths at *Bathe*,
" And made, therefore, two burning Tuns of Brass,
" And other twain seven Kinds of Salts, that have
" In them inclos'd; but these be made of Glass;
" With Sulphur fill'd, Wild-Fire emixt there was.
" And in four Wells those Tuns so placed Heat, for aye
" The Water springeth up before it pass away.

" Which Waters Heat, and cleansing perfect Power,
" With Vapours of the Sulphur, Salts, and Fire,
" Hath Virtue great to heal, and cleanse, and scower
" The bathed Sores therein, that Health desire.
" If of the Virtues more thou dost require
" To know, I will recite what old Experience tells,
" In Causes cold, the noble Virtues of those Wells.

" The Baths to soften Sinews Virtues have,
" And also for to cleanse and scower the Skin;
" From Morphews white and black to heal and save;
" The Bodies freckled, faint, are bath'd therein,
" Scabs, Lepry, Sores are old, and fester'd in
" The Scurf, Botch, Itch, Gout, Pox, swell'd Joints, and Humours fell,
" The Milt and Liver hard it heals, and Palsey well.

" I must confess, by learned Skill I found
" These native Wells, whence Springs that Help for Men.
" But well thou know'st, there runs from under Ground
" Springs, Sweet, Salt, Cold, and Hot, even now as then,
" From Rock, Salt Peter, Allum, Gravel, Fen,
" From Sulphur, Iron, Lead, Gold, Silver, Brass and Tin,
" Each Fountain takes the Force of Vein it coucheth in.

" Then whoso knows by Nature's Work in these
" Of Metals or of Mines the Force to heal,
" May sooner give his Judgment in Disease
" For curing by the Bath; and surer deal
" With sickly People of the Publick Weal:
" And also find of Fountains Salt, or Hot, or Cold,
" And for to heal by them the Sick, with Honour be bold.

" The City eke of *Bathe* I founded there,
" Renowned far by Reason of the Wells:
" And many Monuments that Antient were,
" I placed there, Thou know'st the Story tells, &c.

About the same time also *John Harewell*, the 17th Bishop of *Bath*, became a great Benefactor to his Church; and *Bristol* rivaling *Bath* in the Woolen Trade, the *Bristonians* not only set up a Fair on the Feast Day of St. *Calixte*, i. e. the 24th of *October*, the very Day on which the *Bathonians* held their Fair of *Berton*; but forbid all their Townsmen, upon certain Pains, to bring any Wares to the Fair of *Bath*; for which the Inhabitants, in the 50th Year of *Edward* the 3d, A. D. 1377, complained to Parliament, and prayed for Remedy against such an Invasion of their Rights and Privileges.

In the Year 1443 *Thomas Beckington* became the 23d Bishop of *Bath*, and in the two and twenty Years that he enjoyed the See he layed out vast Sums of Money in adorning and improving the City with Buildings: Soon after his Death *Bath* gave the Title of Earl, to *Philebert de Chandew*, born in *Bretagne*, in *France*; that Honour having been conferred upon him by King *Henry* the Seventh, in the Year 1485: And *Oliver King* having been translated from the See of *Exeter* to that of *Bath*, upon the 6th of *November*, 1495, that Prelate upon his coming to his new See to Institute Prior *Bird* into his Office, who was thereunto elected on the 31st of *August*, 1499, had a Vision or Dream, which caused him to resolve to rebuild the Church of St. *Peter* in the most correct Manner, and with a Magnificence becoming the greatest Prince; for which Work no one was better qualified, both in respect to Knowledge and Ability, than Bishop *King*; he having been principal Secretary to *Edward* the fourth, *Edward* the fifth, and *Henry* the seventh, at a Time when the *Gothick* Architecture was arrived to its highest Perfection in *Britain*.

Of the Dream, or Vision of Bishop *King*, Sir *John Harrington* tells this Story, " The Bishop, says he, having been
" at *Bath*, imagined as he one Night lay meditating in Bed,
" that he saw the Holy Trinity, with Angels ascending and
" descending by a Ladder; near to which there was a fair
" *Olive* Tree, supporting a Crown: The Impression was so
" strong, that the Bishop thought he heard a Voice which
" said, Let an *Olive* establish the Crown, and let a *King* re-
" store the Church. This had such an Effect upon the
" good Prelate, that he instantly formed a Design to rebuild
" the Church of Saint *Peter*, set the Work immediately in
" Hand, and, as Sir *John* concludes, caused his Vision to be
" represented on the Outside of it, under the Title of *De*
" *Sursum est*; it is from on high:"

The

Chap. IX. A Description of BATH.

The Bishop began by pulling down Part of the old Church; but he did not live to see the Work so begun perfected, tho' he pursued it with all the Vigilance in his Power, and declared his Disregard to any extraordinary Expence, so that he could but see it finished; for he died before the South and West Parts of the Building were covered in; or even all the Walls were raised to their proper Height.

The City having been almost maintained by making of Cloth since the Trade was first set up in it, that Business appears, by *Leland*, to have flourished exceedingly about this time by the Industry of three eminent Clothiers, whose Names were *Style*, *Kent* and *Chapman*; and the Priors of *Bath* pursuing the Work of the Church, after the Bishop's Decease on the 24th of *January* 1502, they, in about thirty Years time, compleated it, though not in the elegant Manner it was intended by the Founder: Prior *Bird*, who first engaged in the Work, expended so much Money as impoverished him, and made him die very poor; and *Leland* informs us, that his Successor, Prior *Gibbs*, alias *Holeway*, spent a great Sum in perfecting the Fabrick; which he had scarcely done before he, with *John Pitt* Sub-Prior, *Thomas Bathe* Cannon, and fourteen others subscribed to the Supremacy; this they did upon the 22^d of *September* 1534; and upon the 27th of *January*, 1539, Prior *Holeway* divested himself of the whole Monastery, by a Surrender of it to the Crown; the King's Commissioners thereupon making the following Provision for the Maintenance of him, and the rest of his House, during their respective Lives.

" PENSYONS

" Assigned to the Prior and Bretherne of the late surrendred
" Howse of *Bathe*, by the Commyssioners, to have each of
" them half a Years Pensyon at *Lady-Day*, 1539, and so
" half yearly."

" Furst, to *Will. Holeway* Prior, for his yerely Pensyon,
" in Mone 80 *L*. more is appoynted to hym for his dwelling
" Howse, one Tenement sett and lying in *Stubbs Strete* within
" the South Gate of *Bath*, wherein one *Jeffry Stayner*
" lately dwellyd, being of the yerelie Rent of 20 S. To
" *John Pitt* Supprior, 9 *L*. To *Richard Griffith* Prior of
" the Cell of *Dunster*, *Thomas Bathe* Impotent, *Nicholas*
" *Bathe*, B. D. 8 *L*. each; *Alysaunder Bryslow*, *John Bekenton*, *L* 6. 13. 4. each; *Richarde Lincolne*, *John Arleston*,
" 6 *L*. each; *Richard Gules*, *Thomas Worceter*, *Will. Clement*,

" *John*

" *John Edger, Edward Edwey, Patricke Vertue, John Hu-*
" *mylyte, John Gabriell, Will. Bowachyn, John Benett,*
" *L* 5. 6. 8. each; *Thomas Powell*, 5 *L. John Pacyence,*
" *L* 4. 13. 4.
" Sign'd,
" *Thomas Crumwell.*
" *Jo. Tregonwell.*
" *Will. Petre.*"

AFTER this the annual Pension of *Thomas Powell* was advanced to 6 *L.* and several others were admitted Pensioners, Mr. *Willis* giving us an Account of no less than eight that remained on the List of the Convent, A. D. 1553, whose Names are not mentioned in the above List, to wit, *Alexander Bull L* 6. 13. 4; *John Browne, John Bygge* 6 *L.* each; *John Style, Patrick Archer, Thomas Stylbond, John Bewsham L* 5. 6. 8. each; and *John Long L* 4. 13. 4. Our Author telling us likewise that the Prior had, besides his Pension, some Perquisites out of the Revenues of the Baths.

THE King's Commissioners, after setling these Pensions, made an Offer of St. *Peter*'s Church to the Citizens of *Bath*, for 500 Marks; but they utterly refused it, upon an Apprehension, that if they bought it so cheap, they should lie under the Imputation of cheating the King, and be deprived of their Bargain; whereupon, as Sir *John Harrington* writes in his Brief View of the State of the Church of *England*, certain Merchants bought all the Glass, Iron, Bells, and Lead of this Fabrick, and so left nothing but the Skeleton remaining. The Lead on the Roof was so thick that every superficial Foot must have weighed 20 Pounds, since the whole was reckoned to amount to 480 Tun; the Value of which was 4800 *L.* for Pigg Lead was then worth 10 *L.* a Tun.

THE poor Remains of this Church, with all the other Buildings within the Site, Inclosure, Circuit, Compass and Precinct of the Monastery or Priory of *Bath*; and also part of the Lands belonging to it; together with such Court Leets, View of Frankpledge, Assize or Essay of Bread, Wine and Beer, Knights Fee, Ward, Marriage, Escheats, Nets, Heriots, Fairs, Markets, Tolls, Customs, Commons, Free Warrens, Goods and Chattels, Waifes, Strays, Profits, Commodities, Emoluments and Hereditaments whatsoever as the Abbots and Priors of the said Monastery or Priory ever held or enjoyed, were sold to *Humphry Colles*, Gentleman, by Patent,

Patent, bearing Date the 16th Day of *March*, A.D. 1542-3; the Year after which, an Act of Parliament paffed for the Dean and Chapter of *Wells* to make one fole Chapter for the Bifhop: And thus the City of *Bath* after its having been, for above two thoufand Years, a Place of Habitation for Men who devoted themfelves to the Service of Religion, began to fall into the Hands of the Laity, about four hundred and two Years after the Period of its Reftoration, by *Robert*, the fecond Bifhop after *John of Tours*, *William Knight* then fitting in the Epifcopal Chair, as the thirtieth Bifhop that enjoyed the See of *Bath*.

SIR *William Dugdale* affures us in his *Monafticon Anglicanum*, that the Value of the Abbey of *Bath*, at the Time of its Diffolution, was *L* 617. 2. 3. a Year; and that the Value of the Hofpital of St. *John* the *Baptift* amounted to *L* 22. 16. 9¼ *per Annum*: To which if we add the Income of the Bifhoprick, reckoned worth 1843 *L*. a Year, the whole will amount to *L* 2483. 19. 0½ *per Annum*.

JUST before the Diffolution of Monafteries, King *Henry* the Eighth, created *John Bourchier, Lord-Fitz-Warin*, Earl of *Bath*, by Letters Patent bearing Date at *Weftminfter, July* 9th 1536; who dying three Years after, was fucceeded by *John* his Son, and he died in the third Year of Queen *Elizabeth*, A. D. 1561: The Title next defcended to his Son *John, Lord-Fitz-Warin*; and then to his Iffue, *William*; who dying *July* 12th 1623, was fucceeded in Honour and Eftate by *Edward*, his only Son then living; but he having no Male Iffue that furvived him, the Title, upon his Death, came to Sir *Henry Bourchier*, as Son to Sir *George Bourchier* (who was the third Son of *John, Lord-Fitz-Warin*, the fecond Earl of *Bath* of that Name) and he dying without Iffue on the 15th of *Auguft*, A. D. 1654, the Title became Extinct in that Family, and lay Vacant 'till the Reftoration of King *Charles* the fecond.

CHAP. X.
Of the Additional Works to BATH, between the Removal of the Epifcopal See to WELLS and Vefting the City in the Hands of the Laity.

NOTHING feems more probable than that fome of the Gymnaftick Exercifes attended the Ufage of the hot Waters in every Age, downward, from the Time that the

Baths were restored under *Agricola*'s Government; even when the Monastery was dissolved, a Tennis Court continued, for Ages, on the East Side of the Area of the *King*'s Bath; and this Court is marked with the Letter L in Doctor *Jones*'s View of the City: It was seven and twenty Feet broad in the Clear, by eighty one Feet in Length; and part of it still remains within nine Feet of the Rails of the Bath.

SHOULD my Information be true, this and the two other natural Baths of the City were under the Care and Management of a Bath Keeper at the time of the Dissolution of the Monastery; and the chief Profits of the hot Waters arose from the Tennis Players bathing themselves in the *King*'s Bath; for whose Use there was a Door on the West Side of the Court that opened into the Slip at the North East Corner of the Bath: But upon the Death of Prior *Gibbs*, the Corporation of the City became Lessees of the Baths under a small Annual Rent; and when they took Possession of them, they were divested of all manner of publick Conveniences, as the State of those Baths recorded by *Leland*, in the second Volume of his *Itinerary*, sufficiently demonstrates.

"THE Hot and *Cross* Baths, says our Author, are situated
"in the Middle of a little Street; they are common to poor
"People; and the latter is much frequented for its Tempe-
"rature and Pleasantness, by such as are diseased with the
"Leprosy, Pokkes, Scabs, and great aching Pains: It takes
"its Name from the Cross standing in the Middle of it, and
"it has eleven or twelve Arches of Stone in the Sides, for
"Men to stand under in time of Rain; but the hot Bath
"hath but seven of the like Arches, and is less in Compass
"within the Wall than the other. As for the *King*'s Bath,
"it is very fair and large, and Gentlemen resort to it: It
"stands in an Area encompassed with an high Stone Wall;
"the Brim of the Bath is surrounded with a little Wall;
"two and thirty Arches appear in the Walls of the Cistern
"for Men and Women to stand separately in; and in all
"the three Baths a Man may evidently see how the Water
"bubbleth up from the Springs."

AT every Angle of the *King*'s Bath and *Cross* Bath, there was a Place, in *Leland*'s time, to enter the Water; and it consisted of a small Flight of Steps, with a little Cell at the Head of them: Each Place went under the pittyful Name of a Slip, as the Remnant or Branch of one of the antient Conveniencies, marked with the Letter A, Plate N° 8, 9, for

entering

Chap. X. A Defcription of BATH. 199

entering and re-entering a Bath; and of thefe Slips there feems to have been one, and only one at each End of the hot Bath.

THE Site of the Priory when fold to Mr. *Colles,* as above, extended to the very Wall that made the South Side of the *King's* Bath; bounding, at the fame time, to the Eaft, the Area in which that Bath ftood: This Area was likewife bounded to the North with a Yard belonging to *Stall's* Church; to the Weft with the Houfes on the Eaft Side of *Stall Street*; and a Paffage of nine Feet in Breadth on the North, Eaft, and Weft Sides of the Ciftern was every Inch of Land that remained to the *King's* Bath, for its publick Accommodation, when the Baths came into the Hands of the City!

KING *Edward* the Sixth having by a Patent bearing Date the 12th Day of *July,* 1552, Granted to the Corporation fuch Lands and Tenements within the City, and its Suburbs, as formerly belong'd to the Priory, and were then in the Poffeffion of the Crown, for the Maintenance of ten poor aged People, and for the Inftruction of the Youth of the City, by a proper Mafter, in the *Latin* Tongue; the Patentees forthwith turned fome Rooms over Weft Gate into a School-Houfe, and then began a new Structure for the fame Purpofe, together with Apartments for the ten poor People to be maintained by them: This Work was compleated in the Beginning of Queen *Mary's* Reign, and, in Complement to her, the Building was named Saint *Catherine's* Hofpital, after the Name of her Mother: But, at the fame time, the Corporation ordered the poor People to wear fable Garments, as a publick Mark of Lamentation for the Lofs of the Royal Founder of the Charity, in the Flower of his Youth.

THE Site of the Priory coming to the Poffeffion of *Edmonde Colthurfte,* Efq; upon the Death of his Father the Beginning of the Year 1560, that Gentleman immediately after made the City a Prefent of the Carcafs of Saint *Peter's* Church, with the Ground upon the Eaft, Weft, and North Parts of it: And the Woolen Manufacture ftill flourifhing in the City, the Baths lay neglected; fo that Doctor *William Turner,* Dean of *Wells,* and chief Phyfician to King *Edward* the Sixth, compofing a Book of the Baths of *England, Germany* and *Italy,* during the time of his Banifhment under Queen *Mary,* for his ftrong Attachment to the reformed Religion, he therein infinuates to us that the Baths of *Bath* were in very little Efteem; even in lefs than thofe of *Buxton* in *Derbyfhire*;

and

and People of Fortune, that required the Use of hot Medicinal Waters went to Foreign Baths for it;

"How many use to Bathes abrode
"Far hence with Cost to range,
"Whereby they may their lothsome Lims
"To helthful Members change,"

are the Words of *Thomas Lupton*, a Poet of that Age: But by Doctor *Turner*'s giving the Baths of *Bath* the Priority, even to the Baths of *Germany* and *Italy*, the *British* Subjects, upon the Publication of his Book in the Year 1562, began to frequent their own hot Fountains, and our Baths thereupon got into such Reputation, that the *Cross* Bath was soon reserved for the better Sort of People; the hot Bath, called sometimes the Common Bath, sometimes the Long Bath, having been the only Cistern that remained for common Use, when the celebrated Antiquary Mr. *Lombarde* was collecting his Notes in the City, for his Topographical and Historical Dictionary of *England*.

IMMEDIATELY after this, the hot Bath was rescued from the common People; but, at the same time, a new Cistern was made on the West Side of that Bath to receive the overflowing Water of it, and to serve as a Bath for the Use of the lame and diseased poor People that had been expulsed from the *Cross* and hot Baths: This Cistern is about ten Feet in Length from North to South, by eight Feet in Breadth from East to West; it took the Name of the *Leper*'s Bath; and it was accommodated with a small Room for the Bathers to strip and dress themselves in, which in Process of Time was called the *Leper*'s Hospital.

THIS Bath and Room seems to have been preceded by a House erected in the Year 1568, on the North Side of West Gate, for the Use of the Poor who were to be relieved by the Corporation of the City out of the Church Lands: And Doctor *Jorden* assures us, that Sir *Edward Carne*, Embassador from Queen *Elizabeth* to Pope *Julius* the third, and *Paul* the fourth, having been at *Rome* about the Year 1570, when *Andreas Baccius* was writing his elaborate Work, intitled *De Thermis*, he gave that Author the short Account of our Baths which he inserted in his Book.

THUS the hot Waters of *Bath* began to be celebrated abroad in the Writings of the Learned; and in the Year 1572 Doctor *John Jones* began to celebrate them at home, by his Treatise entitled, *The Bathes of Bathes Ayde:* This he published

published immediately after Mr. *Peter Chapman*, the eldest Son of the Clothier of that Name, spoken of by *Leland*, as above, had so far repaired the East End of the North Isle of St. *Peter*'s Church, as to secure it from the Inclemency of the Weather; and while West Gate was rebuilding: And the Year after that Queen *Elizabeth*, consolidating the Churches of *Bath* into one Cure, vested the Presentation to them, and to S. *John*'s Hospital, in the Corporation of the City: She likewise granted the Citizens a seven Years Brief to raise Money to restore St. *Peter*'s Church, and to rebuild St. *John*'s Hospital; and while the Work was carrying on, and the Citizens were industriously pursuing their Trade in the Woolen Manufacture, Sir *Thomas White* named Bath as one Place that should be intitled to a yearly Donation of 104 *L.* which commenced, A. D. 1577, in favour of four and twenty Towns that are to take their Turns for ever as they stand in the List: This Money is to be lent to the Artificers of such Places, without Interest, to enable them to set up, or carry on their Trades; and the first Payment to the Corporation of *Bath* was made in the Year 1595; the second A. D. 1619; and the subsequent Payments fell in the Years 1646, 1670, 1694, 1718 and 1742: So that the Chamber is now in the Possession of 728 *L.* for this Charity; since the Money is not to be lent without sufficient Security to preserve the Capital for the Benefit of Posterity.

THE Money collected by the seven Years Brief, at least what was paid into the Hands of the Citizens, was not any thing near sufficient, after rebuilding the Hospital, to compleat the Church, the whole Sum having been expended in a Timber Roof, covered with blue Cornish Slate, over the East, the North, and some of the South Part of the Fabrick; and in roofing and flooring the Tower; tho' " the rest might have " been finished with the Money that was gathered, if the " Avarice of some Persons, says Mr. *Camden*, had not led " them to convert it to other Uses, and made them envy " the City the Glory of a finished Piece of Work."

HOWEVER, when the Church was so far perfected as the Money arising by the Brief would go, *Thomas* Earl of *Sussex*, Lord Chamberlain to Queen *Elizabeth*, set a glorious Example to the Nobility and Gentry of the Nation, who had found, or should receive Benefit by the hot Waters, of each Person's doing something towards compleating the Building: He began by glazing the uppermost Windows on the North Side of the Choir;

Choir; and was followed by *Walter Callcut* of *Williamscote* in *Oxfordshire*, Gent. who gave the Sum of 10 *L.* towards glazing the opposite Windows in that part of the Church: But the Earl of *Sussex* dying soon after, the Example set by that noble Peer subsided; and the Work stopping with his Death in the Year 1584, it was not resumed till after the *Spanish* Invasion was over; and then *William* Lord *Burleigh*, Lord High Treasurer to Queen *Elizabeth*, and *Thomas Bellot*, Esq; Steward of her Household, revived it.

BATHING in the hot Waters was the principal Use that was made of them at the Beginning of the Reign of Queen *Elizabeth*; at which time they were drank by a few whose Diseases required them inwardly; and those People were supplied with Water laded out of the full Cisterns early in the Morning, after the Baths were clean, and before the Bathers went into them; Doctor *Jones* laying it down as a Rule, in his *Bathes of Bathes Ayde*, that Patients, immediately after drinking the Water, should walk gently, a few Paces, in a temperate Air: He also laid it down as a Rule that Bathers should approach the hottest Part of the Bath by little and little; and directed that they should instantly rise out of the Water upon the least Symptoms of fainting.

AFTER the Doctors, *Turner* and *Jones*, had thus used their Endeavours to give Reputation to the hot Mineral Waters of *Bath*; the Court of *France* began to restore the Baths of *Bourbon l'Anci*; *Henry* the third, of that Kingdom, sending thither his chief Architect, the Comptroller of his Buildings, and his head Physician to direct, and superintend the Works; and his Queen, *Louisa* of *Lorrain*, repairing, at her own Expence, one of the Fountains, called afterwards the *Queen's Bath*, in Honour of her.

THESE Baths are supposed to have been magnificent Works of the *Romans*, who, as *Morery* takes notice, knowing the Usefulness of the Waters spared nothing to beautify them; but by the unlucky Events of Time they fell, and lay buried in their own Ruins. The bathing Cisterns are five in Number, and are filled with Water, by different Channels, from ten Fountains, seven of hot Water and three of Cold; by which Means the Baths are warmed and tempered to what Degree of Heat is required. The ten Fountains are inclosed in a Court of 180 Feet in Length; and the Royal Bath, of a round Figure, joins on to the North Side of it: Three of the other Baths are built in a long Square; and the fifth Bath is

situated

Chap. X.   A Defcription of BATH.   203

fituated by the Side of it. All thefe Baths and Fountains, with their Pavements, are compofed of white and grey Marble; and while the Walls of the whole Work were faced with the fame kind of Stone, of different Colours, the Statues that adorned the Baths were made of that which was perfectly White.

WHILE the Reftoration of thefe Works were in Hand, by the Order of *Henry* the third of *France*, Queen *Elizabeth* feems to have been no lefs defirous of reftoring the publick Works of *Bath*; and for that End fhe, befides confirming the Leafe of the Baths to the Corporation, made that Body of Citizens, and their Succeffors, perpetual Guardians of the City and hot Waters, by a Charter bearing Date the 4th of *September*, A. D. 1590, wherein *William Sherfton* is declared the firft Mayor; and he having then rented *Berton* Farm, in the Parifh of *Waldcot*, of the above-mentioned *Edmonde Colthurfte*, juft before he fold it to Sir *George Snigg*, *Berton* Houfe was the firft that was honoured with the new Regalia of the City; and, by the Artifices of Mr. *Sherfton*, the whole Farm was included in the Perambulation which the Citizens were then impowered, for the time to come, to make: The Site of the Priory was taken into the fame Perambulation; and the Court of Record as well as Court Leet, then granted to the Corporation, were extended over the Precincts of the diffolved Monaftery, notwithftanding the Rights and Privileges of that Houfe had been fold to Mr. *Colles* by King *Henry* the Eighth, in the Year 1542, as above.

THUS the City fell intirely into the Hands of the Laity; its Bounds were artfully extended into the Hundred of *Bathforum*, as well as over the Precincts of the diffolved Priory; and the private Intereft of the whole Body of Citizens became materially concerned in promoting the publick Works of the Place; the Baths efpecially, as the hot Waters were every Day gaining Reputation, and their Ufes increafing, as well as the Trade in the Woolen Manufacture; by which, and the great Refort of Strangers, Mr. *Camden* declares the City to have been a flourifhing Place about the time that it fell into the Hands of the Lay Inhabitants.

THE Royal Grants that were made to the City between the Years 1552 and 1590, were obtained by the Intereft of the above-mentioned *Peter Chapman*, who was born, A. D. 1506; and entering into the military Service of King *Henry* the Eighth, he was of the Re-inforcement which that Monarch

fent

sent to *Calais*, the latter End of the Year 1540: After this Mr. *Chapman* served at the Siege of *Boulogne*, which was invested the 26th of *July* 1544; and there remained till the King's Death: He was then relieved; but continued in the Army during the Reign of *Edward* the Sixth, of *Philip* and *Mary*, and within a Year of the Death of Queen *Elizabeth*; in whose Reign he was sent to *Tilbury* Camp, under the Command of the Earl of *Leicester*, when the Queen was guarding against the *Spanish Armado*.

To that Camp Mr. *Chapman*, under the Rank of a Serjeant Major, or Major of a Brigade, bravely led eight hundred veteran Soldiers when he himself was in the 82d Year of his Age, and in the Enjoyment of an affluent Fortune acquired, for the most part, by his Father in the Practice of the clothing Trade; the gallant Behaviour of this old experienced Soldier, in his military Atchievements, gaining him very little besides an Addition to his Coat of Arms of a Canton of the second, with an armed Hand, holding a broken Lance, with a Wreath upon it, for a Crest: And with this he was satisfied, since his publick Services had procured his native Place such Advantages as must transmit his Name down to the latest Posterity.

He had two Sons, *William* and *Richard*; the latter dying on *May Day*, 1572, was buried in the Isle on the North Side the Choir of St. *Peter's* Church, which then took the Name of *Chapman's* Isle, and still retains it; *William* was buried in the same Place on the 7th of *November* 1586, and leaving two Sons, *William*, born A.D. 1571, and *George*, born A.D. 1576, the former survived his Father about 61 Years, he dying on the 16th of *June* 1647; but the latter departing earlier, and on the 22d of *July* 1644, left two Sons, *Simon* and *Robert*: The first, inheriting the military Principles of his great Grandfather, served his Country as a Captain of Horse; but the second was educated in the Business of a Surgeon and Apothecary; he was born A.D. 1623; and, taking up his Abode in *Bath*, he served the Office of Mayor of the City in the Years 1668, 1678, and 1689.

The Memoirs of *Bath*, preserved in this Family, fell into the Hands of Alderman *Robert Chapman*, memorable in the City for the uncommon Favours which King *James* the second bestowed upon him for his Care of the Queen, as her Apothecary, during her Course of Bathing in the Year 1687: And this eminent Man, in his Profession, dying on the 20th

of

of *March*, A. D. 1700-1, the Male Line of the Elder Branch of the *Chapman*'s Family thereby became Extinct: But before his Death the Memoirs, preserved in it, were copied by one from whom I had great Part of what I have already, or may hereafter insert in this Essay, concerning the History of *Bath*, from the End of the fourteenth Century to my own Time.

CHAP. XI.
Of the Additional Works to BATH, between Vesting the City in the Hands of the Laity and the Election of its present Titular King.

THE poor Shift that was made in Doctor *Jones*'s time to supply Drinkers, before People went into the Bath, gave Rise to an Invention to come at the Water, at any Hour of the Day, pure as it arose out of the Bowels of the Earth, and entirely separated from the Water of the Bath: This was a Conduit placed over one part of the Spring in the *King*'s Bath; and the Machine appears in *Speed*'s Draught of that Cistern, printed A. D. 1610; Doctor *Johnson* copied it in the Year 1634; and Doctor *Peirce* gives us the following Description of it, in his *Bath Memoirs*, Page 255.

" IT was, says he, a pyramidal Stone, hollow in the Middle, artificially placed over one of the largest Springs, on the South East Part of that Wooden Conveniency, now standing in the *King*'s Bath, and was taken away to make Room for that Structure. A square Wall was made about this Spring, the Hollow of which was about eighteen Inches Diameter, and near upon the same Depth. The top Stone had a Mortice proportionate to the Tennon of the pyramidal Stone which went in, and held so close, that none of the extraneous Water could get into its Hollow; and the Strength of the Spring was so great, that it forced itself up through the Cavity of the pyramidal Stone, which was a Foot and more above the Water, when the Bath was at fullest. This Water discharged itself at a Copper Spout, about three Inches above the highest Water Mark, and to this Spout some set their Mouths and drank, while others put Cups and received the Water sincere from the Spring."

THIS Conduit was erected soon after the Date of the Charter of A. D. 1590; and as an early Instance that the

Property of the hot Waters were, by that Charter, no further vested in the Corporation of the City, than as Guardians of them for the Use of the Publick, an Act of Parliament received the Royal Assent in the Year 1597, giving the diseased impotent poor People of *England* a Right to the free Use of the Baths of *Bath*; and impowering the Justices of the Peace, in the several Counties, not only to Licence them to travel to the healing Fountains for their Cure; but to limit the Money which they should carry with them to defray their Charges.

This Act was continued by two other Acts passed in the first Year of the Reign of King *James* the First; by a third Act made in the third Year of the Reign of King *Charles* the First; and by a fourth Act passed in the sixteenth Year of the same King, which expired and became extinct in the twelfth Year of the Reign of Queen *Anne*, A. D. 1714.: And two Years after that a new Provision for the Poor took its Rise in the General Hospital lately built in the City.

It was about the time of the Commencement of this Law, that the two great Officers of Queen *Elizabeth*'s Court, the Lord High Treasurer, and the Steward of the Houshold, resumed the Work of St. *Peter*'s Church; and for the Benefit of such poor People as the Legislature had given the free Use of the Baths and hot Waters of the City, Mr. *Bellot* purchased a Piece of the Priory Land, joining on to the South Side of the *King*'s Bath, and made a Cistern by the Side of that Bath for those People to bathe in a temperate Water. The Cistern thus made received the overflowing Water of the *King*'s Bath, and taking the Name of the *New Bath*, retained it till the Year 1615, when it was joined to the *King*'s Bath by the Means of an Aperture in the Partition between the two Cisterns; and then it was dignified with the Title of the *Queen*'s Bath on this remarkable Occasion.

As *Anne*, the Queen of King *James* the First, was one Day bathing in the *King*'s Bath, there arose from the Bottom of the Cistern, just by the Side of her Majesty, a Flame of Fire, like a Candle, which had no sooner ascended to the Top of the Water than it spread itself upon the Surface into a large Circle of Light, and then became Extinct: This so frighted the Queen that notwithstanding the Physicians assured her the Light proceeded from a natural Cause, yet she would bathe no more in the *King*'s Bath, but betook herself to the *New* Bath, where there were no Springs to cause the like Phænomena; and from thence the Cistern was called the *Queen*'s

Queen's Bath; it was soon enlarged; and the Citizens erecting a Tower or Cross in the Middle of it, in Honour of the Queen, finished it at the Top with the Figure of the Crown of *England* over a Globe, on which was wrote in Letters of Gold,

ANNA REGINA SACRUM.

WHILE the Work of the *New* Bath was in Hand a large Pond was made in a Garden upon the South Side of Saint *James*'s Church to receive the waste Water of the *King*'s Bath; and this was for some time used as a Bath for Horses, and called the *Horse* Bath.

MR. *Bellot* had no sooner began the *New* Bath, than he founded and built an Hospital for the Entertainment of twelve of the most indigent Men that should be licensed to come to the City, allowing every Man a Room in it, during the Months of *April*, *May*, and *September*, with four Pence a Day in Money: And that the poor People of *England*, thus far provided for, might not be destitute of proper Instructions how to use the Waters on their coming to *Bath*, Dame *Elizabeth* Viscountess *Scudamore*, in the Year 1652, settled a Salary on a Physician to be elected Yearly, on the 15th of *April*, by the Mayor and Aldermen of the City, to assist them with his best Advice, without any Fee or Reward from them; and a Brass Plate was, and still remains fixed against the Wall of a House on the West Side of the *Queen*'s Bath, with an Inscription engraved upon it, to advertise the Publick of that Provision.

THE making of this Bath was succeeded by the rebuilding of the *Cross* and hot Baths; and in the Execution of the Work the Arches for Shelter in the new Walls of the Cisterns were altered from Oven-like-Niches to square Recesses: And at the same time that the *Cross* Bath was rebuilt, a large House was erected on the North Side of it for the private Accommodation of the Bathers in it; and this was finished, A. D. 1602. Doctor *John Sherwood*, renting the Abbey-House, made a Communication between that Structure and the *King*'s Bath, for the private Use of his Patients and Lodgers, particularly Queen *Anne*, from whom the Slip at the North East Corner of the Bath took the Name of the *Queen*'s Slip; in the Year 1615; and three Years after that a House was rebuilt and enlarged on the West Side of the *Queen*'s Bath for the private Use of such as should bathe in that

that Cistern; in the Battlements of which House the Letters of the Inscription on the Cross in the Middle of the Bath supplied the Place of Ballusters, or other Ornaments in the Dado, where they continued for almost 120 Years.

THE Zeal of People of Rank and Fortune in the Reign of Queen *Elizabeth* for the Interest of their Country, by restoring the publick Works of *Bath*, and extending the Uses of the hot Waters to prevent the *British* Subjects from flying abroad to the like medicinal Fountains, at the Hazard of their Lives in crossing the Seas, and at a great Expence, to the Impoverishment of the Kingdom, and to the Enrichment of other Nations, stirred up *Henry* the *Great* of *France* to pursue the Works of *Bourbon*, begun by his Predecessor; the King, in the Year 1602, committing the Care of it to Mr. *Beaulieu*, his Secretary of State; and six Years after that Mr. *Descures* had the Conduct of the Work vested in him; who, in the Year 1609, discovered the seventh hot Fountain of the Place, and that which now bears the Name of *Descures*.

WHEN the Work of Saint *Peter*'s Church at *Bath* was resumed by my Lord *Burleigh*, and Mr. *Bellot*, they began with compleating the Choir so as to make it fit for Divine Service to be performed therein; and for that End, after separating it from the other parts of the Church, with proper Partitions, they fitted it up with Seats, Galleries, Pulpit, and Font; Mr. *Bellot*, at his own Expence of 60 *L.* repairing and glazing the great Window at the East End of the Church, and giving a handsome Sum towards the Ornaments and other Necessaries for Divine Service; previous to the Performance whereof, if I am rightly informed, the Church was consecrated and dedicated to the Names of Saint *Peter* and Saint *Paul*.

MR. *Bellot* gave the further Sum of 200 *L.* towards compleating the South Wing, which seems to have been left low to join a Cloister to it; and after paving the Floor of the Nave of the Church from North to South, he presented the Citizens with 30 *L.* towards the Purchase of a Bell, which they, after a general Collection among themselves and Strangers, bought at *Cainsham*: The Prime Cost of this Bell was 80 *L.* and the new casting it came to 27 *L.* more; the Collection for it was begun in *Stall*'s Parish, and therein *William Ford* and *George Gibbs* gathered 10 *L. John Baker* collected in St. *Mary*'s Parish 11 *L. John Sherston* gathered in Saint *James*'s Parish 12 *L.* the Parishioners of St. *Michael* without the City Gate

Gate gave L 8. 18. 2; and the Benefactions of Strangers amounted to about 40 L. more.

Mr. *Bellot's* Benefaction towards compleating the South Wing was followed by another from Doctor *William Powell*, Arch-Deacon of *Bath*, who, on the 25th of *May* 1603, gave the Sum of 10 L. towards that Work, and four Years after he contributed 7 L. more; *Walter Chapman, Thomas Wiat,* and *Peter Sherston*, all Inhabitants of the City, gave and collected towards the same Work, in the Autumn of the Year 1603, the Sum of L 44. 8. 0; *Edward Horton* of the same City, Esq; gave 6 L. and by his Will left 50 L. more; *John Still*, D. D. Bishop of *Bath* and *Wells*, gave 20 L. Sir *William Paston* of *Norfolk*, Knt. coming to *Bath* in the Year 1604, gave 100 L. for which his Arms were set up in the great Window at the End of the North Wing; and Mr. *Daniel Walters* of the same County, with divers others, gave such considerable Sums, that the Benefactions together amounted to L 514. 14. 0.

To this we may add 12 L. paid by Alderman *Rowland Backhouse* of *London*, as the Legacy of Mr. *Bartholomew Barns* of the same City; who had such a strong Idea that Contributions would be raised to finish the whole Church, that he ordered his Body to be richly entombed in it: This Confidence Sir *John Harrington* much admired, and very much commended, in his Epistle to Prince *Henry*, as it shews the Ideas of a Man of Business, to whom no laudable Design, to be accomplished by Industry, can appear insurmountable. Alderman *William Sherston*, eight times Mayor of *Bath*; and serving that Office the first under Queen *Elizabeth's* Charter, had no less an Idea than Mr. *Barns* that the Church would in time be perfected; and therefore he bequeathed to the Work the Sum of 100 L. to be paid by 40 Shillings yearly, for fifty Years, out of the Parsonage of *Lyncomb*.

The South Wing of the Church having been raised up with the Benefactions, as above, *Edward* Earl of *Worcester* gave the further Sum of 20 L. to compleat and beautify the arched Cieling of it: The Citizens of *Bath*, at their own Charge, arched the Cieling under the Tower; after which, with the Help of some Friends, they not only repaired and beautified the arched Cieling of the North Wing, but the Cieling of the Choir.

The Isle on the South Side of the Choir was paved at the sole Charge of *Francis Allen*, an eminent Clothier of the City;

and *Thomas Power*, Mayor of *Bath*, contributing by his laſt Will 10 *L.* towards the Repairs of this Iſle; *Nicholas Hide*, Eſq; Recorder of the City, giving 5 *L. Thomas Leyſon*, one of the Phyſicians, bequeathing 3 *L.* and the Widow *Gold* of *Dorcheſter*, giving 5 *L*; theſe Sums together amounted to 23 *L*; and the whole was expended in repairing part of the arched Cieling; in new building the Wall at the Eaſt End; and in making the Door and Window therein: And the other part of the arched Cieling was repaired and beautified at the only Coſt of one *Hugh Bagley*, a famous Bone Setter, and at that time an Inhabitant of the City.

THE arched Cieling of the Iſle, on the North Side of the Choir, and then bearing the Name of *Chapman*'s Iſle, was repaired and beautified at the Coſt of *Miles Jackſon* of *Combhay*, in the County of *Somerſet*, Eſq; *Jeffery Flower* of *Philips Norton*, Gent. expended *L* 22. 10. 0. in erecting a Wall at the Eaſt End of this Iſle, and in making a Door and Window therein; and the above *Francis Allen* bequeathed 10 *L.* to be employed in building two Buttreſſes on the Outſide of that Wall, to make the North Corner of the Eaſt Front of the Church uniform with the South Corner, which was accordingly done in the Year 1616: The Lady *Elizabeth Boothe*, an Inhabitant of *Bath*, paved the greateſt Part of the Floor of this Iſle; and what ſhe left undone was compleated by three Seafaring Men, whoſe Names were *Richard Stanley, John Smith*, and *Ellis Wood*.

WE now come to the Weſt End of the Church; and this part of the Building having been open and uncovered in the Year 1609, Doctor *James Montague*, Biſhop of *Bath* and *Wells*, afterwards Biſhop of *Wincheſter*, one of the Lords of his Majeſty's Privy Council, and Prelate of the moſt noble Order of the Garter, was moved in that Year to give the Sum of 1000 *L.* towards covering it; *Francis* Earl of *Rutland* gave 20 *L.* more; and *William* Lord *Compton*, afterwards Earl of *Northampton*, added 40 *L.* to theſe Benefactions; with which three Sums, twenty Trees given by *Gilbert* Earl of *Shrewſbury*, and fifty Tuns of Timber preſented by *Thomas* Earl of *Suffolk*, the ſame was compleatly roofed. Then the Biſhop gave the paved Floor of the Nave, which coſt him *L* 43. 6. 8. after that he ſet up a Stone Pulpit, at the Expence of 32 *L.* and upwards, and in the laſt Place he expended 4 *L.* in cutting the Words, *Domus Mea*, over the North Window, and *Domus Orationis* over the South Window,

Chap. XI.   A Description of BATH.   211

at the West End of the Church, and in gilding the Letters with Gold.

THE Isle on the North Side the Nave was paved by the Contributions of *John Webb* of *Swinefwick*, Gentleman; *Richard Davis* Rector of the same Place; *Thomas Cox* of *Corston*, Gentleman; *John Attwood* one of the Aldermen of Bath; Mrs. *Margaret Mannering*; and Lady *Boothe*. The whole Expence of this Work is not mentioned; but Mr. *Webb*'s Benefaction towards it was 10 *L*. The Isle on the South Side of the Nave was paved by the Contributions of *John Kerry* of *Weston*, Esq; Sir *Augustine Nichols*, Knt. one of the Judges of the Common Pleas; and *John Taylor* Vicar of *Cold Aston*: The Work came to *L* 16. 2. 0. of which Mr. *Kerry* gave 10 *L*. and the other gentlemen gave between them the remaining *L* 6. 2. 0.

THE Stair Cases at the West End of the Church were covered and pinacled by three worthy Benefactors; that next the North was done by Mrs. *Oldfield* of *London*, and cost her, besides Stone and Carriage, 20 *L*. that next the South was done by Sir *Francis Jones*, Knt. Alderman of *London*, and *Henry Southworth* of *Wells*, Esq; at the Expence of *L* 31. 10. 0. of which the former paid 22 *L*.

THE Stair Cases at the East End of the Church were compleated like those at the West End by the Bounty of Sir *Hardwick Heale* of *Wenbury*, in *Dorsetshire*, Knt. *Edward Rogers* of *Cannington*, in *Somersetshire*, Esq; and Sir *John Hipesly* of *Masson*, in the same County, Knt. This last Gentleman, at the Expence of 30 *L*. finished the Stair Case next the South; and the two former, at their joint Charge of 30 *L*. perfected the Stair Case next the North.

SIR *Henry Montague*, Knt. Lord Chief Justice of the *King's Bench*, and Brother to the noble Bishop, as above, laid out 40 *L*. in beautifying the great Doors at the West End of the Church; and *John Hall* of *Bradford*, Esq; having given a Piece of Ground for a Vestry to this Structure, Sir *Nicholas Salterns* of *London*, Knt. gave the Sum of *L* 47. 9. 4. to build and finish the same; wherein there is a small Collection of Books began by Dr. *Arthur Lake*, Bishop of *Bath* and *Wells*; and continued by *Richard Lowe* of *Calne*, in *Wiltshire*, Barrister at Law; Mr. *George Lowe* his Son; Mr. *Isaac Tullie*; *William Rouse* of *Halton*, in *Devonshire*, Esq; Mr. *Thomas Radcliffe* of *University* College, in *Oxford*; Sir *William Waller*, Knt. Mr. *Edward Bisse* of *Sparge*, in *Somer-*
E e 2   *setshire;*

setshire; Mr. *Thomas Hayne* of *Alborne*, in *Wiltshire*; *William Prynne* of *Swinefwick*, in the County of *Somerset*, Esq; Recorder of *Bath*; *John Harrington* of *Kelson*, Esq; Son of the above-mentioned Sir *John Harrington*; *Robert Creighton* Bishop of *Bath* and *Wells*; Doctor *Guidott* of *Bath*; Sir *Edward Greaves*, Bart. and divers others.

The Window over the Vestry Door was set up by the Company of Taylors of *Bath*; and *Richard Beacon*, an honest Tyler and Plaisterer of the City, after his having slated the East, the North, and the South Parts of the Church, generously paid for the North Window on the West Side of the South Wing. The Remainder were glazed, the first on the East Side by Sir *Maurice Berkley* of *Bruton*, in the County of *Somerset*; the second by *George Speake* the Younger, of *White Lackington*, in the same County, Esq; and the Window opposite to this by Sir *Hugh Smith* of *Longashton*, likewise in the same County, Knt.

The Windows in the North Wing of the Church were glazed, the first on the East Side next the Tower by Sir *James Ley* of *Beckington*, in the County of *Somerset*, Knt. and Attorney General of the Court of Wards; the second at the joint Cost of *Robert Baynard* of *Lackham*, and *Edward Reade* of *Corsham*, in the County of *Wilts*, Esq; and the opposite Windows by ————

In the Year 1612, *Francis James*, LL.D. Chancellor of the Diocese of *Bath* and *Wells*, glazed the great Window at the West End of the Church: The five Windows on the South Side of the Nave were glazed, the first by *Francis* Earl of *Rutland*; the second by *Francis* Lord *Norris*; the third by *Elizabeth* Baroness of *Hundsdon*; the fourth by *John May* of *Charter House*, in the County of *Somerset*, Esq; and the fifth by *John Kerry* of *Weston*, Esq; And the five Windows on the North Side of the Nave were glazed, the first by *Anne* Countess Dowager of *Dorset*; the second by Sir *Robert Rich*, Knight; the third by Sir *Francis Seymour*, Knight; the fourth by Sir *Edward Rodney* of *Rodney-Stoke*, in the County of *Somerset*, Knight; and the fifth by *Francis Bat* of *Chew*, in the same County, Esquire.

The lower Windows in the West Part of the Church were glazed, that over the North small Door by *Philip Welch* of *London*, Glazier; the first in the North Isle by *James Biss* of *Batcombe*, in the County of *Somerset*, Esq; the second by *Thomas Norreys* of *Bath*, Esq; the third by *William Plumby*

of

Chap. XI.   A Description of BATH.   213

of *Newton Saint Lo*, Gentleman; the fourth by *William Saint Barbe*, Prebendary of *Hereford*; and the fifth by *Michael Mallet* of *Warwick*, Esquire. The second Window in the South Isle, the first being darkened by the Abbey House, was glazed by Sir *John Stafford* of *Thornbury*, in the County of *Gloucester*, Knight; the third by *John Barker* of *Bristol*, Merchant; the fourth by *William Blanchard* of *Catherine*, in the County of *Somerset*, Esq; and the fifth by *William Basset* of *Claverton*, in the same County, Esquire.

The Lady *Jane Rodney* of *Pilton*, in the County of *Somerset*, and her Son-in-Law, Sir *Theodore Newton* of *Barrow*'s Court, in the same County, Knt. gave to this Church a Chair Organ; *Anne* the Wife of *Matthew Randall*, one of the Aldermen of *Bath*, gave 5 L. towards erecting the Gallery over *Bird*'s Chapel; Lady *Hopton* of *Wytham*, in the County of *Somerset*, and several of her Family, gave to the Amount of 100 L. towards the Great Bell in the Tower, which was perfected by the City at the further Expence of 60 L. Towards the other Bells, *Robert* Earl of *Essex* contributed 40 L. Sir *Henry Slingsby* of *Scriven*, in the County of *York*, Knt. 20 L. Sir *Clement Throckmorton* of *Coughton*, in *Warwickshire*, 10 L. Sir *Rowland Lacie* of *Shipton*, in *Oxfordshire*, Knt. 5 L. *Arthur Duck*, LL.D. Chanceller of the Diocese of *Bath* and *Wells*, L 6. 13. 4.; *Henry* Lord *Morley*, 5 L. *John Kerry* of *Weston*, in the County of *Somerset*, Esq; 20 L. Sir *John Scudamore* of *Holm Lacie*, in *Herefordshire*, Knt. 5 L. *George* Lord *Berkley*, 20 L. *Edward Hungerford* of *Corsham*, in the County of *Wilts*, Esq; 20 L. and Sir *Francis Popham* of *Littlecot*, in the same County, Knt. 15 L. making together the Sum of L 206. 13. 4.

I was willing to be thus particular in enumerating the Contributors to repair the Devastations committed upon this Church, since there is scarce a Part of it but what claims a particular Benefactor among People of the first Rank; whose Bounties were obtained partly by the Instance of Sir *John Harrington*, and partly by the Instance of the Reverend Mr. *John Pelling*, at that time Rector of *Bath*; to whose Memory the City, in the Year 1621, erected a Monument in the North Isle of the Church, for his singular Services to it.

The Work of this Fabrick was succeeded by the Rebuilding of the *Guild Hall*, and making a Council House therein, according to a Draught presented to the City by *Inigo Jones*; this Structure was compleated just after the Accession of King

Charles

Charles the firſt to the Crown, in the Year 1625; and the Court of Juſtice in it, for more than 20 Years, ſerved alſo for the common Theatre of the City, for Players to act their Plays and Interludes in.

WHILE this Fabrick was about, Sir *Francis Stoner* of *Stoner*, in *Oxfordſhire*, received ſuch an extraordinary Cure by the hot Waters, that he, in the Year 1624, generouſly gave the Corporation of the City a Sum of Money to beautify the *King*'s Bath, by paving the Paſſage on the North Side, as well as at the Eaſt and Weſt Ends of it; and then ſurrounding the Ciſtern with handſome Rails inſtead of the low Wall it had been environed with: So that Dr. *Venner*, four Years after, declares in his Treatiſe intitled, *The Baths of Bath*, that the publick Baths of the City appeared ſo fairly built, and fitted with ſuch Conveniency for bathing, as the like was not elſewhere to be found.

THE Conveniency the Doctor ſpeaks of was only Private, and conſiſted of ſuch a Communication between a few lodging Houſes about the Baths, and the Slips or Ways into them, as enabled Bathers to go directly from their Beds into the hot Waters, and return to them again: As for Publick Accommodations there was not ſo much as a Hovel, even by the *King*'s Bath, wherein a Guide or a poor Perſon could depoſit his Clothes, while in the Bath; and they were obliged to leave them in the common Slips till a Cabbin was made for that Purpoſe over a Slip at the South Eaſt Corner of the *King*'s Bath.

THE Private Conveniency of the Baths did very well while the Houſes immediately ſurrounding them were ſufficient to entertain all the Bathers that came to the City; tho' it was attended with this ill Conſequence, that the Perſon intereſted in any ſuch Houſe promoted the Uſe of the Bath near which it was ſituated, whether proper or not for the Patient; and this Cuſtom, as a moſt groſs Abuſe of the Baths, Dr. *Venner* explodes under the Title of Baths Technologie, with ſuch as for the Health of their Bodies reſorted to the City.

THE free Uſe of the hot Waters, and the Private Conveniencies about the Baths, were not only ſoon attended with a wrong Application of the Waters, but all manner of Order or Government was laid aſide in the Uſage of them; and in that dangerous Situation the numerous Benefactors of thoſe Days to the City, reſolved to Petition King *James* the firſt for a Power to reform the Abuſes of the Baths, and put them under

under such good Regulations as would fairly enable the Publick to receive the Advantages of the Waters in all succeeding Times; the Corporation of the City, as Guardians of the Baths, voluntarily joining with them in that Petition: But the King's Death happening just after the Petition was presented, their good Designs were thereby frustrated, and the Abuses complained of continued and increased.

For on the 23^d of *April* 1631, we find Doctor *Jorden*, in his Epistle Dedicatory of a Discourse of natural Baths, complaining to Sir *Francis Cottington*, Chancellor of the *Exchequer*, that those of *Bath* could not display their Virtues, and do that Good for which God hath sent them to us, for want of such good Government as other Baths then enjoyed; declaring, at the same time, that the City had done all in their Power to remove the Abuses.

Such were the early ill Effects of Private Property, so near the Bounds of the Cisterns at the Heads of the hot Springs; and the *King*'s Bath, which had been retire and private, became exposed and publick to every Body.

Doctor *Jorden* tells his Reader that he is sorry he could not presume to commend the inward Use of the hot Waters as they deserved, because he could hardly be persuaded that, by the Conduit in the *King*'s Bath, People could have the Waters pure as the Spring yielded them, without mixing with the Waters of the Bath: " If this Doubt, says he, was cleared, " I should not doubt to commend them inwardly:" To this Doubt we may therefore attribute the Custom that still prevailed, of sending the Invalids of *Great-Britain*, that required the inward Use of hot Mineral Waters, to the Fountains of *Bourbon* to drink of them.

But notwithstanding this learned Doctor could not commend the inward Use of the hot Waters of *Bath*, yet he promoted and improved the external Application of them, then in its Infancy, by pouring them on the lame and afflicted Parts of Patients, while in the Baths, by the Means of Buckets; which was thus performed before the Doctor practised at *Bath*. Two of the tallest and strongest of the Guides, stood with the Patient in the hottest Part of the Bath, and lifting up a full Bucket as high as they could, they then let the Water fall leisurely upon the Part affected: But the Doctor finding that this Method did not Heat some sufficiently, as the Water was taken from the Surface of the Baths, he therefore caused Pumps to be erected to draw it as

hot

hot as possible from the Spring. He names the Persons that were at the Charge of erecting five of these Pumps for the Use of the Publick; four of which were fixed in the four principal Baths, in Recesses made for that Purpose, and called Wet Pumps, from their wet Situation; and one was placed in a little Room built over part of a Slip at the End of the hot Bath, and named a Dry Pump, from its dry Situation.

To make room for the Wet Pump in the *King*'s Bath, the South Side of that Cistern was almost all taken down; and Wet and Dry Pumping having been thus introduced, and established at *Bath*, as the second outward Use of the hot Waters, in Process of Time one Dry Pump was placed in a Room built over the Slips on the West Side of the *Queen*'s Bath; and another was fixed in a Room erected over the South East Corner of the *King*'s Bath; which, at present, is the chief Dry Pump of the City, and, by Way of Eminence, it is stiled The Dry Pump.

Doctor *Jorden*, in the 90th Page of his Discourse, confirms Doctor *Jones*'s Rule for Bathers to proceed gradually, to the hottest Part of the Baths; and at their rising out of the Water he advises them to have their Bodies well dried. Our Author sets forth the Usefulness of covered Baths; tells us that most of the Baths of *Europe* are roofed over; and wishes that the *Queen*'s Bath and *Cross* Bath were covered, and their Slips made close and warm: He adds, that the right Honourable, the Earl of *Marlborough* had, of his own accord, undertaken the covering of the *Cross* Bath, and then concludes, that "If some other would do the like for the *Queen*'s Bath, they " would do much Good to many, and gain a thankful Re- " membrance of their Names for ever."

The Doctor survived the Publication of his Book but little more than one Year; however it brought the hot Waters into such Esteem with the Court of King *Charles* the first, that his Queen, as *Rushworth* informs us, was desirous of making Use of them for her Health, after she had been delivered of the Princess *Henrietta*, in the Year 1644. She afterwards made Use of the hot Waters of *Bourbon*, in *France*; to the Baths of which Place she was attended by Sir *Alexander Frayser*; and about the time that the Queen went there, all kinds of Disorders were grown to their highest Pitch in *Bath*; insomuch that the Streets and publick Ways of the City were become like so many Dunghills, Slaughter-Houses, and Pig-Styes: For Soil of all sorts, and even Carrion, was cast and laid

Chap. XI.   A Description of BATH.   217

laid in the Streets, and the Pigs turned out by Day to feed and rout among it; Butchers killed and dressed their Cattle at their own Doors; People washed every kind of thing they had to make clean at the common Conduits in the open Streets; and nothing was more common than small Racks and Mangers at almost every Door for the baiting of Horses: The Baths were like so many Bear Gardens, and Modesty was entirely shut out of them; People of both Sexes bathing by Day and Night naked; and Dogs, Cats, Pigs, and even human Creatures were hurl'd over the Rails into the Water, while People were bathing in it.

THESE Disorders coming to this Pitch, the Corporation assembled together upon the 7th Day of *September*, 1646. and framed a Body of By-Laws not only to remove every Kind of Nusance the City was then subject to; but to establish good Order in it; and the Laws so made had their intended Effect, in Regard to the Removal of Nusances, and establishing good Order in the City: So that they were confirmed by the Corporation, who met upon the 28th Day of *October*, 1650, for that and other Purposes. Then People began to flock to *Bath* for Recreation as well as for the Benefit of the Waters; the Citizens beautified St. *Peter*'s Church with the present Battlements and the small Pinacles which adorn the Top of the Structure; and the Cloathing Trade flourished so exceedingly that, in the Parish of St. *Michael* without the North Gate, there were no less than sixty broad Looms at the Time of the Restoration.

UPON the Coronation of King *Charles* the 2d on Saint *George*'s Day, the 23d of *April* 1661, he created *John Granville*, Son of Sir *Bevil Granville*, Baron of *Hilkhampton* and *Bediford*; Viscount *Granville* of *Lansdown*; and Earl of *Bath*. And about the latter End of *September* in the Year 1663, the King brought his Royal Consort, Queen *Catherine*, to *Bath*; Sir *Alexander Frayser*, as chief Physician, attending them hither; who upon finding the hot Waters to be from the same Minerals as those of *Bourbon*, and that they could be pumped up directly from the Spring, began to advise the inward Use of them, sending all such Patients to the hot Fountains of *Bath*, as he had before ordered to those of *Bourbon*, whereby the Fatigue and Expence of a long Journey from the *Britannick* Island to the Heart of *France*, as well as the Danger of crossing the Sea, was avoided, to the private Advantage of the Subjects of *Great-Britain*; and to the publick Advantage of the Kingdom.

F f   FROM

FROM this Period the Drinking of the hot Waters of *Bath*, may be very juftly faid to have been eftablifhed; and from the fame Period the Trade of the City began to turn from the Woolen Manufacture, to that of entertaining the Strangers that came to it for the Ufe of the hot Waters.

CAPTAIN *Henry Chapman* was no fooner elected Mayor of the City, on the 29th of *September*, 1664, than he took down an old Stone Tower built over the Spring in the *King*'s Bath, erecting, in its Stead, the Wooden Conveniency fpoken of by Doctor *Peirce*, as above, and then fet up a Table againft the Dry Pump Room on the Weft Side of the *Queen*'s Bath, with an Infcription wrote in Gold Letters upon it, acknowledging the Waters to be entirely free for the Publick, by the Bounty of God, and the Charters of the King; and declaring artificial Baths of little Worth, as being the Works of Man, while there were natural Baths at *Bath* prepared by Almighty God.

MR. Mayor placed another Table againft the Side of the *Crofs* Bath, with an Infcription upon it importing, that the Bath had loft it's Name of *Crofs*, and that it fhould from thenceforth be called Queen *Catherine*'s Bath. The firft Table ftill continues, but the laft was taken down upon the famous *John* Earl of *Rochefter*'s under writing the Mayor's Infcription with Lines which made Mr. *Chapman* the Chang'ling, and not the Bath.

SIR *Alexander Frayfer* coming a fecond Time to the City, in the Year 1673, to drink the Waters for an old Cough, and Cachectick Habit of Body, he contrived the Method that is now made Ufe of to draw the Water pure from the Spring; and then Pumps were placed as well in the Baths as out of them, for People to drink at; or rather the Dry Pump by the Side of the *Queen*'s Bath, and the Dry Pump by the End of the hot Bath, were, by additional Spouts, made Drinking Pumps; but their high Situation was, and is ftill of exceeding bad Accefs for poor Cripples; and the Dry Pumping, as well as the Drinking of the Waters were, from the firft, rendered incommodious for Want of proper Room about the Baths.

THE Work was begun in the fecond Mayoralty of Capt. *Chapman*, who, on the 13th of *November*, 1673, publifhed his Defcription of the City, under the Title of, *Thermæ Redivivæ*, with a View chiefly, as he himfelf confeffeth, to blazon the Virtues of the hot Waters, and refcue them from a Sort of State of Oblivion in which they had till then lain.

IN

Chap. XI. A Description of BATH.

IN this Work Mr. *Chapman* advertised the Publick of the Method contrived, and then executing, to draw up the Water, in its utmost Purity, from the Spring before it can mix with the Water of the Bath; and from thenceforward People drank without the least Hesitation.

MR. *Chapman* takes Notice that the hot Waters, at the time of his Writing, were carried in Bottles and Runlets to *Bristol*, *Gloucester*, *Worcester*, nay to *London* itself; and this Trade soon extended all over *England*, to *Scotland*, and to *Ireland*; from whence a certain Profit arose to the Guardians of the Baths, whose Interest in them was so inconsiderable before, that whatever was done to extend their Uses was performed by the publick Spirit of People of Fortune that had found Benefit by the Waters.

THIS Extention was begun by *Robert* Lord *Brook*, an elder Brother of *Fulk* Lord *Brook*, the Great-Grandfather of the Right Honourable *Francis* now Earl *Brook*; for that Nobleman having drank the Water of the *Cross* Bath, with Success, for a Diabetes, in the Year 1673, he afterwards sent for them Weekly to his Seat near *Salisbury*, to his House in *London*, and to his Seat at *Warwick*: His Case was so remarkable, that all the Physicians of any Note in the Kingdom were consulted upon it; it was, says Dr. *Peirce* in his Book Memoirs, Page 312, talked of all the Nation over; and his Lordship testified the Benefit he had received, by erecting a Stone Gallery, at the North End of the *Cross* Bath, in the Year 1674, and by setting up a handsome Chimney Piece, at the same time, in the Dining-Room of the House wherein he resided in Remembrance of it.

THAT House was rebuilt by me in the Year 1727, for the late Duke of *Chandos*; and I have reserved the chief Ornaments of the Chimney, to this Hour, because it is a Testimony of the Fame that ensued to our hot Waters; a Fame that stirred up the grand Monarch of *France* to compleat the Works of *Bourbon*, which was done at a great Expence in the Year 1680; the King sending Mr. *Motheau*, one of his Physicians, and Intendant of the mineral Waters of *France*, to direct and manage the Work; and ordering the Money to be furnished by the Collectors of the States of *Burgundy*.

THE rising Fame of the hot Fountains of *Bath*, soon induced the Corporation to extend their Bye Laws, for the better Regulation of the Baths; and upon the 28th of March 1676, they assembled together to put an End to a Custom which

then

then prevailed of fmoaking Tobacco in the bathing Cifterns, finging Songs, and making fuch Difturbances in them as rendered the Baths like fo many Bear Gardens: So that what by the Labours of the Learned, and what by the good Regulations of the Place, with the Succefs of the Waters upon Perfons of the higheft Rank, the City grew into great Efteem; People began to make their Houfes more commodious for Strangers than they had ever been; and *Bath* becoming famous as well for its Buildings, as for the Company that came to it, it induced Mr. *Jofeph Gilmore* of *Briftol* to make a Survey of the City, as above, and in the Year 1694, to publifh a Draught of it on four Sheets of Paper; which he adorned with the Elevations of the public Buildings, and thirty of the chief Houfes, as well old as new. He alfo publifhed a fmaller Draught on a fingle Sheet of Paper, and by thofe Draughts it appears, that the Gravel Walks at the Eaft End of St. *Peter*'s Church; the old Bowling-green on the South Side of thofe Walks; the new Bowling-green a fmall Matter to the Weftward of St. *Michael*'s Church, without the North Gate of the City; the Cock Pit on the South Side of the Saw Clofe, or Timber-green; and the Fives Court juft without the Weft Gate, were Places fet apart for the Diverfion of the Company: Befides which a Stable by the Abby Gate was appropriated for a Theatre; and the Council Houfe of the Guild Hall ferved for a Ball Room.

The public Amufements of fuch as came to *Bath* about this Time, confifted, for the moft Part, in Bowling and Walking in the Summer Evenings; People in thofe Days feldom coming to the City but in the Summer Time, when the Roads were dry and paffable, for they were, in effect, unpaffable in the wet Seafons of the Year; and it was not above a Year or two after Mr. *Gilmore* publifhed his Draughts of the City, that Safh Windows were introduced in *Bath*, by one *Philip Taylor*, a Chairman.

The Pump, by the Side of the *Queen*'s Bath, fupplied the Drinkers with the Water of the chief hot Spring for more than thirty Years, and all Degrees of People, in all forts of Weather, flocked to it, notwithftanding the expofed Situation of the Machine rendered them liable to catch Cold; " the immediate Confequence of which, fays the late Doctor " *Oliver*, was fuch cold Rheum and Catarrhs, as very much " difturb the whole Animal Œconomy, and render the Wa- " ters of very little Ufe while they laft:" For this Reafon the

Doctor concluded, that it would be better to drink the Waters at some Distance from the Pump, or even cold, rather than the Patient should expose himself to the Inconveniencies of the Fountain: Inconveniencies still attending the Poor; but the better Sort avoided them, in some Measure, by retiring to the Gallery belonging to the Abbey House, erected over the Passage at the South End of the Tennis Court, in the Year 1615, for a Communication between that House and the *King*'s Bath; and in that Gallery they not only exercised themselves by Walking, but amused themselves by looking upon the Bathers in the Bath below.

From this Gallery some Steps descend, on the West Side of the Tennis Court to the *Queen*'s Slip at the North East Corner of the *King*'s Bath, and under those Steps a Cabbin was formerly made, for some of the Bath Guides to deposite their Cloaths in; but this reduced the Passage at the East End of the Bath to half its former Breadth; and thereby a little Convenience to the Guides introduced a great Inconvenience to the Publick.

Queen *Anne*, and her Royal Consort, the Prince of *Denmark*, coming to *Bath* in the Year 1702, and 1703, brought such a Concourse of People to the City, for the Use and Benefit of the hot Waters, that the drinking Pumps could not supply them; all the neighbouring Villages were filled with People of Rank and Fortune that flocked to *Bath* for Health, for Pleasure, or for any other Purpose; and Lodgings were then so scarce, that many were obliged to Pay a Guinea a Night for their Beds.

It was now that the abovementioned Dr. *Oliver* first put Pen to Paper on the Subject of the Bath Waters; and after composing an Essay on them, he subjoined it to a Treatise of Fevers, &c. published A. D. 1704: This Essay was three Years after altered to a Practical Dissertation, and under that Title it then appeared in Print: " The new Notion, says our " Author, of the first and latter Season for drinking the hot " Waters is ridiculous; infallible Experience telling us, that " they may be drank at any Time of the Year with Success, " if the Case requires it; and there ought to be two Hours " at least allowed for the drinking of them; for if taken too " fast, they pass off too quick, or else purge by Stool, and " then the Benefit of the Waters is often lost. Very mode-
" rate Exercise is required all the Time of drinking between " each Glass, lest Nature should be disturbed; and that
" thrown

" thrown off by Sweat, which naturally should have been
" discharged by Urine; and all the Objection I know against
" drinking the Waters in Winter is, the Danger of catching
" Cold, upon the Use of them in cold Weather, one of the
" worst Accidents that can happen to any Body in the Course
" of drinking *Bath* Waters."

The Guardians of the hot Fountains having been duly sensible of what our Author wrote, soon came to a Resolution to build a handsome Room on the North Side of the *King*'s Bath, and to set up a new Pump in it, that People of Rank and Fashion might drink the Waters, and walk about, at all Seasons of the Year, without that Danger of catching Cold, which the exposed Situation of the old Pumps made them liable to; and they were much encouraged in their Design by Doctor *Bettenson*, who generously gave them one hundred Pounds towards the Expence of the Work.

But as the Passage on that Side the *Bath* was no more than nine Feet broad, the Corporation resolved to place the Pump Room over it, and extend the Edifice to the Fronts of some Shops then standing on the South Side of the Yard that had formerly belonged to *Stall*'s Church: The Shops were therefore purchased, and while Matters were preparing for the Execution of the Work, Mr. *Nash*, commonly called *Beau Nash*, came to the City; and the Sovereignty of *Bath* was soon decreed to him, in the room of Captain *Webster*.

CHAP. XII.

Of the Additional Works to BATH, between the Election of its present Titular King and The Year MDCCXXVII.

THE Vernal Equinox having formerly opened the Spring Season at *Bath*, and the Dissolution of the Parliament, in the Year 1705, immediately following it, the greatest Physician of the Age forthwith conceived a Design to ruin the City, by what he called casting a Toad into its Medicinal Waters, in Revenge for an Affront that was put upon him by some of the Inhabitants: But unluckily for the Doctor the wonderful Effect of Musick, on such as were bit by the Tarantula, was then recent in every Body's Mind, from the Accounts that had been published in the Memoirs of the Academy of Sciences, at *Paris*, for the Year 1702: Mankind
were

were amazed that a Perfon without Senfe or Motion, and brought to the Point of Death, by the Poifon of the Spider, fhould, by an Air of Mufick, begin to fhew Signs of Life, then by little and little move his Limbs, and at laft rife up and Dance, with an increafe of Activity and Force, till his Senfes returned, as if waked out of a deep Sleep: And therefore Mr. *Nafh* finding that a Fiddle was capable of difpelling the rankeft Poifon, he immediately fet up that Inftrument againft the Doctor's Reptile, furnifhed with all its Venom; and by declaring that he would fiddle the Amphibious Creature out of the hot Waters, whenever it fhould be caft into them, and, by the Harmony of his Cremona, charm every Body on whom the Toad fhould fpit his Poifon, into fuch a Dance as fhould drive out the Venom, and turn Languifhment itfelf into Gaiety, he allayed the Doctor's Wrath; then triumphed; and the Sovereignty of the City was decreed him by the Suffrages of all Ranks of People.

IT was then that the Sons of the Mufes began to erect a regular Theatre on that Spot of Ground which once contained the Prætorium of the *Roman* Camp; the Year after that, the Pump Houfe was compleated; and the Fountain was then opened with a Revival of the following Song:

GReat BLADUD born a Sov'reign Prince,
But from the Court was Banifh'd thence,
 His dire Difeafe to fhun,
The Mufes do his Fame record,
That when the Bath his Health reftor'd,
 Great *Bladud* did return.

This Glorious Prince of Royal Race,
The Founder of this happy Place,
 Where Beauty holds her Reign,
To *Bladud*'s Mem'ry let us join,
And crown the Glafs from Springs Divine,
 His Glory to maintain.

Let Joy in every Face be fhewn,
And Fame his Reftoration crown,
 While Mufick founds his Praife,
His Praife, ye Mufes, fing above,
Let Beauty wait on *Bladud*'s Love,
 And Fame his Glory raife.

Though

Though long his Languish did endure,
The Bath did lasting Health procure,
   And Fate no more did frown,
For smiling Heaven did invite,
Great *Bladud* to enjoy his Right,
   And wear the Imperial Crown.

May all a fond Ambition shun,
By which e'en *Bladud* was undone,
   As antient Stories tell,
Who try'd with artful Wings to fly,
But towering on the Regions high,
   He down expiring fell.

The Pump House was immediately put under the Care of an Officer that bore the Name of the Pumper; he is the only Tenant of the hot Waters, all other Officers being complimented with their Places; and the Rent, from time to time, paid by him to the Corporation, seems to me to have been no more, after discharging the chief Rent to the Crown, and keeping the Baths in Repair, than a reasonable Interest for the Money expended by the City in making the Conveniencies, already mentioned, for the Usage of the hot Waters: It is at this Day a mere trifle in respect to the Rent that is paid for the Water of St. *Vincent*'s Well at *Bristol*; and, upon the most moderate Computation, it can't amount to the fiftieth Part of what the Invalids, that make use of the hot Waters at the Fountain Heads, pay the Gentlemen belonging to the Faculty of Physick for Directions how to use them, and for Medicines to promote their Efficacy.

The Beginning of the Year 1706, a Row of new Houses was begun on the South Side of the Gravel Walks; before which a handsome Pavement was then made, with large flat Stones, for the Company to walk upon: No less than seventeen or eighteen hundred Pounds, that was raised by Subscription, was laid out, during the Summer of this Year, in repairing the Road to *Lansdown*, that the Invalids might conveniently ascend that Hill, to take the Benefit of the Air upon it: And in the Autumn, an Application was made to Parliament for a Power to amend the principal Roads leading to *Bath*; to pave, cleanse, and light the Streets, Lanes, &c. of the Town; and to regulate and licence a sufficient Number of Chairmen, that nothing might be wanting for the publick Utility of the City.

In this Act the Invalids were exempted from all Manner of Toll, as often as they shou'd go out of the City for Air, or Recreation; the Legislature shewing thereby the strictest Regard for the free Use of the hot Waters; and not permitting the Afflicted to have the least addition to their Afflictions, even by so small a Taxation, as that of the Duty for passing the Turnpikes.

The Pump House, tho' built and finished at a very considerable Expence, was so far from rendering the inward Use of the hot Waters perfectly convenient, that the abovementioned Dr. *Oliver* declared in his Practical Dissertation, printed in the Year 1707, that the Inconveniencies attending the old Pump were only much lessened since the erecting the new one: And the Doctor having in his Work recommended it to the Citizens to make a cold Bath for the Service of the Publick, Mr. *Thomas Greenway*, one of the Free-stone Masons of the City, directly engaged in the Work; and made a handsome Bath, in one of the Rooms of a House built by him upon the *Beach*, at the Foot of *Beaching-Cliff*.

Twenty Years had now been spent in improving the private Buildings of the City; in the Course of which Improvements, thatch'd Coverings were exchanged to such as were tiled; low and obscure Lights were turned into elegant Sash Windows, as soon as Mr. *Taylor* had set the Example; the Houses were raised to five and more Stories in Heighth; and every one was lavish in Ornaments to adorn the Outsides of them, even to Profuseness: But in the midst of all this Splendour, the Company were driven to the Necessity of meeting in a Booth to drink their Tea and Chocolate, and to divert themselves at Cards, till Mr. *Thomas Harrison*, at the Instigation of the new King of *Bath*, erected a handsome Assembly-House for those Purposes.

This House was begun in the Spring of the Year 1708; to which Mr. *Harrison* added Gardens for People of Rank and Fortune to walk in: But his Works were soon looked upon as prejudicial to the Gravel Walks, and as an Invasion of the Liberties of the City; as such the Corporation opposed them with the Power of Men determined by Might to overcome all Manner of Right; and the Citizens, in general, were so uneasy at the Sight of every new House that was begun, that, in the utmost Despair, they cry'd out,

O Lord! *Bath* is undone; 'tis undone; 'tis undone.

But notwithstanding this Mr. *George Trim*, a worthy Member of the Corporation, thought it expedient to augment the Buildings of the City, and, in the Year 1707, that Gentleman began a new Street at the North West Corner of it: His Example stirred up another Citizen to purchase a Lease of some Land at the South East Corner of the Town, and promote Building there: So that as the City now began to shew graceful Suburbs, the Inhabitants were desirous of promoting a Trade, for the better Support of it; and with this View, they not only proposed to make the River navigable to *Bristol*, but, the latter End of the Year 1710, they applied to Parliament for a Power to carry their Design into Execution, and obtained an Act accordingly.

The following Year, the Title of Viscount *Granville* of *Lansdown*, and Earl of *Bath*, conferred by King *Charles* II. upon *John*, the eldest Son of Sir *Bevil Granville*, became extinct in that Family; for this Nobleman dying A. D. 1700, his eldest Son *Charles*, enjoy'd the Title but one Year; and he leaving only one Son, named *Henry William*, this third Earl dyed without Issue, A. D. 1711.

Charles, the Son of *John* Earl of *Bath* was, for his singular Service in the War of *Hungary* against the *Turks*, created an Earl of the sacred *Roman* Empire, by the Title of Earl of *Lansdown*, and permitted to Bear his paternal Coat on the Breast of the *Roman* Eagle: And immediately after the Decease of the Issue of this great Peer, Queen *Anne*, upon the 31st of December 1711, created *George* the Son of *Bernard*, the second Son of Sir *Bevil Granville*, Lord *Lansdown* of *Bediford*; but he dying without Male Issue, the Title expired with him.

Seven and twenty Days before the Date of this Nobleman's Patent, a fraudulent Lease of the Lands and Tenements of Saint *John*'s Hospital, obtained by one *Tobias Ruslat*, and bearing Date the 29th of May 1665, determined by the Decease of the last Life, for which that Lease was granted; and the Reverend Mr. *William Clement* having been then the Master of that Hospital, He forthwith granted his own Son *Thomas*, an Attorney at Law, a Lease of the Estate under his Guardianship for the same Rent Mr. *Ruslat* had paid, viz. L 130. a Year: But Mr. *Clement* scarcely surviving his Grant, and the Reverend Mr. *John Chapman* becoming his Successor, he instantly preferr'd a Bill in Chancery against the Lessee, and set his Lease aside; Sir *John Trevor*,

Chap. XII. A Defcription of BATH.

Trevor, Knt. Mafter of the Rolls, determining the Suit upon the 13th of February 1716-7; and directing, at the fame time, that the Lands and Tenements of the Hofpital fhould not be leafed out again for lefs than *L* 163. 15. 2. per annum, nor for a lefs Fine than *L* 3922. 0. 1½.

He alfo directed that all future Fines fhould be certain, and never raifed above the Sum by him ftipulated, without the Direction of the Court of Chancery; and this was fuch an Encouragement to the Tenants of that Eftate, that they forthwith began to improve, and enlarge their Houfes upon it; and St. *John*'s Chapel was rebuilt with Part of the Money arifing by the Fines.

The Improvements carried on at the South Eaft Corner of the City, induced the Inhabitants of St. *James*'s Parifh to repair and enlarge their Church, the Tower of which was raifed and finifhed in the Year 1716; and in that Year Mr. *Humphrey Thayer*, a wealthy Druggift of *London*, and afterwards one of the Commiffioners of the Excife, purchafed the old Bowling-green, and Abbey Orchard, with a View to improve each Piece of Ground by Building, at the Expiration of the under Tenant's Leafes.

The fame Year a Street was begun to be erected upon the new Bowling-green, the Inhabitants of *Bath* having been animated by the great Concourfe of Strangers to the City, the Year before, to increafe the private Accommodations of the Place: The Author of a Book intitled, Memoirs of a Man of Quality, was at *Bath* in the Year 1715, and he affures us, that on his Arrival in the City, the Strangers were computed to be near eight Thoufand in Number; *William Jellicut*, alias *Bengy*, was then Tenant of the old Bowling-green; and as foon as the Buildings were begun on the new Bowling-green, he procured a Leafe of fome Ground on the South Side of his own Green, upon which he forthwith erected two of the firft Rate Houfes of the City.

About this Time the two chief hot Springs of *Bath* were threatened with inevitable Deftruction; for the Profits of the Water fent abroad, excited the Proprietors, or rather Poffeffors of the Lands about the Baths, to fearch the Bowels of the Earth for hot Springs, that they might difpofe of the Water, as their own juft Right and Property. Mr. *William Skrine* having then had the Poffeffion of the Ground on the Weft Side of the hot Bath, proceeded fo far as to draw Water from that Bath, and fold the fame for his own Benefit; and his

his Example stirred up Mr. *William Swallow*, a Tallow Chandler, to dig for hot Water within the Limits of his House, situated at the South End of the Tennis Court: He proceeded to a very considerable Depth; but his Tryal having been made where a Mill had formerly stood, and he meeting with a Mill-Stone in the Progress of his digging, it discouraged him from the further Pursuit of his Design.

Thus the traditional Religion, which the late Dr. *Oliver* tells us he found subsisting among the Inhabitants of *Bath*, not to dig any where too deep for fear of disturbing or interrupting the hot Springs, was intirely laid aside; and these modern Instances may serve, as Precepts, to teach us how necessary it is to expell all private Property to a proper Distance from the Heads of our Sovereign Fountains, and to enlarge the Bounds of the Baths, to preserve the Springs for the Benefit of Posterity.

Mr. *Swallow*'s Attempt don't appear to me to have been intended to intercept the Spring that fills the *King*'s Bath, but to discover another Spring that antiently supplied the Prior's private Bath: " There is a Bath in *Hadnett*'s Tenement " which was for the Prior's private Use; but it is now filled " up with Rubble, and covered with Earth, and of no Use; " but there be many of the Town that do remember when " it was of great Use, for there is as hot a Spring in it, " as in any of the Baths, and a little Charge will repair it " to its former Virtue, and fit for Use," are the express Words in a Particular of the Priory Estate made just before the Sale of it in the Year 1614.

The Works carried on for three or four Years before the Year 1720, consisted of little more than the Rebuilding and enlarging a few Houses fronting some of the Streets or other publick Parts of the City; but that memorable Year produced great Designs: Mr. *Harrison* then added a large Ball Room to his Assembly House; and my Lord *Lansdown* caused a Monument to be erected on the Northern Brow of *Mons Badonca*, in Memory of his Grandfather, Sir *Bevil Granville*; and this was placed as near the Spot whereon Sir *Bevil* was killed in the Civil Wars, in the Reign of King *Charles* the First, as could be well discovered at such a Distance of Time.

The Poetical Genius of the illustrious Author of this Work hath excited the Curiosity of Multitudes to go to View it; People have almost daily visited the Monument since the time

Chap. XII. A Defcription of BATH. 229

time of its firft Erection; and if the Architecture of it had been equal to the reft of the Defign, no Memorial, of the fame Kind, within my Knowledge, would have exceeded this. The Trophy confifts of two Quadrangular Pedeftals, fet upon each other, but without any Proportion in, or Harmony betwixt them, and thefe being furmounted by a kind of Attick Bafe, a Cap of Dignity, bearing the Figure of a Griphon Paffant, whofe Breaft is fupported by a Shield, finifhes the Top of the Monument, and raifes it to the Altitude of about five and twenty Feet, from a Bafe of about feven Feet Square.

THE Arms of *England*, refting upon the joint Arms of *George* Duke of *Albemarle*, and *John* Earl of *Bath*, with military Ornaments under them, all cut in Free Stone, adorn the Right Side of the Body of the upper Pedeftal, and were intended to allude to the Reftoration of King *Charles* the Second: And the following Infcriptions, cut on Slabs of Grey Stone, and fixt on the Front and Back Part of the fame Pedeftal, were intended not only to fet forth the Fall of Sir *Bevil Granville* and his Friends, in that Place; but to revive the Memory of the Valour of Sir *Bevil*'s Grandfather, the renowned Sir *Richard Granville*, in the remarkable Inftance of his fighting, with a fingle Ship, the whole *Spanifh Armada*, at the *Azores*, in the Year 1591.

THE Infcription on the FRONT of the Pedeftal is an Abftract from Lord *Clarendon*'s Hiftory, and ftands in thefe Words, tho' not legible, without clofe Infpection, from the Grey Colour of the Stone on which they are flightly cut.

" IN this Battle, on the King's Part, there were more
" Officers and Gentlemen of Quality flain than common
" Men; and more hurt than flain: But that which would
" have clouded my Victory, and made the Lofs of others
" lefs fpoken of, was the Death of Sir *Bevil Granville*. He
" was indeed an excellent Perfon, whofe Activity, Intereft
" and Reputation, was the Foundation of what had been
" done in *Cornwall*; and his Temper and Affection fo pub-
" lick, that no Accident which happened could make an
" Impreffion in him; and his Example kept others from
" taking any thing ill, or at leaft to do fo. In a Word, a
" brighter Courage, and a gentler Difpofition were never
" married together, to make the moft chearful and innocent
" Converfation." " *Clarendon*'s Hiftory, Vol. II."

UNDER

Under this Inscription there is a Scutcheon with the Arms of Lord *Lansdown, Granville* and *Villers,* carved upon it: But the Inscriptions on the Back of the Pedestal fill the whole Surface of the Stone, in the following Words slightly cut, and not legible without a closer Inspection than even the Inscription on the opposite Side of that part of the Monument.

" When now the incensed Rebel proudly came,
" Down like a Torrent without Bank or Dam:
" When undeserv'd Success urg'd on their Force,
" That Thunder must come down to stop their Course,
" Or *Granville* must step in, then *Granville* stood,
" And with himself oppos'd, and check'd the Flood.
" Conquest or Death was all his Thought, so Fire
" Either o'rcomes, or does itself expire.
" His Courage work'd; like Flames cast Heat about,
" Here, there, on this, and that Side none gave out:
" Not any Pike in that renowned Stand,
" But took new Force from his inspiring Hand.
" Soldier encourag'd Soldier, Man urg'd Man,
" And he urg'd all; so much Example can:
" Hurt upon Hurt, Wound upon Wound did call,
" He was the Butt, the Mark, the Aim of all.
" His Soul this While retir'd from Cell to Cell,
" At last flew up from all, and then he fell.
" But the devoted Stand enrag'd the more,
" From that his Fate ply'd hotter than before,
" And proud to fall with him, sworn not to yield,
" Each fought an honour'd Grave, and gain'd the Field.
" Thus he being fallen, his Action fought anew,
" And the Dead conquer'd; whilst the Living flew."
                        " *William Cartwright,* 1643."

" Thus slain, thy valiant Ancestor did lye,
" When his one Bark a Navy did supply.
" When now encompass'd round He Victor stood,
" And bath'd his Pinnace in his conquering Blood,
" 'Till all his Purple current dry'd and spent,
" He fell, and made the Waves his Monument.
" Where shall the next fam'd *Granville's* Ashes stand?
" Thy Grandsire fills the Seas, and thou the Land.
                        " *Martin Llewellin,* 1643."

" To

Chap. XII.   A Defcription of BATH.   231

" To the Immortal Memory of
" His renowned Grandfather and valiant *Cornifh* Friends
" Who conquer'd, dying in the Royal Caufe,
" *July* 5th 1643.
" This Column was dedicated
" By the Rt. Honourable *George Granville* Lord *Lanfdown*,
" In the Year 1720,
" *Dulce eft pro patria mori.*"

THE Left Side of the Body of the Pedeftal is adorned with a Bas Relief, in Free Stone, alluding to the Actions of *Charles* Earl of *Lanfdown* in *Hungary*; and this piece of Sculpture confifts of a Trophy compofed of Military Ornaments and Labels, with *Granville's* Arms, born on the Breaft of the *Roman* Eagle, in the Middle of it: The Infcription, *Vienna obfidione foluta*, filling one Label, and the Date, *September* the 12th 1683, filling another.

THE noble Lord that caufed this Monument to be erected is ftill charged with not paying the Undertaker, one *John Harvey* a Painter Stainer, and Stone Cutter of *Bath*, and the fecond of that Name, fo much as a fingle Shilling for it: But this Scandal arofe from an Equivocation in the Undertaker to evade paying the Workmen that were concerned under him; and particularly Mr. *John Pitcher*, the Mafon that performed the Free Stone Work, who he amufed, to the Day of his Death, with a Promife of Payment as foon as he fhould receive his Money of Lord *Lanfdown*; protefting, at the fame time, that he had not received a Shilling of his Lordfhip; when in Truth he had had the full Value of the Monument from him in three Blocks, or more, of fine Marble, which his Lordfhip procured for him from abroad.

WHILE this Work was about, Dr. *Bettenfon* began a Court of Houfes at the South End of the Body of the City, on a Piece of Ground, formerly Part of the Priory, and by Indenture bearing Date the 20th of Auguft 1583, leafed to one *John Hull*, a Shoemaker, from whom it is now corruptly called the *Bull Garden*; and the abovementioned *Thomas Greenway* began another Court of Houfes, on the Town Mixen, upon the Weft Side of the Timber Green, to which he gave the Name of St. *John*'s Court: Part of the firft Houfe that was built in it became the Palace of the King of *Bath*; and it was the richeft Sample of Building, till then executed, in the City.

IN

In the same Year an Application was made to Parliament, and an Act was obtained, not only to enlarge the Term for amending the Roads leading to the City, for paving, cleansing, and lighting the Streets, and for regulating the Chairmen, but to explain and make the former Act more effectual; and upon the 27th of May 1724, a Subscription was opened by Mr. *John Hobbs*, a Deal Merchant of *Bristol*, for carrying the Navigation of the River into Execution: So that when I found the Work was likely to go on, I began to turn my Thoughts towards the Improvement of the City by Building; and for this Purpose I procured a Plan of the Town, which was sent me into *Yorkshire*, in the Summer of the Year 1725, where I, at my leisure Hours, formed one Design for the Ground, at the North West Corner of the City; and another for the Land, on the North East Side of the Town and River.

AFTER my Return to *London*, I imparted my first Design to Mr. *Gay*, an eminent Surgeon, in *Hatton Garden*, and Proprietor of the Land; and our first Conference was upon the last Day of December 1725: The 31st of March following, I communicated my second Design to the Earl of *Essex*, to whom the Land, on which it was proposed to be executed, then belonged: And in each Design, I proposed to make a grand Place of Assembly, to be called the *Royal Forum* of *Bath*; another Place, no less magnificent, for the Exhibition of Sports, to be called the *Grand Circus*; and a third Place, of equal State with either of the former, for the Practice of medicinal Exercises, to be called the *Imperial Gymnasium* of the City, from a Work of that Kind, taking its Rise at first in *Bath*, during the Time of the *Roman* Emperors.

WHILE these Designs were under Consideration, a terrible Fire broke out in *Horse Street* in *Bath*; it began on the 6th of May 1726, between twelve and one o' clock at Noon; and the Flames consuming the principal Part of the old low thatch'd Hovels fronting the Street, the rebuilding them into larger Houses was the last Addition the City received before The Year M.DCC.XXVII.

The End of the SECOND PART.

Milton Keynes UK
Ingram Content Group UK Ltd.
UKHW021110200224
438164UK00006B/716